Beginning FORTH

Beginning FORTH

Paul M. Chirlian

Professor of Electrical Engineering
and Computer Science

Stevens Institute of Technology

Matrix Publishers, Inc.
Beaverton, Oregon

10 9 8 7 6 5 4 3 2 1

Library of Congress Cataloging in Publication Data

Chirlian, Paul M.
Beginning FORTH.

  Includes index.
  1. FORTH (Computer program language) I. Title.
II. Title: F.O.R.T.H.
QA76.73.F24C48 1983   001.64'24   83-7253
ISBN 0-916460-36-3

Production: Vicki L. Tobin
Printing: Pantagraph Printing
In-house Editor: Nancy L. Morrice

Printed in the United States of America

Matrix Publishers, Inc.
8285 S.W. Nimbus
Suite 151
Beaverton, Oregon 97005

To Barbara, Lisa, and Peter

Preface

This is an introductory text on FORTH. It is intended for readers who have essentially no programming experience. This book can be used by college or junior-college students or by those who are interested in teaching FORTH to themselves.

The different aspects of FORTH are presented in a simple manner so as not to confuse the beginner. The book discusses the editing and running of programs. It is assumed that the user is working with a small computer. However, most of the ideas presented here can be used with FORTH implementations on large computers.

No only is the FORTH language discussed, but the topic of debugging is also presented. Basic ideas of structured programming are also considered. It is important for beginners to be aware of these ideas.

The subject of FORTH is rather thoroughly discussed. Standard FORTH-79 as distributed by the FORTH Interest Group is considered in detail. In addition, enhancements such as those provided by the MMSFORTH system are also discussed. (MMSFORTH is a high-performance 79-Standard FORTH system with many applications programs.) A glossary of FORTH words is included.

The book is organized so that a beginner can start running programs almost immediately. Many varied exercises are included at the end of each chapter.

Many thanks are due to A. Richard Miller for his many helpful comments. Much loving gratitude and heartfelt thanks are again due my wife Barbara, who not only provided me with constant encouragement, but who also typed the final drafts of the manuscript and copyedited the text.

Table of Contents

Chapter 1

Introduction to FORTH Programming

This book discusses the FORTH programming language and how to write programs in this versatile language. The discussion begins with some very basic ideas and then builds up to complex procedures.

The modern digital computer can do remarkable things. In a matter of seconds or minutes it can perform jobs that would have taken days or years to perform by hand. The computer can control industrial processes or monitor a hospital operating room. However, the computer cannot think. It can only follow a detailed set of instructions called a *program*. In this book we shall discuss a language called FORTH that is used to program computers. In the first chapter we shall discuss some introductory computer concepts and compare FORTH to other programming languages. Simple ideas of FORTH programming will be introduced in this chapter so that you can start programming without delay.

1-1. SOME BASIC IDEAS OF COMPUTER OPERATIONS

Before discussing programming in FORTH we shall consider the makeup of a digital computer. Although the examples that are used here apply to a microprocessor-based computer, the basic ideas apply to large computers as well.

The microprocessor contains the *central processor* which performs all the arithmetic and logical operations. For instance, it can add two numbers or compare them to see if they are equal. Computers also have a *main memory* which is used to store both the program that directs the computation and the data that is used by it.

The main memory can supply data to the computer at a very rapid rate, often in a fraction of a microsecond (millionth of a second) for each item. However, such memory is relatively expensive and its size is limited by the hardware of the computer. For this reason the main memory is not used to store extremely large amounts of data. For instance, you might have several different programs that you run occasionally. It would not be an efficient use of memory to store all of these programs in the main memory, since it would soon become full. You would also have to keep the computer turned on since all the information would be lost once it was turned off. (Some computers have main memories that can store data even if the computer is turned off. However this is usually not the case with small computer.) A similar situation applies to data storage. Suppose that a certain bank has 100,000 depositors. Their computer would require an enormous main memory to store all their account information. For these reasons computers utilize magnetic storage. A great deal of information can be stored on *magnetic tape.* Small computers often use an ordinary tape recorder for this purpose. Many programs can be stored on a single tape; when you want to run one of these programs it is read from the tape and stored in the main memory. Both *hard* and *floppy disks are also used for information storage. Magnetic bubble* memories are also being used for data and program storage.

If a computer is to be useful we must have a way to put in programs and data and take out the results. With most small computers, input and ouput of information is done using a *video terminal.* The input is entered using a keyboard that resembles a typewriter keyboard. The output appears on a screen that is similar to an ordinary television set. (In fact, it can be a television set.) Often there is a line printer that is connected to the computer. This produces a printed, or *hard* copy of the output.

1-2. PROGRAMMING LANGUAGES

All of the information stored in a digital computer is in the form of numbers. These numbers consist only of the digits 0 and 1. Such numbers are called *binary* numbers. For instance, 0110 is a binary number that represents the ordinary (decimal) number 6. You do not have to know all about binary numbers to program a computer in FORTH. One reason that languages such as FORTH are used is to avoid the need for using binary numbers in programming.

Digital computers can be instructed by what is termed a *machine language* program. The instructions in this language are relatively simple; one might direct the computer to add two numbers together or to store a number in a particular memory location. The commands consist of long sequences of 0's and 1's. It is extremely tedious to write programs in machine language. A simple multiplication problem might require a lengthy sequence of machine language instructions. To make the programmer's work much easier, special programs are written that translate simpler, understandable statements or symbols into a machine language program.

One such class of programs is called *assembly language* programs. These are similar to machine language, but the instructions are in the form of mnemonics rather than binary numbers. In machine language the programmer must keep track of the memory locations where the data is stored. In assembly language, names, which are easier to remember, are assigned to memory locations. In many ways assembly language is just a more easily used form of machine language.

A special class of programs called *programming languages* or *higher-level* languages is available. These can greatly simplify the programmer's work since they translate simple statements or symbols into a sequence of machine language statements. For instance, in most programming languages the symbol * (asterisk) is translated into a sequence of machine language commands that perform multiplication. The programmer is not concerned with the details of the translation from the * to the sequence of machine language commands. The programming language program takes care of this.

In general, programming languages are more limited than assembly or machine languages. When you program in assembly or machine language you can utilize all the commands that are built into the microprocessor. When you program in a high-level language you are limited to the commands that have been written into that language. However, most programming languages are reasonably versatile and are *much* more easy to use than assembly languages. In this book we shall study the very powerful FORTH programming language.

1-3. A COMPARISON OF FORTH AND OTHER PROGRAMMING LANGUAGES

FORTH is one of many programming languages that is used by people working on small computers. Other languages that are commonly used are BASIC, FORTRAN, Pascal, and to a lesser degree, COBOL. FORTH is actually very different from these others. This can be illustrated by writing a program, in both BASIC and FORTH, which adds the numbers 3 and 4 and prints the result 7. (A very simple example has been chosen to illustrate some ideas. We assume that at this point many readers will have no knowledge of programming.) The BASIC program is

```
10   A = 3
20   B = 4
30   C = A + B
40   PRINT C
```
(1-1)

The FORTH program that performs the same operation is

```
3  4  +  .
```
(1-2)

We can immediately see some of the advantages and disadvantages of FORTH. The BASIC program looks very familiar while the FORTH program appears strange. However, the FORTH program is very short. If you are writing long programs the compactness of FORTH can be a great help since you do not have to write as much. In addition short programs require less storage space and may execute faster. On the other hand longer programs are often self-documenting. That is they can, if written properly, explain themselves to you and to other programmers. We shall see that by adding comments to a FORTH program it can also be made self-documenting.

In the last section we mentioned that assembly or machine languages were more versatile than programming languages. FORTH has aspects that resemble assembly language and hence gains some versatility without giving up convenience.

Before considering some other aspects of FORTH we must discuss some general ideas about programming languages. Often a program written in a high-level programming language is translated into machine language by a program called a *compiler.* The process of translation is called *compilation.* After a program is written, it is supplied to the compiler, and compilation then takes place. The resulting program is still not ready to be run. There are other subprograms that must be combined with the compiled one. For instance suppose that your program contained several multiplications. The compiler would not write a lengthy sequence of machine language instructions for each multiplication. Instead a multiplication routine would be stored in a *library* of programs that is supplied with the compiler. After your program is compiled it contains instructions that *call* or reference the multiplication subprogram from the library.

The library subprogram must then be combined with the compiled program. This combination procedure is called *linking*.

The process of compilation and linking can take a significant amount of time. On a small computer a moderately-sized program might take five minutes to compile and link if you were using a language such as FORTRAN. A new program usually contains a few *bugs* or errors. Thus, the process of compilation and linking may have to take place many times as you attempt to remove the bugs. In such cases the five minute wait can be unbearable. The compilation process can be speeded by dividing your program into many short subprograms. These can be compiled quickly. One subprogram is added to the program at a time and debugged. Only the latest subprogram need be compiled, since the others have already been compiled. Hence, time is saved. However the linking must still be performed. Therefore, at each step there may be several minutes delay. One of FORTH's advantages is that it can be broken into very short subprograms so that compilation delay is short. More importantly, *the linking time is essentially nonexistent*. Thus, the process of writing programs can be greatly speeded up by using FORTH.

Some programming languages such as BASIC are often *interpreted* instead of compiled. In this case, the operation is somewhat different. When a program is compiled and linked a machine language program results. You run this program to obtain the desired data. When a program is interpreted a machine language program is never obtained. When the program is run another program called an *interpreter* converts individual statements into machine language instructions that direct the computer. This is done every time that the program is run, one (or several) statements at a time. No time is lost in compiling and linking. However, interpreted programs run very slowly, often ten to thirty times more slowly than a compiled program. In some cases the program runs so quickly that this increased time is not significant. For instance, it probably does not matter it it takes 0.01 seconds or 0.2 seconds for a program to run. On the other hand, the difference between thirty seconds and ten minutes can be significant. Thus, interpreted programs can be troublesome. Programs written in BASIC can be debugged using an interpreter. Once the program is completely debugged it can be compiled into a faster running version. This is often the best possible procedure. However, the slow running time can delay debugging. One of interpreted BASIC's greatest weaknesses is that the programmer cannot write isolated subroutines. Interpreted programs have a great advantage in that errors can be detected very quickly, and the programs run in a relatively short time.

The FORTH language has some of the properties of an assembly language, while it also has similarities to higher-level languages. If we consider machine language to be at one level and assembly language and higher-level languages to be at the second and third levels, then FORTH is at a *fourth* level. Incidentally, the name FORTH was originated by Charles H. Moore (the developer of FORTH) when he was working on a third generation computer. The new language seemed to give it the power of a fourth generation computer so Moore decided to call it FOURTH, but the computer could only accept five letter names. Thus, FORTH was used.

When we compare FORTH with the other programming languages we find that it is somewhat harder for the beginner to learn and it is not as easily self-documenting. On the other hand, very short, easily debugged subprograms can be written in FORTH, and the compiling and linking time required is much less than that of other compiled languages. The running time of FORTH programs is much less than that of interpreted BASIC programs. The running time of FORTH programs may be somewhat longer that that for compiled FORTRAN programs, but the compiling and linking times will be much shorter with FORTH. One of the main advantages of FORTH is that it is *extensible*, that is, the programmer can actually add to the FORTH language. We shall discuss this subsequently.

Another advantage of FORTH in comparison with other programming languages is that FORTH requires substantially less main memory. This can be an advantage when small computers are used.

When we deal with large mainframe computers the advantages of FORTH are not as apparent. These computers are, in general, very fast and have a great deal of memory. The time required for compilation and linking may be so small that the time saved may not be significant to the programmer. Similary, the reduction in memory requirements may not longer be a significant factor. The extensible nature of FORTH is still an advantage.

1-4. GETTING STARTED—THE STACK—POSTFIX NOTATION

We shall now discuss some fundamental ideas so that you can start programming in FORTH. Let us begin by writing a very simple FORTH program that adds 3 and 4 and prints the result, 7. A FORTH program that accomplishes this is

3 4 + . (RETURN)   (1-3)

Note that (RETURN) means that you hit the RETURN (or ENTER) key. Let us consider the details of typing in this program and then see how it works. A 3 is typed, followed by a space, and then a 4 and a space. Next, a plus sign is typed followed by a space and after that a period is typed. After all this is done hit RETURN. Your computer will respond

7 ok   (1-4)

Note the blank spaces. In most programming languages, blanks are ignored. This is *not* the case in FORTH. Blanks are used to *delimit*, i.e., separate, quantities. Thus, *blank spaces are very important in FORTH.*

If your computer is running FORTH and you are actually typing in this program, then you must "bring up" the FORTH system in accordance with the instructions supplied by the manufacturer. These will be in your FORTH manual.

Now let us consider the details of program (1-3). We start by entering the values 3 and 4 as data. These are stored by the computer in a set of memory locations called the *stack*. Next the instruction + is encountered. This causes the two values 3 and 4, which were stored on the stack, to be added. The 3 and 4 are then removed from the stack and are replaced by their sum, 7. Finally the instruction . (period, which is pronounced dot) is encountered. In FORTH, this causes the value on the top of the stack to be output to the screen or printer. We shall go over these ideas in detail.

Let us start by taking a closer look at the stack. It is a sequence of locations in the main memory of the computer. A stack is illustrated in Figure 1-1. In Figure 1-1a the stack is empty. That is, no information has been entered into the memory locations set aside for the stack.

Now suppose that program (1-3) is *executed*. That is, the program is run. Consider that it is scanned from left to right. The 3 is encountered first. This is data and it is stored on the stack. We say that 3 has been *pushed* onto the stack. This is indicated in Figure

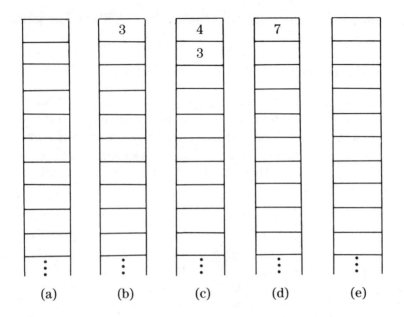

Figure 1-1. An illustration of stack manipulation. (a) an empty stack; (b) the stack after 3 is pushed on; (c) the stack after 4 is pushed on; (d) the stack after + is executed; (e) the stack after . (period) is executed.

1-1b where 3 is on the *top* of the stack. Now let us continue scanning program (1-3). The 4 is encountered next. It, too, is data so it is pushed onto the stack. This is indicated in Figure 1-1c. Note that the 3 has been "pushed down" the stack and the 4 is now on the top of the stack. In general, as new data is pushed onto the stack, the existing data is pushed further down.

Now let us continue the left-to-right scanning of program (1-3). We next encounter the + symbol. This is not data. In fact, it is called a FORTH *word* or command. Many FORTH words are used to define operations. In the body of the text of this book, we shall use boldface type to indicate FORTH words. The word + causes the following to occur—the top two items on the stack are removed. They are said to be *popped* off the stack. (The item on the top of stack is popped off first.) Next the word + causes the two popped numbers to be added. The sum is then pushed onto the stack. This is illustrated in Figure 1-1d. Note that the 3 and 4 are gone and only their sum 7 remains.

Finally the left-to-right scanning encounters the . (period). This is a FORTH word that causes the number on the top of the stack to be popped and output to your terminal. The stack is now empty, see Figure 1-1e. After the number 7 is printed on your terminal FORTH prints "ok" to indicate that no errors were discovered and it is waiting for additional instructions.

We have discussed instructions that involve pushing data on the stack or popping it off the stack. The last data pushed on the stack is the first data popped off. This is called a *Last In First Out,* or LIFO, operation. Once data is removed from the stack it is lost and cannot be used again. In subsequent chapters we shall discuss procedures that will allow us to reuse data.

In FORTH we enter the data and then the symbol, for instance 3 4 +. The FORTH order may appear strange. However, it is a very efficient way of programming and is used by some calculators. The FORTH order of operations is called *postfix notation* or *reverse Polish notation.* (This is named after the Polish mathematician J. Lukasewcleicz.) The ordinary notation is called *infix notation.* One advantage of postfix notation is that parentheses are not needed, whereas infix notation often requires parentheses. For instance, suppose that we want to add 3 and 5 and then multiply their sum by 10. Using infix notation we would have to write

$$(3 \ + \ 5) \ * \ 10 \hspace{5cm} (1\text{-}5)$$

Note that the * (asterisk, which is pronounced times) is the symbol used by FORTH and most other programming languages to signify multiplication. The parentheses are needed in (1-5) since, if they were omitted, we would add 3 to the product of 5 and 10, which yields a different result.

Now let us see how (1-5) would be written using postfix notation. We shall illustrate this with a simple FORTH program.

$$10 \ 3 \ 5 \ + \ * \ . \ (\text{RETURN}) \hspace{3cm} (1\text{-}6)$$

Note that no parentheses are needed. Let us explain program (1-6) using Figure 1-2 which illustrates the stack. In Figure 1-2a the stack is shown after 10, 3, and 5 have been pushed on in that order. Next the + is executed. The top two numbers, 5 and 3, are popped off the stack, in that order, and added. Their sum 8 is then pushed on the stack, see Figure 1-2b. Next the FORTH word * is executed. This causes the top two numbers to be popped off the stack and their product figured. This product is then pushed on the stack, see Figure 1-2c. Note that two numbers were popped off while only one was pushed onto the stack. The remaining numbers are then moved up

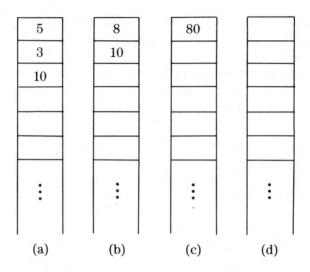

(a)   (b)   (c)   (d)

Figure 1-2. The stack during execution of program (1-6). (a) after 10, 3, and 5 have been pushed onto the stack; (b) the stack after + is executed; (c) the stack after * is executed; (d) the stack after . is executed.

the stack (see Figure 1-2b). Finally the FORTH word . is executed. The top number 80 is pushed off the stack and printed.

The numbers we have used are whole numbers or *integers.* That is, they have no fractional part. For the time being, we shall restrict ourselves to integer arithmetic.

In this section we have introduced the important concepts of the stack and postfix notation. These are basic to programming in FORTH. We have also introduced the FORTH words for addition, multiplication, and the printing of data. You should now be able to use this information to write simple FORTH programs.

1-5. RUNNING FORTH PROGRAMS

We have considered some simple FORTH programs. These were entered from the keyboard and executed when **RETURN** was typed. At that point the program was lost. If you wanted to run it again you would have to retype the entire program. It would be handy to be able to store programs so that they can be run many times. In this section we shall discuss the storage of programs on disk or tape. We cannot be too specific here since the procedures that we discuss are not part of the FORTH language, but are part of the operating system that you are using. Thus, you must refer to the manual that came with your FORTH system for specific details. However, most FORTH systems use similar techniques for entering, editing, and storing programs. We shall present a general overview of these procedures in this section. In addition, we shall consider the actual details of running the programs.

Lengthy programs are almost always typed in using an *editor*. This, as its name implies, is a program tht allows you to enter text material (your program) and, if necessary, correct it. Most FORTH editor systems are based on a *screen* of text. Nominally a screen is the amount of text that will fill your monitor screen. Typically this is 1024 characters, although many video screens can display more characters. The text material is often arranged in 16 (or 24) lines, each containing 64 (or 80) characters.

The programs are stored on tape or floppy disks. Each screen is called a *block*. The blocks are numbered. The blocks correspond to locations on the disk or tape. The exact details of your numbering scheme should be obtained from the manual for your FORTH system. Suppose that you want to write a program on block 120. Typically, you would type

120   EDIT   (RETURN)   (1-7)

Now you can type in text material. (If you are writing on a block that has not been used before you may have to delete any extraneous material that is present before starting.) We shall assume here that the material is to be stored on a floppy disk. The material that you type in would not be immediately placed on a disk. It would temporarily be stored in the computer's memory. The area of memory that is reserved for the storage of the text that you are entering is called a *buffer*. After you finish entering the text you type a symbol that causes you to leave the editor and marks the buffer for *updating*. (Once a buffer is so marked it will subsequently be stored on the disk.) At this point you could edit another block. For instance, if the program was too long to fit on one block you could continue it on the second block. When you type the symbol that exits the editor and marks the block for updating, you would have two blocks stored in two buffers. Now if you enter

SAVE-BUFFERS(RETURN)   (1-8a)

or in some FORTH systems

FLUSH(RETURN)   (1-8b) the material in the blocks that were marked for updating will be stored on the disk.

The number of buffers that are available is limited. Consult your FORTH manual to see how many you have. Usually, when you attempt to use more buffers than are available the buffers marked for updating will be written to the disk automatically. This will free the buffers so that they can store the additional material.

Many FORTH systems use the block numbers to specify the location of the block on the floppy disk. In this way no directory is needed. Since the operating system is written in FORTH you can always modify it to include directories. We shall discuss such procedures in Chapter 8.

Suppose that you want to modify the program that you have typed in using the editor. Again let us assume that it is on block 120. You would again type (1-7). The material from block 120 would be read from the floppy disk and stored in the buffer. (If it were already in a buffer then the disk would not have to be read.) The material in block 120 would also appear on your screen. You can now perform operations such as insertion or deletion of characters or lines, or you can change characters. In this way you can modify your program without retyping it completely. There is a *cursor* that indicates where on the screen the operation (e.g., entering or deleting text) will occur. There are commands that allow you to move the cursor to any point on the screen. The commands for editing vary and you should consult your FORTH manual to determine the specific editing commands for your system. It is a good idea to practice some editing at this point.

You are now ready to run your program. Let us again assume that it is on block 120. We also assume that you have exited the editor and that the block has been marked for updating. Now type

120   LOAD(RETURN)   (1-9)

The program will be executed (i.e., run). Note that the program does not have to be in the buffer. Suppose that the program had already been written and stored on the disk in block 120. If you type 120 LOAD(RETURN) the program will automatically be read from the disk, stored in a buffer, and executed. This assumes that the disk is mounted on the proper disk drive. Note that when the block is loaded it is first compiled into machine language and then run.

Often a program will occupy more than one block. In such cases you want to load several blocks. For instance, suppose that the program is on blocks 120 and 121. You could make the last line of block 120

121 LOAD   (1-10)

Now when block 120 is executed it will direct the FORTH system to load block 121. Note that this statement must not interfere with your FORTH program. We shall consider specific procedures for doing this in Chapter 8. Different operating systems have additional procedures for loading multiple blocks. Again, your FORTH operating manual should be consulted for these procedures.

In this section we have discussed some basic ideas of editing and loading programs. In Chapter 8 we shall consider this material in greater detail. However, the material covered in this section, in conjunction with your FORTH manual, will enable you to write, edit, and run FORTH programs.

1-6. PROGRAMMING ERRORS—DEBUGGING

Almost all programs are originally written with some errors. This may be discouraging to the beginning programmer, but it should not be. Experienced programmers know that removing errors, or *bugs* as they are called, is a part of programming. In this section we shall consider some basic procedures for eliminating bugs.

The simplest type of error that can occur is a mistake in *syntax*. That is, you have not followed the rules of FORTH. For instance, in program (1-6), if the space between the + and the * were omitted, a syntax error would occur. When you attempt to run this program an error message that indicates something about the error would be printed. In most FORTH systems, the program would not run and the ok would not be printed. The error messages will vary with the FORTH system. If you are attempting to load a block, the error message may point out the number of the line with the error. Usually the compilation will stop when an error occurs so that only the first error will be detected. In any event, edit the program to remove the error and then load the block again. The program may run all the way through or the next syntax error will be detected. Once the approximate location of a syntax error is pointed out, you can usually find it by rereading the program.

Another type of error is the *logical* error. In this case the program is written in perfectly good FORTH, but it does not calculate what you intend it to. For instance, suppose that in program (1-6) you inadvertently typed a plus sign instead of an asterisk; the program would obtain the sum of the three numbers. The program would run properly but *the wrong answer* would be obtained. Whenever you write a program, no matter how simple, you should *always* check your result. For instance, you might check the result using a hand calculator. This should be done with several different sets of data. This point cannot be emphasized too strongly. *Always check your programs.*

Debugging of logical errors can be accomplished in a number of ways. Start by rereading your program. You will often catch typographical errors this way. You should go through your program, step by step, just as the computer does. This often shows you the errors in logic. That is, you may find out that you are not calculating what you thought you were. Draw diagrams, such as those in Figures 1-1 or 1-2 to illustrate the stack for each step in the program. This can also show you your mistakes. Some FORTH systems have commands that allow you to print out the stack without changing it. This can be a great help in debugging, since you can use these values to see if the program is computing the things that it should. Remember that the . will cause the top item to be popped off the stack so that adding a . will change the remainder of the program. In the next chapter we will look at a way to avoid this problem.

One of the great advantages of FORTH is that it allows you to write a long program that consists of a set of short subprograms. Logical errors can most easily be eliminated from short programs since the amount of material to check is limited. Each subprogram is debugged as it is written. Thus your debugging is always confined to relatively simple programs. We shall discuss the writing of these subprograms in the next chapter.

EXERCISES

1-1. Describe the functions of the components of a computer.

1-2. What is the difference between a machine language and an assembly language?

1-3. What is the difference between an assembly language and a high-level language?

1-4. What is a compiler?

1-5. What is a linker?

1-6. What is an interpreter?

1-7. What are the advantages and disadvantages of FORTH? Do the advantages outweigh the disadvantages?

1-8. Write a FORTH program that adds five numbers.

1-9. Write a FORTH program that performs the following operation

$$(3+4+5)6$$

1-10. Repeat Problem 1-9 for

$$(5+6+7+20+21)(8)(9)$$

1-11. Repeat Problem 1-9 writing the program using your editor. Run the program.

1-12. Repeat Problem 1-10 writing the program using your editor. Run the program.

Chapter 2

Basic FORTH Operations

This chapter will expand upon the FORTH procedures that were introduced in the first chapter, beginning with a discussion of basic arithmetic operations. The stack and stack manipulations shall also be considered. In Chapter 1 we introduced the idea of FORTH words or commands; in this chapter we shall discuss these ideas more fully and show you how to define your own FORTH words. This will let you break your program into a sequence of short subprograms. You should then be able to write relatively complex FORTH programs. Remember that in the body of the text (not in programs) we shall write FORTH words in boldface type. This will separate the FORTH words from the rest of the text.

2-1. ARITHMETIC OPERATIONS

In this section we shall consider the basic operations of addition, subtraction, multiplication, and division. In order to emphasize important concepts some of the material that was introduced in the last chapter will be repeated. Some convenient notation that illustrates the stack behavior will also be introduced.

Addition

Let's start by considering addition. The FORTH word that results in addition is **+**. As we discussed in the last chapter, **+** results in the two top numbers in the stack being popped off and their sum being pushed onto the stack. Let us see how we can indicate the stack. Suppose that there are three numbers n_3, n_2, and n_1, where

n_3 is on the top of the stack, n_2 is next, etc. This is illustrated in Figure 2-1. To represent this stack we simply write

$$n_1 \ n_2 \ n_3 \qquad\qquad\qquad\qquad\qquad\qquad (2\text{-}1)$$

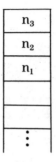

Figure 2-1. A stack containing three numbers.

Note that the stack is characterized by a sequence of numbers separated by blanks. *The rightmost character represents the top of the stack.* We can use this notation to characterize the + word.

$$n_1 \ n_2 \ \rightarrow \ n_{sum} \qquad\qquad\qquad\qquad\qquad (2\text{-}2)$$

where n_{sum} is the sum of n_1 and n_2. Relation (2-2) shows the stack before and after the operation, in this case +, is performed. The terms to the *left* of the arrow represent the stack *before* the FORTH word has been executed while the terms to the *right* of the arrow represent the stack *after* the FORTH word has been executed. The entire stack need not be shown, just the pertinent values. As an example, let us write a program that adds five numbers and prints their sum.

$$23 \ 45 \ 6 \ 78 \ 1 \ + \ + \ + \ + \ . \ (RETURN) \qquad\qquad (2\text{-}3)$$

The computer will respond with

153 ok

The stack, at various stages, is illustrated in Figure 2-2. In Figure 2-2a the stack is shown after 23, 45, 6, 78, and 1 have been pushed on, in that order. When the first (leftmost) + is executed, the top two numbers are popped off the stack and are replaced by their sum.

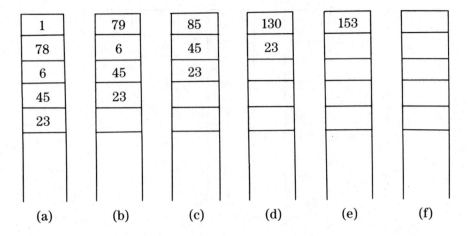

Figure 2-2. The stack for program (2-3) at various stages of execution. (a) after 23, 45, 6, 78, and 1 have been pushed on; (b) after the execution of the first +; (c) after the execution of the second +; (d) after the execution of third +; (e) after the execution of the fourth +; (f) after the execution of ..

Since two numbers are replaced by one, the remaining numbers are moved up the stack. This is illustrated in Figure 2-2b. In a similar way Figures 2-2c, 2-2d, and 2-2e show the stack after the execution of the second, third, and forth + words. Finally, the . word is executed, the result is printed, and the stack is empty, see Figure 2-2f. (This assumes that the stack was originally empty.)

Subtraction

The FORTH word that indicates subtraction is −. We can symbolically represent this by

$$n_1 \; n_2 \; \rightarrow \; n_{diff} \tag{2-4}$$

where n_{diff} is equal to n_1 minus n_2. Note that the number on the *top* of the stack is subtracted from the *second* number on the stack. For instance, a program that subtracts 3 from 5 and returns the result 2 is

$$5 \; 3 \; - \; . \; (RETURN) \tag{2-5}$$

The stack for various stages of this program is shown in Figure 2-3.

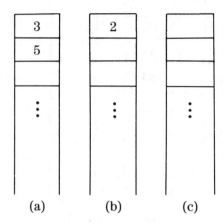

Figure 2-3. The stack for program (2-5) at various stages of execution. (a) after 5 and 3 are pushed onto the stack, in that order; (b) after the - is executed; (c) after the . (period) is executed.

The minus sign can be included with a number to indicate that it is negative. Note that in this case the minus sign is not the FORTH word for subtraction; it is "part" of the number. For instance, the program

    2 −5 − . (RETURN)   (2-6)

will result in the answer 7 being printed. Note that there is *no space* between the minus sign and the 5.

Remember that all the numbers that we are dealing with are integers. That is, they are whole numbers with no fractional parts. They must be written without commas or decimal points. The integers are restricted in magnitude. They must lie in the range between −32768 and 32767, inclusive. If your program calculates a number that does not lie in this range, a *wrong* answer will result. We shall consider procedures for working with numbers of greater magnitude in Chapter 5.

Multiplication

The FORTH word for multiplication is * which is the asterisk and in FORTH is pronounced times. When it is executed, the top two numbers on the stack are popped off and multiplied. Their product is then pushed onto the stack. This is symbolically indicated by

    n_1 n_2 → n_{prod} (2-7)

Here n_{prod} is the product of n_1 and n_2. Let us write a FORTH program that does the following arithmetic operation (5-3)24.

24 5 3 – * . (RETURN)   (2-8)

The stack for this program at various times during the execution is shown in Figure 2-4. In Figure 2-4a we illustrate the stack after 24, 5, and 3 have been pushed onto the stack, in that order. When the – is executed the top two numbers are popped off the stack and the number that was at the top of the stack is subtracted from the second one. The resulting 2 is pushed onto the stack, and 24 is moved up the stack since two numbers were popped off and only one was pushed on. This is shown in Figure 2-4b. When the * is executed, the top two numbers are popped off the stack and their product (48) is obtained. This number is then pushed onto the stack, see Figure 2-4c. Finally, when the . is executed the top number is popped off the stack and printed. The stack is then empty, see Figure 2-4d.

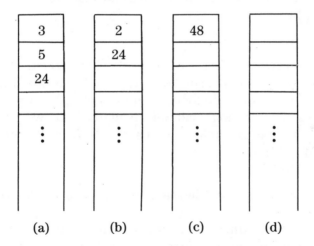

(a)   (b)   (c)   (d)

Figure 2-4. The stack for program (2-8); (a) after 24, 5, and 3 have been entered, in that order; (b) after - has been executed; (c) after * has been executed; (d) after . has been executed.

Division

Up to this point the fact that we were dealing with integers made the situation less complicated. However, the use of integers in division must be considered in detail. Let's consider $5/2 = 2.5$. The division of two integers can result in a noninteger answer. Let us see what happens in FORTH in such a case. The noninteger part will be *truncated*. That is, it is thrown away. For instance, the result of the above division problem in FORTH will be 2. The factor of $0.5 = 1/2$ is not lost because FORTH has a provision for obtaining the remainder, which in this case is 1. (There are ways of working with decimal fractions in FORTH and some systems actually work with numbers that have decimal points. We shall consider this in Chapter 5.) When we work with negative numbers the results are similar. For instance, suppose we have $-14/3 = -4 \ -2/3$. The result of the division is -4 and the $-2/3$ is truncated. The remainder is -2. If we consider the apparently equivalent division $14/(-3)$, somewhat different results are obtained. We can write $14/(-3) = -4 + (2/-3)$. In this case the truncated result of the division is still -4; however, the remainder is now 2. You should experiment with your system to see how it functions with negative numbers.

Actually we have not considered the FORTH command for division is is / which is pronounced divide. We can again represent the stack operation by

$$n_1 \ n_2 \ \rightarrow \ n_{quot} \tag{2-9}$$

Here the top two numbers are popped off the stack. The quotient n_1 divided by n_2 is then pushed onto the stack. The number that was *second* on the stack is divided by the number that was on the *top* of the stack. There is no remainder calculated here (we shall consider it after a simple example). Let us divide 5 by 3 and print the truncated quotient.

$$5 \ 3 \ / \ . \ (RETURN) \tag{2-10}$$

In Figure 2-5 we illustrate the stack for this program at various stages in its execution.

We have not obtained the remainder in the division problem. In fact the FORTH word / does not result in a remainder being computed. However, the FORTH command **MOD** does cause the remainder to be calculated. We can characterize it by the stack description

$$n_1 \ n_2 \ \rightarrow \ n_{rem} \tag{2-11}$$

In this case n_{rem} will be the remainder of the division n_1/n_2. (Remember that n_2 was at the top of the stack before the division.) The sign of n_{rem} will be the same as that of n_1, according to

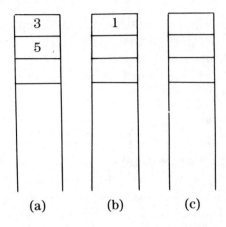

(a)   (b)   (c)

Figure 2-5. The stack for program (2-10). (a) after 5 and 3 have been entered, in that order; (b) after / has been executed; (c) after . has been executed.

FORTH-79. Let us now consider a FORTH program that obtains the remainder of the division problem 5/3.

5 3 MOD . (RETURN)   (2-12)

The stack, for various times during the execution of the program, is shown in Figure 2-6.

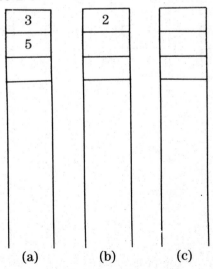

(a)   (b)   (c)

Figure 2-6. The stack for program (2-12). (a) after 5 and 3 have been entered, in that order; (b) after **MOD** has been executed; (c) after . has been executed.

Can we calculate *both* the quotient and the remainder? The answer is that there is FORTH word that leads to the calculation of both quantities. It is **/MOD** which is pronounced divide-mod. Note that there are no spaces in this word. When this word is executed the stack is characterized by

$$n_1 \; n_2 \rightarrow n_{rem} \; n_{quot} \tag{2-13}$$

Here we divide n_1 by n_2 and pop these numbers off the stack. The remainder n_{rem} and the quotient n_{quot} are pushed onto the stack. Note that, originally, n_2 was on the top of the stack and, after **/MOD** is executed, n_{quot} will be on the top of the stack. As an example we shall divide 5 by 3 and obtain the quotient and the remainder.

$$5 \; 3 \; /MOD \; . \; . \; (RETURN) \tag{2-14}$$

The stack at various times during the execution of the program is shown in Figure 2-7. Note that after **/MOD** is executed the quotient is printed and popped off the stack. The 2 is then moved up the stack. After the second . is executed the quotient is printed and popped off the stack. The 2 is then moved up the stack. After the second . is executed, the remainder is popped off the stack and printed.

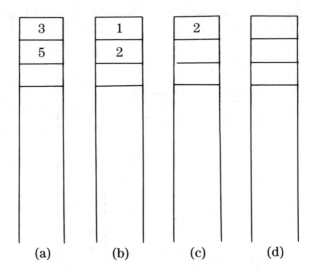

Figure 2-7. The stack for program (2-14). (a) after 5 and 3 have been entered, in that order; (b) after **/MOD** has been executed; (c) after the leftmost . has been executed; (d) after the second . has been executed.

Thus, after program (2-14) is run the following will be printed

1 2 ok

As a final example let us write a program that computes the quotient and remainder of $3016/(12 + 3 + 14)5$. (Note that the 5 is in the denominator.) The program is:

3016 5 14 3 12 + + * /MOD . . (RETURN)   (2-15)

The stack for various stages of execution is shown in Figure 2-8. In Figure 2-8a we show the stack after 3016, 5, 14, 3, and 12 have been pushed on, in that order. In Figure 2-8b the stack is shown after the top two numbers have been popped off and their sum 15 has been pushed on. Note that 14, 5, and 3016 have been moved up the stack. Figure 2-8c shows the stack after the second + has been executed. Figure 2-8d shows the stack after the top two numbers 29 and 5 have been popped off and their product has been pushed on to the top of the stack. Again note that 3016 has been moved up the stack. Figure 2-8f illustrates the stack after 145 and 3016 have been popped off and /**MOD** is executed. The remainder 116 and the quotient 20 are pushed onto the stack, with the quotient on top. Figures 2-8e and 2-8f illustrate the stack after the first and second periods, respectively, have been executed. In this case, the result that is displayed on your terminal is

20 116 ok

Note the order in which the data is entered. We want to add 12, 3, and 14. Next we want to multiply this sum by 5 and, finally, we want to divide 3016 by the result of the previous calculation. We want 3016, therefore, on the bottom of the stack, since it is to be used last. Hence, the 3016 is entered first so that it is pushed down the stack as other data is entered. Similarly, the 5 is to be used next-to-the-last, so it is entered second. Then, 14, 3, and 12 are entered. Now consider the FORTH commmands. In the execution of the program, we start by obtaining the sum of the three top numbers on the stack. Thus we start with two + words. Next, we want to multiply this sum by 5. Hence, the * is the next FORTH word. The next arithmetic operation we perform is /**MOD**. Therefore, this FORTH word is next. Finally, we conclude with two periods which display the two numbers which are the result of this program.

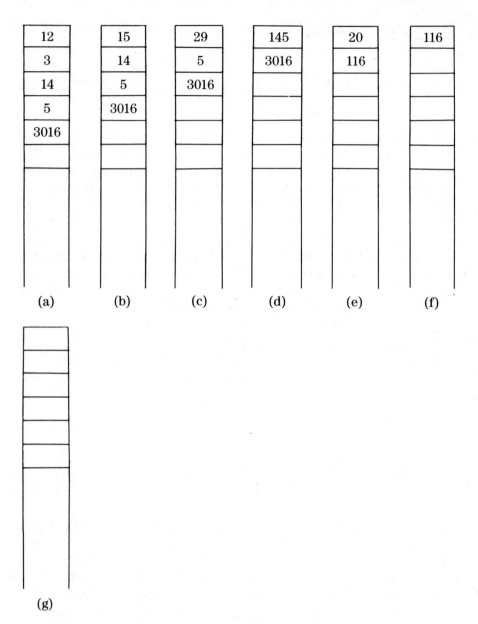

Figure 2-8. The stack for program (2-15). (a) after 3016, 5, 14, 3, and 12 have been entered, in that order; (b) after the first; (leftmost) + has been executed; (c) after the second + has been executed; (d) after * has been executed; (e) after /**MOD** has been executed; (f) after the leftmost . has been executed; (g) after the second . has been executed.

2-2. STACK MANIPULATION

In this section we shall discuss some FORTH words that allow us to manipulate the stack. Let's consider some reasons why we might want to perform such manipulations. Suppose that we want to print the top item without removing it from the stack. We cannot do this using only the FORTH words that have been introduced so far. Also, we cannot perform the operation $(12+3+4)*5/6$ using the previously developed FORTH words unless we intermix data and symbols. This can be done, but it makes it impossible to define our own FORTH word to perform the operation. (This will be discussed in the next section.) It may seem as though this operation could be easily performed without mixing data and symbols. However, on attempting it, we soon find that the 6 cannot be placed on top of the stack and so we cannot perform the required division. We need to know how to manipulate the stack.

DUP—A word that duplicates the top number on the stack is **DUP** (which is pronounced dupe). The stack operation is described by

$$n \rightarrow n \ n \qquad\qquad (2\text{-}16)$$

As an example Figure 2-9 illustrates the stack for various stages in the execution of

$$5 \ 6 \ 9 \ DUP \ (RETURN) \qquad\qquad (2\text{-}17)$$

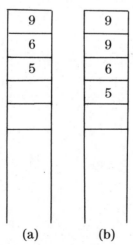

Figure 2-9. The stack for program (2-17); (a) after 5, 6, and 9 have been entered, in that order; (b) after **DUP** has been executed..

Suppose that we want to print the top number on the stack, without removing it from the stack. The following will accomplish this:

DUP . (RETURN)   (2-18)

Note that **DUP** causes the top number to be duplicated. Then, when .is executed the duplicated top number is popped off and printed. Thus, the top number on the stack has been printed without changing the stack.

DROP—The FORTH word **DROP** causes the top item on the stack to be popped off. All the other numbers on the stack are moved up one position. **DROP** can be characterized by the stack relation

n →   (2-19)

In Figure 2-10 the stack is illustrated at various stages in the execution of

2 5 1 DROP (RETURN)   (2-20)

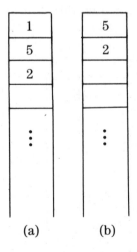

(a)   (b)

Figure 2-10. The stack for program (2-20). (a) after 2, 5, and 1 have been entered, in that order; (b) after **DROP** has been executed.

It may seem as though there is no real use for **DROP**, but we shall demonstrate its use soon.

There are cases where a program will continuously add numbers to the stack. This can be disastrous. The stack represents a set of memory locations. If you keep adding items to the stack it will eventually become full. If you attempt to add more items to the stack these will be stored in memory locations *not reserved for the stack*. This is called *stack overflow*. It is possible that you will then write over the memory locations that contain the FORTH system, in which case, computation will cease. Often, your only recourse in such cases is to "boot" the system. All the data that you have entered may then be lost. The **DROP** word should be used to remove unneeded data from the stack, reducing its size, and thereby avoiding stack overflow.

SWAP—The FORTH word **SWAP** causes the top two items on the stack to be interchanged. The stack relation that describes the **SWAP** by computing the quotient and remainder for the expression $(12+3+14)5/6$. A FORTH program that accomplishes this is

6 5 14 3 12 + + * SWAP /MOD . . (RETURN)   (2-22)

The stack at various stages during the operation of this program is shown in Figure 2-11. This follows the details of previously discussed programs. Look at Figures 2-11d and 2-11e. The **SWAP** word has caused the top two items on the stack to be interchanged. Note that **SWAP** only affects the top *two* items on the stack. If there are more than two numbers on the stack, **SWAP** will still only affect the top two numbers.

OVER—Another useful stack manipulating word is **OVER**. This *duplicates* the second number on the stack onto the top of the stack. **OVER** is described by the stack relation

$n_1 \ n_2 \rightarrow n_1 \ n_2 \ n_1$ (2-23)

The following illustrates the use of the FORTH word **OVER**.

2 3 4 5 OVER (RETURN)   (2-24)

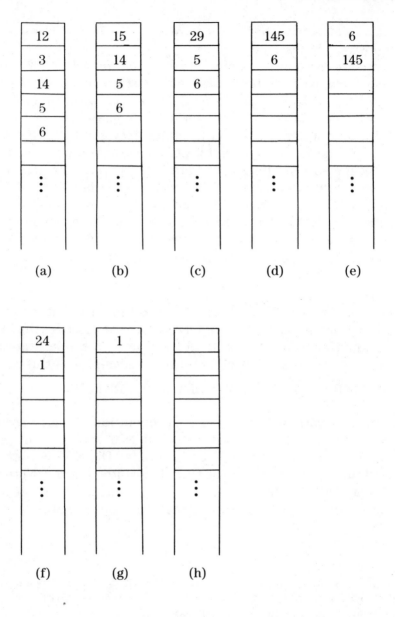

Figure 2-11. The stack for program (2-22). (a) after 6, 5, 14, 3, and 12 have been entered, in that order; (b) after the first + has been executed; (c) after the second + has been executed; (d) after * has been executed; (e) after **SWAP** has been executed; (f) after /**MOD** has been executed; (g) after the first . has been executed; (h) after the second . has been executed.

Figure 2-12 shows the stack at various stages during the execution of program (2-24). We shall consider other examples of the word **OVER** later.

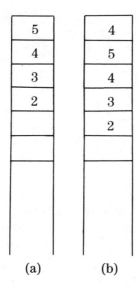

(a)   (b)

Figure 2-12. The stack for program (2-24). (a) after 2, 3, 4 and 5 have been entered, in that order; (b) after **OVER** has been executed.

PICK—PICK is a generalized form of **OVER**. **PICK** allows you to *duplicate* any number on the stack as the top item in the stack. When PICK is executed, the number that is on the top of the stack is popped off. This popped number determines which number is to be duplicated, from the *remaining* stack. We can illustrate this with the stack relation

$$n_1 \rightarrow n_{n_1} \tag{2-25}$$

Let us illustrate the use of **PICK** with the following program

$$32 \ 345 \ 567 \ 189 \ 764 \ 3 \ \text{PICK (RETURN)} \tag{2-26}$$

The stack during various stages of the execution is illustrated in Figure 2-13. The number 3 on the top of the stack is popped off when **PICK** is executed. A number equal to the third item on the *remaining* stack is then pushed onto the top of the stack. The top

3		567
764		764
189		189
567		567
345		345
32		32
(a)		(b)

Figure 2-13. The stack for program (2-26). (a) after 32, 345, 567, 189, 764, and 3 have been entered, in that order; (b) after **PICK** has been executed.

number on the stack is used by the word **PICK** and thus, does not "count" as part of the stack. Note that **2 PICK** is equivalent to **OVER**.

ROT—The FORTH command **ROT**, which is pronounced rote, moves the third item on the stack to the top of the stack. This is characterized by the stack relation

$$n_1\ n_2\ n_3\ \rightarrow\ n_2\ n_3\ n_1 \qquad\qquad (2\text{-}27)$$

Let us illustrate **ROT** with the following program

$$23\ \ 45\ \ 11\ \ 34\ \ 55\ \ \text{ROT}\ \ (\text{RETURN}) \qquad\qquad (2\text{-}28)$$

In Figure 2-14 the stack is shown at various stages during the execution of this program. In Figure 2-14a we have the stack after 23, 45, 11, 34, and 55 have been entered. In Figure 2-14b we show the stack after **ROT** has been executed. Note that the third number has been removed and pushed onto the top of the stack. There is no duplication of numbers, and the amount of numbers on the stack is unchanged.

ROLL—The word **ROLL** is a generalization of **ROT**. You can use **ROLL** to move any number on the stack to the top. There is no

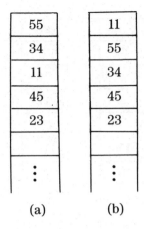

Figure 2-14. The stack for program (2-28). (a) after 23, 45, 11, 34, and 55 have been entered, in that order; (b) after **ROT** has been executed.

duplication here. When **ROLL** is executed, the number on the top of the stack is popped off and that number determines which item of the remaining stack is to be brought to the top. The stack relation that characterizes the **ROLL** command is

$$n_1 \rightarrow n_{n_2} \tag{2-29}$$

ROLL is illustrated by the following program

41 456 23 17 56 34 4 ROLL (ENTER)   (2-30)

The stack during various stagers of operation is shown in Figure 2-15. Figure 2-15a is a picture of the stack after 41, 456, 23, 17, 56, 34, and 4 have been pushed on, in that order. In Figure 2-15b we illustrate the stack after **ROLL** has been executed. The number on the top of the stack, 4 in this case, is popped off the stack and controls the **ROLL** operation. The fourth number in the remaining stack, 23, is moved to the top position, and the resulting space is closed up. Note that **3 ROLL** is equivalent to **ROT**.

DEPTH—There are times when we want to know how many numbers there are in the stack. The FORTH command **DEPTH** pushes a number that supplies this information onto the top of the stack. The number that is pushed does not "count itself."

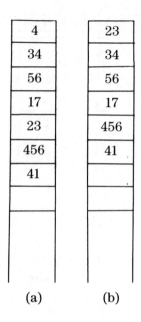

4	23
34	34
56	56
17	17
23	456
456	41
41	

(a)   (b)

Figure 2-15. The stack for program (2-30). (a) after 41, 456, 23, 17, 56, 34, and 4 have been entered, in that order; (b) after **ROLL** has been executed.

The stack relation is

$$\rightarrow \quad n_{depth} \tag{2-31}$$

Note that n_{depth} gives the depth of the stack before n_{depth} was pushed onto the stack. Let us illustrate the use of **DEPTH** with the following sequence of operation

```
23  46  57  (RETURN)
52  437  56  78  (RETURN)
DEPTH .  (RETURN)
```
(2-32)

The stack at various times in the operation is shown in Figure 2-16. We start by entering 23, 46, and 57, in that order. The resulting stack is shown in Figure 2-16a. Next 52, 437, 56, and 78 are entered, in that order. The numbers that were on the stack are pushed farther down and the result is shown in Figure 2-16b. Next **DEPTH** is executed. Since there are seven numbers on the stack a 7 is pushed onto the stack, see Figure 2-16c. Finally the . causes the 7 to be

57		78		7		78
46		56		78		56
23		437		56		437
		52		437		52
		57		52		57
		46		57		46
		23		46		23
				23		
:		:		:		:
(a)		(b)		(c)		(d)

Figure 2-16. The stack for program (2-30). (a) after 23, 46, and 57 have been entered, in that order; (b) after 523, 437, 56, and 78 have been entered, in that order; (c) after **DEPTH** has been executed; (d) after . has been executed.

popped off the stack and appear on your terminal. The resulting stack is shown in Figure 2-16d. Note that Figures 2-16b and 2-16d are identical. That is, executing **DEPTH** and then printing the depth of the stack leaves the stack unchanged.

2-3. WRITING FORTH WORDS

We have, thus far considered FORTH words that are supplied with almost any FORTH system. One of the most important aspects of FORTH is that you can write *your own* words and add them to the FORTH language. In this section, the writing of FORTH commands will be discussed. We shall then be in a position to write more complex programs.

The FORTH commands : and ; are used to define your own FORTH words. Let's illustrate this with an example. We'll write a FORTH word called, **ADD3**, that adds three numbers and then prints the resulting sum. To do this we type

   : ADD3 + + . ; (RETURN)   (2-33)

Let's take a close look at what we've just done. We started with the command : which is *followed by a space*. This is followed by the name of the FORTH word that we are defining, in this case **ADD3**. After this the desired operations are typed, separated by one or more spaces. Then we typed a space followed by ;. Once the operations indicated by (2-33) are performed, **ADD3** is a FORTH word. When we subsequently type

ADD3 (RETURN)   (2-34)

it is as though we typed all the text following the FORTH name that we defined, up to but not including the semicolon. Note that when we define a FORTH word, it ends with a space ;. Note that the semicolon is separated from the rest of the work by a blank space. When we define a word as in (2-33), the operation is called a *colon definition*. Now we can use **ADD3** just as any other FORTH word. If we reboot the system **ADD3** will be lost. We could retype (2-33) again to add **ADD3** to the system. It would be better to use the editor to store the word-defining statement (2-33) into a block. Then, whenever that block is loaded, **ADD3** will become part of the FORTH system.

Now suppose we type

27 34 56 ADD3 (RETURN)   (2-35)

This is equivalent to typing

27 34 56 + + . (RETURN)   (2-36)

In either case the result

117 ok

will appear on your terminal. Note that when you define your own word you must begin with a : followed by a space and you must end with a space;.

You can use either the words that are present when your FORTH system is booted, or words that you have defined yourself when defining *additional* words. Any word that is used in a new colon definition must be part of the FORTH system for the new word to be compiled or executed. Note that a FORTH word is compiled when its defining block is loaded. (Compiled words are added to the FORTH language.) Similarly, a FORTH command is also compiled when you colon-define it from your terminal. For instance if you type (2-33), **ADD3** will be compiled when you type **RETURN**.

If you use your own words to define other words you must first have made them a part of your FORTH system. For instance, if one of your words is defined in a block, then that block must be loaded before you attempt to use the word. The information in any one block is loaded in the order that it is written on the block. Thus, you can define two words in a block and the second word can use the first one. Incidentally, most FORTH systems are such that a basic set of words is included every time that you boot the system. However, blocks with specialized words, called *extension words*, are often included also. These specialized words are *not* included into the FORTH system on during booting. If you wish to use these specialized words, either by themselves or in words that you define, you must load the blocks that contain the specialized words. These words are just like words that you define yourself.

A FORTH program usually consists of many self-defined words. One word uses, or *calls*, one or more previously defined words, which may in turn use other words. This is one reason why FORTH is called a *threaded* language. Each individual colon definition should be kept relatively short so that it can be easily debugged.

As an illustration let us write a program that computes the value of the following expression for various values of x.

$$3x^4 + 2x^3 + 5x^2 + 2x + 4 \qquad\qquad (2\text{-}37)$$

The listing of the FORTH program is shown in Figure 2-17. Look at the numbers from 0 to 15. They are called *line numbers* and are

```
0  ( SQUARE, CUBE, FOURTH, AND POLYNOMIAL )
1  : SQUARE DUP * ;
2  : CUBE DUP    SQUARE  *  ;
3  : FOURTH  DUP      CUBE    *   ;
4
5  : POLYNOMIAL    DUP DUP DUP
6                  FOURTH 3 *
7                  SWAP CUBE 2 * +
8                  SWAP SQUARE 5 * +
9                  SWAP 2 * +
10                 4 + . ;
11
12
13
14
15
```

Figure 2-17. A FORTH program that evaluates the polynomial (2-37) for various values of x; words **SQUARE**, **CUBE**, and **FOURTH** are also defined there.

not part of the FORTH program. In fact, you may not see them when you write or edit your program. However, the numbers are printed when you list the block on which you are working. For example if this program were on block 115, then

115 LIST   (2-38)

would produce the listing in Figure 2-17. The line numbers allow you to discuss the program more easily.

Now let's discuss the program in Figure 2-17. Line 0 is called a *comment*. It is ignored by the FORTH system. The only purpose of comments is to provide information to the programmer or to other readers. Comments explain the program to you or to other readers. Comments can be very helpful when you come back to a program that you have not worked with for some time. Comments can be included at any point in a FORTH word or program. To write a comment, type a left parenthesis (followed by a *space*. All material up to, and including the next right parenthesis) will be ignored when the program is compiled.

Now consider line 1. Here we define a FORTH command called **SQUARE,** which squares the number on the top of the stack. (The square of x is written x^2 and is equal to x times x). **SQUARE** starts by duplicating the number that is on the top of the stack. Then the top two numbers are popped off the stack and multiplied by themselves. The resulting square is then pushed onto the stack.

Now consider line 2 of Figure 2-17. Here we define the word **CUBE** that causes the number on the top of the stack to be popped off and be replaced by its cube. (That is, it is multiplied by itself three times.) The first operation duplicates the number on the top of the stack. Now **SQUARE** is run. The number on the top of the stack is now the square of the original number. Note that **SQUARE** does not change the rest of the stack. The second number in the stack is the original number. Then when * is executed, these two numbers are popped off the stack and multiplied. The resulting cube of the original number is pushed onto the stack.

Now consider line 3 of Figure 2-17. The word **FOURTH** causes the number on the top of the stack to be popped off and be replaced by its fourth power. The operation of **FOURTH** is very similar to that of **CUBE** except that **FOURTH** uses **CUBE** in the same way that **CUBE** used **SQUARE**.

Notice that we have left line 4 blank. As far as the FORTH compiler is concerned, one blank or a sequence of many blanks are the same, in that they simply serve as a delimiter. Blanks are included in programs to improve the readability for humans. For instance, as long as we separated them by at least one blank, we could have squeezed the subprograms for **SQUARE, CUBE,** and **FOURTH,** onto two lines. The FORTH compiler does not care about readability and it treats a sequence of lines, in one or more blocks, as continuous text. Thus, extra spaces are not needed. However, *spaces should be included to make the program readable.* This is an important debugging tool. In fact, it helps to prevent errors.

In line 5 of Figure 2-17 we define the command **POLYNOMIAL**, which is used to evaluate expression (2-37) with $x = 5$, we would type

5 POLYNOMIAL   (2-39)

Now consider **POLYNOMIAL**. We start by duplicating the number on the top of the stack three times. Thus the number in question is in the top *four* positions of the stack. We execute **FOURTH** and the number on the top of the stack is popped off and replaced by its fourth power. Next 3 is pushed onto the stack. The top two numbers are popped off and their product is pushed on the stack. Thus, the number on the top of the stack is $3x^4$. Next, in line 7 we execute a **SWAP**. The original number is brought to the top of the stack. Then **CUBE** is executed so that x^3 is now at the top of the stack. Now 2 is pushed onto the stack and * is executed. At this point $2x^3$ is on the top of the stack and $3x^4$ is the second number on the stack. When the + is executed, these two numbers are popped off the stack and their sum $3x^4 + 2x^3$ is pushed on. Note that the second number on the stack is now equal to the original number. In line 8 we again execute a **SWAP** which brings the original number to the top of the stack. When **SQUARE** is executed this number is popped off the stack and is replaced by its square. Now 5 is pushed onto the stack and * is executed. Thus, $5x^2$ is on the top of the stack. When + is executed the top two numbers are popped off the stack and are replaced by their sum, $3x^4 + 2x^3 + 5x^2$. In line 9 a **SWAP** is executed again bringing the original number to the top of the stack. It is multiplied by 2 and added to the second number on the stack. Finally, in line 10 we add 4 to obtain the final answer and the result is printed.

After the block in Figure 2-17 is loaded we can use not only the command **POLYNOMIAL**, but we can also use **CUBE, SQUARE,** and **FOURTH**. For instance, if we type

5 CUBE . (RETURN)

the terminal will output

125 ok

Remember that *once the block represented by Figure 2-17 is loaded,*
we can use the FORTH words defined there in the same way as any
other FORTH word.

2-4. MORE ON FORTH WORDS

In the last section we discussed the basic ideas involved in writing
FORTH commands. In this section we shall consider some additional
details about FORTH words. Every FORTH word that can be used
(i.e., one that is in the system from the start or one that you have
loaded) is stored in the main memory of the computer. The
instructions for each individual word are stored in a sequence of
consecutive memory locations. The amount of memory occupied
by a FORTH word depends upon its complexity. Every time that you
execute a FORTH word, the program's control is directed by the
instructions for that word stored in the computer's memory. These
instructions are stored in an area of memory which in FORTH is
called the *dictionary.* Each *entry* in the dictionary contains a
number of items. In addition to the instructions for a particular word,
each entry contains a representation of the name of that word. This
is how the word is identified. In addition, the dictionary entry also
contains the starting address for the word that was compiled just
prior to the one in question. The FORTH system only "remembers"
the address of the dictionary entry for the last word that was
compiled. It may seem as though the system would only find the
last dictionary entry. However, remember that each item in the
dictionary also contains the address of the previous entry. When
you execute a FORTH word, the system checks the name part of
the last dictionary entry to see if its name is the same as the word
being executed. If it is, then control of the program is transferred
to the instructions for that word. If the word to be executed is not
the same as the word specified in the last dictionary entry, then
the next-to-last dictionary entry (whose memory address is specified
in the last dictionary entry) is checked to see if its name is the same
as that of the word being executed. The dictionary is searched
backward in this way until the desired word is found. This is called
a *dictionary search.* If the word is not in the dictionary, then an
error message will be printed and compilation will cease. It may seem
as though a dictionary search would take a long time, but actually

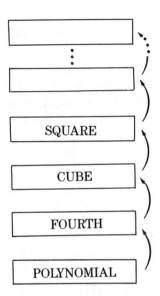

Figure 2-18. A representation of the dictionary.

it is very fast. In Figure 2-18 we show a representation for part of
the dictionary when the block of Figure 2-17 is loaded. Note that
POLYNOMIAL is the last entry and **FOURTH** is the next to last
entry. **CUBE** is the entry before **FOURTH**, etc. When the FORTH
system is executing a program, it encounters both words and data.
This is how FORTH distinguishes between a word and data. Data
is not a FORTH word.

Every time that a word definition is encountered, a new dictionary
entry is made. The FORTH system dictionary will warn you about
duplication, however, it will tolerate duplicate names. If you are
careful, duplicate words can be managed. They can also be a
problem. Let us consider some of the aspects of duplicate words.
Suppose that we are working on the block of Figure 2-17, which
we assume is BLOCK 115, Let us assume that, when the program
was written, there were bugs. We would edit the block and then
load it again. Each time that we do this, new definitions for
SQUARE, CUBE, FOURTH, and **POLYNOMIAL** would be put into
the dictionary. This would not bother us because we would always
reference the definition that was used last. Thus, if we ignored the
messages about duplicate words we could proceed with our
programming. There is, however, a problem that could occur. Suppose

that we have a great deal of trouble debugging the program. We
might have to edit it many times. This would result in BLOCK 115's
being loaded many times. This could cause the dictionary, which
contains all the instructions, to become very large. We might run
out of dictionary space and overwrite part of the FORTH system,
causing computation to cease. If we are debugging, then there are
errors in the programs. Hence, much of the stored material is garbage.
We would like to remove entries from the dictionary and free the
memory used by these words. The FORTH word **FORGET** allows us
to do this. For instance, suppose that BLOCK 115 (see Figure 2-17)
has been loaded. If we now type

FORGET POLYNOMIAL   (2-40)

The word **POLYNOMIAL** would be removed from the dictionary and
the memory occupied by that word's instructions would be free for
other use.

The word **FORGET** is more powerful than we have indicated. If
the FORTH system forgets a word it also forgets all the words that
were defined *after* that word. For instance, if the block for Figure
2-17 is loaded and we type

FORGET CUBE   (2-41)

the words **CUBE, FOURTH,** and **POLYNOMIAL** will be forgotten.
When you are debugging a block it is a good idea to forget all the
words of the block each time you reload it. This can be done
automatically if you add two items to the block. We illustrate this
in Figure 2-19 where Figure 2-17 has been appropriately modified.

```
0  ( SQUARE, CUBE, FOURTH, AND POLYNOMIAL ) FORGET FOO : FOO ;
1  : SQUARE DUP * ;
2  : CUBE DUP    SQUARE  * ;
3  : FOURTH  DUP     CUBE   * ;
4
5  : POLYNOMIAL    DUP DUP DUP
6                  FOURTH 3 *
7                  SWAP CUBE 2 * +
8                  SWAP SQUARE 5 * +
9                  SWAP 2 * +
10                 4 + . ;
11
12
13
14
15
```

Figure 2-19. A modification of Figure 2-17 that causes previously loaded
versions to be "forgotten"; is useful for debugging.

The first two instructions in the block are now

FORGET FOO   (2-42a)

: FOO ;   (2-42b)

In (2-42b) we define a word called **FOO** that does nothing. However, a dictionary entry will be made for **FOO** and some very simple instructions for **FOO** will be set up in memory. The first instruction is to **FORGET FOO**. Hence, if the block had been loaded previously, now the entire block would be forgotten. The first time that you attempt to load the block an error will occur, since there is no word **FOO** to forget. Thus, before you load the block for the *first* time enter

: FOO ; (RETURN)   (2-43)

Now load the block. **FOO** will be forgotten and a new word **FOO** will be established. The next time that you load the block, the instruction **FORGET FOO** will cause the old words to be forgotten. Thus, we will not have the problem of the dictionary and memory being filled with garbage. Note that the only time that you enter (2-43) is before you load the block for the *first* time. Once the program is debugged you can edit the block to remove the **FORGET FOO** and : **FOO** ;.

The word **FORGET** has other uses. Often, when working with a small computer, the program becomes too big for the memory and will not run. With most languages you must then shorten your program or reduce the amount of data it uses. FORTH provides another alternative. You may be able to write your program so words that are used in the beginning of the program are not used at the end of the program. Then you write the program so that only those words that are used at the beginning of the program are loaded. Thus, not too much memory is used. These initially loaded words are used to compute intermediate data. Once this is done, the **FORGET** command can be used to remove the unneeded words from the dictionary and from memory, making that memory available for other use. The remainder of the program is then loaded and the computation is completed. All of this can be done by instructions within your FORTH program and the person running the program need not be concerned with it. For instance, you could load a particular block which contains only those words that are used first. The last instructions on the block could be a **FORGET** and a **LOAD** for the next block. Hence, the old words would be forgotten and the new ones would be loaded. This procedure uses the disk, or tape, storage to effectively increase the size of the main memory. It is called using an *overlay* and the disk or tape is called a *virtual memory*. If we attempt to use a similar technique with other programming languages, it becomes very cumbersome. You would actually have to write separate programs and run them separately. The intermediate data would have to be stored on separate disk or tape files, in most cases. Thus, the person running the program would have to be concerned with these details.

To illustrate the effect of duplicate names, and to further understand dictionary operations, study the FORTH program in Figure 2-20. There are two defined words with the name **TEST1**.

```
0 ( AN ILLUSTRATION OF DUPLICATE NAMES  )
1 : TEST1   2 .   ;
2 : RUNNER1   TEST1   3 .   TEST1   ;
3 : TEST1   4 . ;
4 : RUNNER2   TEST1   TEST1   RUNNER1   TEST1   TEST1   ;
5
6
7
8
9
10
11
12
13
14
15
```

Figure 2-20. An illustration of duplicate names.

For illustrative purposes we have used very simple words. In line 1 we define **TEST1** which simply prints 2. In line 2 we define the word **RUNNER1** that calls **TEST1**, prints 3, and then calls **TEST1** again. In line 3 we define a new word that is also called **TEST1** which prints 4. We can tell which **TEST1** is being executed by noting whether 2 or 4 is printed. Finally, in line 4 we define the word **RUNNER2** that calls **TEST1** twice, calls **RUNNER1**, and then calls **TEST1** twice again. When the block of Figure 2-20 is loaded, line 1 is loaded first, then line 2, etc. If we execute **TEST1** by typing

TEST1 (RETURN)   (2-44)

a 4 will be ouput. That is, the last **TEST1** entry in the dictionary is that from line 3 of Figure 2-20. This will be the *first* dictionary entry that is found when a dictionary search is conducted.

Now suppose that we execute **RUNNER2**. The output will be

4 4 2 3 2 4 4   (2-45)

Note that when **RUNNER1** is executed as part of the word **RUNNER2** it calls on **TEST1**. Now the first **TEST1** is executed. This results in the printing of 2. While **RUNNER1** is being executed, all dictionary searches begin with the word that was defined just *before* **RUNNER1** was compiled. Thus, the first **TEST1** will be executed. On the other hand, when **RUNNER2** is executed, it also calls on **TEST1** after the execution of **RUNNER1** is *completed*. These result in two 4's being printed. That is, once the execution of **RUNNER1** is completed, the dictionary searches begin with the word defined just before **RUNNER2** was compiled. If we type **FORGET TEST1** then it would be as if only lines 0 to 2 of Figure 2-20 existed. Then, when **TEST1** is executed, a 2 would be ouput.

The word FORGET applies to all dictionary entries. For instance, you can type FORGET + . Be careful, if you do things like that your FORTH system may lose most of its memory and you may have to reboot the system to recover it.

2-5. SOME ADDITIONAL STACK MANIPULATION WORDS

In this section we shall introduce some additional stack manipulation words that can be helpful at times. These commands are similar to those that were introduced in Section 2-2 except that they will operate on two stack locations at a time. Let us consider the background of these words. In Section 2-1 we discussed that integers were constrained to lie between − 32768 and 32767. Usually, each of these integers are stored in two memory words, each of which has eight bits. This assumes that we are working with an eight-bit memory word computer. In such cases, FORTH automatically works with two memory words and, as far as the programmer is concerned, the two words are a single entity. For instance, when we discuss an integer stored on the stack, we only consider one stack location, although there are actually two memory words used for each stack location. There are times when we want to work with integers whose magnitudes are greater than 32767. FORTH does have provisions for working with integers that have much larger magnitudes. These are called *double-length* or *double-precision* integers. Each double-length integer occupies two consecutive stack locations. If we want to manipulate the stack and it contains some double-length integers,

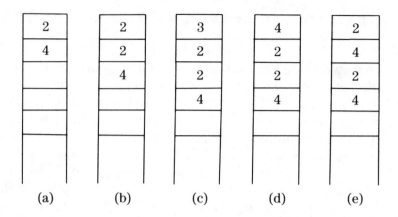

(a)　　　　(b)　　　　(c)　　　　(d)　　　　(e)

Figure 2-21. The stack at various stages during the execution of (2-48). (a) after 4 and 2 have been pushed on, in that order; (b) after **DUP** has been executed; (c) after 3 has been pushed on the stack; (d) after **PICK** has been executed; (e) after **SWAP** has been executed.

we must manipulate a pair of stack locations. For instance, to **DROP** a double-length integer we must apply the **DROP** twice. Double-length integers will be discussed in detail in Chapter 5. The stack manipulation that involve a pair of stack locations are also convenient when dealing with single-length integers. The words that manipulate pairs of integers will usually not be loaded when you boot your system. With most FORTH systems, there will be part of the extension word set that can be used by loading the appropriate block.

　　2DUP—The word that duplicates the top pair of integers is **2DUP** which is pronounced two-dupe. The stack operation is characterized by

$$n_1 \ n_2 \ \rightarrow \ n_1 \ n_2 \ n_1 \ n_2 \qquad\qquad (2\text{-}46)$$

Double-length integers are represented by the letter d just as single-length integers are represented by the letter n. So, we can write relation (2-46) as

$$d \ \rightarrow \ d \ d \qquad\qquad (2\text{-}47)$$

If we compare (2-47) with (2-16), we see that they are the same except that n has been replaced by d. If we wanted to write our own 2DUP we could do it in the following way

: 2DUP DUP 3 PICK SWAP ;   (2-48)

In Figure 2-21 we illustrate the operation

4 2 2DUP   (2-49)

The FORTH word **2DROP** drops the top two single-length integers from the stack. It is characterized by the stack relation

$n_1 \; n_2 \; \rightarrow$ (2-50)

In terms of double-length integers this can be written as

$d \rightarrow$ (2-51)

2SWAP—The FORTH command **2SWAP** interchanges the top two double-length integers. In terms of single-length integers we can write

$n_1 \; n_2 \; n_3 \; n_4 \; \rightarrow \; n_3 \; n_4 \; n_1 \; n_2$ (2-52)

If we want to write our own **2SWAP**, we can do it in the following way

: 2SWAP ROT 4 ROLL SWAP ;   (2-54)

In Figure 2-22 we illustrate the stack at various stages in the execution of

8 17 9 7 2SWAP   (2-55)

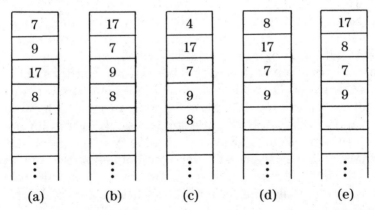

(a)   (b)   (c)   (d)   (e)

Figure 2-22. The stack at various stages in the execution of (2-55). (a) after 8, 17, 9, and 7 have been pushed on, in that order; (b) after **ROT** has been executed; (c) after 4 has been pushed on the stack; (d) after **ROLL** has been executed; (e) after **SWAP** has been executed.

Note that the functions that come with the FORTH system may execute somewhat more rapidly than the ones that we write here.

2ROT—The FORTH word **2ROT** (which is pronounced two-rote) moves the third double-length integer to the top of the stack. In terms of single-length integers we can write

$$n_1 \ n_2 \ n_3 \ n_4 \ n_5 \ n_6 \ \rightarrow \ n_3 \ n_4 \ n_5 \ n_6 \ n_1 \ n_2 \qquad (2\text{-}56)$$

In terms of double-length words we have·

$$d_1 \ d_2 \ d_3 \ \rightarrow \ d_2 \ d_3 \ d_1 \qquad (2\text{-}57)$$

2OVER—The FORTH word **2OVER** duplicates the second double-length integer to the top of the stack. The stack relation, in terms of single-length integers, is

$$n_1 \ n_2 \ n_3 \ n_4 \ \rightarrow \ n_1 \ n_2 \ n_3 \ n_4 \ n_1 \ n_2 \qquad (2\text{-}58)$$

In terms of double-length integers, the stack relation is

$$d_1 \ d_2 \ \rightarrow \ d_1 \ d_2 \ d_1 \qquad (2\text{-}59)$$

Note that all the double-length stack manipulation words introduced in this section are analagous to single-length stack manipulations, which were introduced in Section 2-2.

2-6. THE RETURN STACK

The stack that we have been discussing is actually called the *parameter stack* or the *data stack*, since it stores the parameters or data that the program uses. Most FORTH programmers refer to the parameter stack as the stack. There is also another stack, called the *return stack*. This stack is used by the FORTH system to keep track of its operations. If the return stack is disrupted, computation ceases and you must reboot the system, possibly losing all your data. There are some FORTH words that allow you to manipulate the return stack. It may seem as though you should not used these words since you might lose your system. However, if certain rules are obeyed, you can use the return stack without adversely affecting operations.

The FORTH system does not use the return stack while it is executing one of your own FORTH words. (We shall modify this statement subsequently. However, it is true for all the words that we have discussed so far.) Thus, you can manipulate the return stack as part of your own word *provided that the return stack is returned to its original condition before the execution of your word is completed.*

FORTH programmers use the return stack to temporarily hold data. For instance, suppose that you want to multiply the fifth number in the stack by 7. You could use a **ROLL** to bring the fifth number to the top of the stack and then multiply it by 7. However, you would then have to go through a sequence of operations to get the resulting product back to the fifth position. On the other hand, if you could pop the first four numbers off the stack and store then somewhere, then the fifth number would come to the top of the stack and could be multiplied by 7. The four stored numbers could then be taken from their storage place and pushed back onto the stack. The return stack is often used for the storage space in this type of operation. We shall now consider two FORTH words that allow words to be moved from the stack to the return stack and vice versa. Note that the return stack is a LIFO stack (see Section 1-4). That is, the return stack functions in the same way as does the regular (i.e., parameter) stack.

>R—The FORTH command **>R** (which is pronounced to-R) pops the top word off the stack and pushes it onto the return stack. We can indicate this stack manipulation by the relation

$$n \rightarrow \qquad\qquad (2\text{-}60)$$

In Figure 2-23 an example of the stack and the return stack is shown before and after **>R** is executed. Note that, in our figures we will show the return stack with double lines along its sides.

R>—The FORTH word **R>** (which is pronounced R-from) pops the top number off the return stack and pushes it onto the stack. Note that **R>** is the converse of **>R**. The stack relation is

$$\rightarrow n \qquad\qquad (2\text{-}61)$$

In Figure 2-24 we show the stack and the return stack before and after **R>** is executed. When you write your own FORTH word, there must be an equal number of **>R**'s and **R>**'s in that word. Up to this point, the execution of all our programs has flown in a clear sequence. In subsequent chapters we shall discuss procedures that will allow programs to branch or take different paths. You must be extremely careful to ensure that in each word you define yourself,

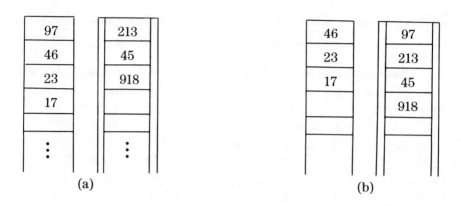

Figure 2-23. (a) The stack and the return stack; (b) the same stacks after >R is executed; note that the sides of the return stack are drawn with double lines.

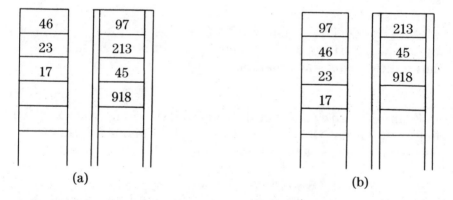

Figure 2-24. (a) the stack and the return stack; (b) the same stacks after R> is executed.

the number of >R's that are executed is the same as the number of R>'s that are executed. In a following chapter we shall discuss nested structures that can lie *within* a word. The number of >R's and R>'s within *each* such nested structure must be equal.
We shall now write a command that multiplies the fifth number on the stack by 7.

: FIVMULT7 >R >R >R >R 7 * R> R> R> R> ;   (2-62)

We start by popping the first four numbers off the stack and pushing them onto the return stack. Then 7 is pushed onto the stack and * is executed. Thus the fifth number on the original stack has been multiplied by 7. Next the top four numbers on the return stack are popped off and pushed onto the stack. The stack is now unchanged except that the fifth integer has been multiplied by 7.

We shall now consider some instructions that copy a number from the return stack and push it onto the stack. These instructions do *not* modify the return stack, so we do not have to take the same precautions that we do with **R>** and **>R**.

R@ or I—The command **R@** (which is pronounced R-fetch) duplicates the number on the top of the return stack onto the top of the stack. The return stack is *unaffected* by this operation. The number is pushed onto the stack. The stack relation is

→ nretl   (2-63)

In Figure 2-25 we illustrate a stack and return stack before and after **R@** has been executed. In some FORTH systems, including MMSFORTH, the word **I** can be used interchangeably with **R@**. According to the FORTH-79 I should only be used to obtain a DO LOOP index. We shall discuss this in Chapter 4. (Note that some FORTH systems may require the **I** rather than the **R@**.)

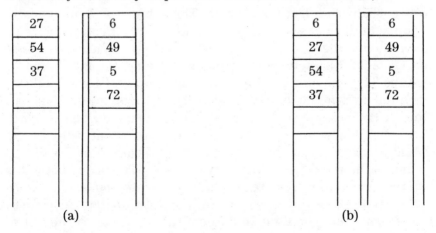

(a)   (b)

Figure 2-25. (a) The stack and the return stack; (b) the same stacks after **R@** is executed.

I'—The FORTH command **I'** (pronounced I-prime) duplicates the second number on the return stack to the top of the stack. The return stack is unaffected by this operation. This is characterized by the stack relation

$$\rightarrow \quad n_{ret2} \qquad\qquad\qquad\qquad (2\text{-}64)$$

Note that **I'** is not part of FORTH-79. It is implemented by MMSFORTH and by other FORTH systems.

J—The FORTH word **J** duplicates the third number on the return stack to the top of the stack. The return stack is unchanged by this procedure. The stack relation that characterizes this is

$$\rightarrow \quad n_{ret3} \qquad\qquad\qquad\qquad (2\text{-}65)$$

Although this is not part of FORTH-79, it is implemented by MMSFORTH and other FORTH systems. Both **I'** and **J** may be implemented in the FORTH-79 in conjunction with DO LOOP. We shall discuss this in Chapter 4.

Let's use some of these instructions to rewrite **POLYNOMIAL** (see Figure 2-17). The modified form is shown in Figure 2-26. We assume here that **SQUARE**, **CUBE**, and **FOURTH**, see Figure 2-17, have been made part of your FORTH system. Remember that we execute **POLYNOMIAL** for x = 5 by entering

5 POLYNOMIAL

Now consider line 1 of Figure 2-26. The value of x, 5 in this case, is popped off the stack and pushed onto the return stack. Then in line 2 the number 5 is duplicated from the top of the return stack to the stack. It is then operated on by **FOURTH** and multiplied by 3. Thus $3x^4$ is now on the top of the stack. In line 4 we duplicate the number from the top of the return stack to the top of the stack. Now **CUBE** is executed; 2 is pushed on the stack; then * is executed. $3x^4 + 2x^3$ is now on the top of the stack. Note that many of the details of operation are the same as those for Figure 2-17. The details of lines 4, 5, and 6 follow the previous ones. The desired result is printed when the * is executed. Now, *before ending the word* **POLYNOMIAL** we must remove any modification that we made to the return stack. The **R>** in line 7 pops the top value off the return stack and pushes it onto the stack. The return stack is as it was before we started. We could end the word **POLYNOMIAL** here but that would leave the stack with the value (5 in this case) that was just pushed on. It is best not to do this to avoid cluttering the stack. Thus we add the **DROP** in line 7. Now we terminate the word.

```
0  ( ALTERNATE POLYNOMIAL )
1  : POLYNOMIAL >R
2                  R@ FOURTH 3 *
3                  R@ CUBE 2 *  +
4                  R@ SQUARE 5 *  +
5                  R@ 2 *  +
6                  4 + .
7                  R>   DROP    ;
8
9
10
11
12
13
14
15
```

Figure 2-26. A modification of the word **POLYNOMIAL** that was defined in Figure 2-17. It is assumed that **SQUARE**, **CUBE**, and **FOURTH** have been made part of the FORTH system.

2-7. SOME ADDITIONAL ARITHMETIC WORDS

We shall now consider some additional FORTH words that are used to perform mathematical operations. There are some simple arithmetic operations that are used so often that standard FORTH words have been written for them.

1+—The word **1+** pops the top number off the stack, adds 1 to it, and then pushes the sum onto the stack. The stack relation is

$$n \rightarrow n+1 \tag{2-66}$$

If we wanted to write our own **1+** it could have the form

$$; 1+ \ 1 \ + \ ; \tag{2-67}$$

Note that the **1+** commands execute more rapidly than the one that we have written ourselves because it is written in machine language.

1 – –the FORTH word **1 –** pops the top number from the stack, subtracts 1 from it, and pushes the result onto the stack. The stack relation is

$$n \rightarrow n-1 \qquad (2\text{-}68)$$

2 + –The FORTH word **2 +** pops the top number from the stack, adds 2 to it, and pushes the sum onto the stack. The stack relation is

$$n \rightarrow n+2 \qquad (2\text{-}69)$$

2 – –the FORTH word **2 –** pops the top number from the stack, subtracts two from it, and pushes the difference onto the stack. The stack relation is

$$n \rightarrow n-2 \qquad (2\text{-}70)$$

2* –The FORTH command **2*** (pronounced two-times) pops the top number from the stack, multiplies it by two, and pushes the resulting product onto the stack. The stack relation that characterizes this is

$$n \rightarrow n*2 \qquad (2\text{-}71)$$

Although this word is not, as yet, part of FORTH-79, it is implemented in MMSFORTH and in other FORTH systems.

2/ –The word **2/** which is pronounced two-divide, pops the top number from the stack, divides it by two, and pushes the resulting quotient onto the stack. The stack relation is

$$n \rightarrow n/2 \qquad (2\text{-}72)$$

Note that there is no **MOD** form of this word. This word is not, as yet, part of FORTH-79 but it is implemented in MMSFORTH and in other FORTH systems.

16* –The FORTH command **16*** (pronounced sixteen-times) pops the top number off the stack, multiplies it by 16, and pushes the product onto the stack. The stack relation is

$$n \rightarrow n*16 \qquad (2\text{-}73)$$

This command is not part of FORTH-79, but it is implemented in MMSFORTH and in FORTH systems.

We shall now consider some words that manipulate pairs of numbers. In general, two numbers will be popped off the stack and the result of the operation will be pushed onto the stack.

MIN—The FORTH word **MIN** pops the two numbers off the stack and pushes the smaller one onto the stack. The stack relation is

$$n_1 \ n_2 \ \rightarrow \ n_{min} \tag{2-74}$$

For instance 2 3 MIN . (RETURN) will result in a 2 appearing on the screen. Similarly 4 − 30 MIN . (RETURN) will result in − 30. In either of these cases, the stack will be empty after the . is executed.

MAX—The command **MAX** pops the top two numbers off the stack and then pushes the larger one onto the stack. The stack relation is

$$n_1 \ n_2 \ \rightarrow \ n_{max} \tag{2-75}$$

We shall now consider two FORTH words that operate on the top number in the stack. In each case that number is popped off the stack and replaced by another number.

NEGATE—The word **NEGATE** pops the top number off the stack, multiplies it by − 1 and pushes the product onto the stack. The stack relation is

$$n \ \rightarrow \ -n \tag{2-76}$$

For instance, if we enter

$$6 \ \text{NEGATE} \ . \ (\text{RETURN}) \tag{2-77}$$

the answer − 6 will be printed. After the . is executed the stack will be empty, provided that it was empty before the operation was begun.

ABS—The FORTH word **ABS** (pronounced absolute) pops the top number off the stack and obtains its *absolute value*. This is then pushed onto the stack. Note that the absolute value of a positive number is simply that number. The absolute value of a negative number is the number multiplied by − 1. The stack relation that characterizes this is

$$n \ \rightarrow \ |n| \tag{2-78}$$

For example, if we enter

-6 ABS . (ENTER)   (2-79)

The result 6 will be printed. At this point the stack will be empty
if there were no other numbers on the stack prior to the operation.

Random Numbers

There are times when we want to simulate a random occurrence
such as throwing a single die or tossing a coin. In the case of the
single die we would want numbers from 1 to 6 to be generated in
a random manner. In the case of a coin we would want the numbers
0 or 1 (or any two numbers) to be generated randomly. In general,
we might want a sequence of numbers, in some specified range, to
be generated randomly. There are computer programs that generate
what *appears* to be a random sequence of numbers. These are
actually not random, but, for most purposes, they suffice. Such
sequences of numbers are called *pseudorandom*. FORTH-79 does
not have a provision for generating random numbers but some
FORTH systems do. We shall discuss the words provided by
MMSFORTH that are concerned with random number generation.

RND—The FORTH word **RND** pops the top number n_1, off the stack
and generates a pseudorandom number n_2 which lies between 1 and
n_1. The stack relation is

$$n_1 \rightarrow n_2 \qquad\qquad\qquad\qquad (2\text{-}80)$$

For instance, 24 **RND** (RETURN) will result in 24 being popped off
the stack and a random number between 1 and 24 being pushed
onto the stack.

The random number generator program uses a particular number
called a *seed number* to generate a sequence of numbers that appears
to be random. If we change the seed number, we change the
sequence produced by the random number generator.

SEED—In order to change the seed number we must use two
FORTH words: one is **SEED** and the other is the exclamation point
!. They are used in the sequence **SEED** !. Note the space. We shall
discuss the significance of the word ! in Chapter 6. For the time being
we shall treat the sequence of the two words **SEED** ! as if it were
a single word. The FORTH word **SEED** ! pops the top number off

the stack and makes it the seed number for the random number generator. The stack relation for the sequence **SEED** ! is

$$n \rightarrow \hspace{8cm} (2\text{-}81).$$

For instance 10 **SEED** ! (RETURN) changes the seed number to 10. We might want to change the seed number in a random way. This can be accomplished by using **RND** to push a random number onto the stack and then using **SEED** ! to pop that number off the stack and make it the new seed number. There is a command that carries out all of these steps. When the word **RN1** is executed, the next random number is generated and used as a seed number. The stack is unaffected by this operation.

The seed number determines the sequence of pseudorandom numbers that is generated. The sequence will always be the same if the seed number is the same. In general, this sequence may be very long but finite and it will always start at the same point. That means that if you write a game program that uses **RND**, it will always play the same way. It would be desirable to vary the point at which you start in the sequnce. There is a FORTH word that accomplishes this.

RANDOMIZE—The word **RANDOMIZE** does not use a number from the stack. Whenever **RANDOMIZE** is executed, it changes your location in the random number sequence. Thus if you execute **RANDOMIZE**, your sequence will start at a different point and thus appear to be different.

Change of Number Base

People who are not concerned with the details of machine language work with the *decimal* system of numbers. This uses the digits from 0 to 9, and is called a base 10 number system. Computers use the *binary* or base 2 system. All numbers that are stored or used by your computer are in base 2. However, the numbers that are input or output are converted to base 10. FORTH allows you to modify this conversion so that you can work in a base other than base 10. Many machine language programmers use base 8 (called *octal*) or base 16 (called *hexadecimal*). You can set up your FORTH system so that the input/output is in another base. (If you are not familiar with other bases, you can skip this material. It is not necessary to know about number bases to understand FORTH.) The words we discussed here are not, as yet, part of FORTH-79. However, they may be in the future. They are implemented in MMSFORTH and in other FORTH systems.

HEX—The word **HEX** changes the base of the input/output numbers to hexadecimal. **HEX** does not modify the stack. Note that **HEX** does not change the values of any numbers that are stored in the stack or elsewhere in the memory. **HEX** only affects input and output. The word **HEX** should be executed by itself. If it is executed as part of your own FORTH word, then that word should not input any numerical data.

DECIMAL—The FORTH command **DECIMAL** functions exactly as **HEX**—except the base is made 10. When your FORTH system boots up you will operate in base 10.

OCTAL—The word **OCTAL** converts the system to base 8, otherwise it operates the same as **HEX**.

BASE—(The word **BASE** that is discussed here is used in conjunction with the FORTH word **!**. Some FORTH systems, such as MMSFORTH, allow you to set the base for input/output at something other than 10, 8, or 16. Two FORTH words used in sequence will accomplish this. They are **BASE !**. This sequence pops the top number off the stack and makes it the number base for input/output. The stack relation is

$$n \rightarrow \qquad\qquad\qquad\qquad\qquad\qquad (2\text{-}82)$$

For instance, 16 **BASE !** is equivalent to **HEX**.

EXERCISES

In the following exercises check all programs and user-written FORTH words by running them on your computer.

2-1. Write a FORTH program that performs the following operations
$$3 + 4 + 5 - 6$$

2-2. Repeat Problem 2-1 for
$$(3 + 4 + 18 - 25)*5$$

2-3. Repeat Problem 2-1 for
$(3+19-4)/6$.

2-4. Write a FORTH program that finds the quotient and
remainder for the following function.
$(3+4+6)/7$

2-5. Repeat Problem 2-4 for
$(3+4*6)/7$

2-6. Write a FORTH program that multiplies the number on
top of the stack by 5, prints the answer, and leaves the
original number on the top of the stack.

2-7. Discuss a use for the word **DROP**.

2-8. Repeat Problem 2-4 for
$(4+5-6*3)/7$
Do not intermix data and FORTH words.

2-9. Compare the FORTH words **OVER** and **PICK**.

2-10. Compare the FORTH words **ROT** and **ROLL**.

2-11. Write a FORTH program that prints the number of items
on the stack.

2-12. Discuss the procedure for writing your own FORTH
words.

2-13. Write your own FORTH command that adds the top four
numbers on the stack and then prints the result.

2-14. Repeat Problem 2-13 leaving the stack unchanged after
the word is executed.

2-15. Write a FORTH word that obtains the average of the first
five numbers on the top of the stack. Print both the
quotient and the remainder.

2-16. Write a FORTH program that allows you to evaluate

$$6x^5 + 3x^4 + 2x^3 - 21x^2 - 17x + 5$$

for different values of x

2-17. Write a FORTH word that allows you to evaluate

$$ax^3 + b$$

for different values of a, b, and x.

2-18. Write a FORTH word that allows you to evaluatae

$$ax^3 + bx^2 + cx + d$$

for different values of a, b, c, d, and x.

2-19. Discuss the FORTH dictionary.

2-20. Discuss the FORTH word **FORGET**.

2-21. Discuss how **FORGET** should be used when you are debugging a program.

2-22. What is meant by a double-length integer?

2-23. Compare the FORTH words **DUP** and **2DUP**.

2-24. Write your own FORTH word that implements **2DROP**.

2-25. Write your own FORTH word that implements **2ROT**.

2-26. Write your own FORTH word that implements **2OVER**.

2-27. What is the primary function of the return stack?

2-28. What problems can arise if you use the return stack in your own FORTH commands? How can you avoid these problems?

2-29. Write a FORTH word that multiplies the first five numbers on the stack by five but does not otherwise change the stack. Use the return stack in your program.

2-30. Why do you have to exercise much more care when you use >R and R< than when you use R@?

2-31. Discuss the FORTH words I, I, and J.

2-32. Repeat Problem 2-18, but now use the return stack.

2-33. Why is it desirable to use **DROP** to remove any unneeded data from the stack?

2-34. Use the FORTH words introduced in Section 2-7 to write a FORTH word that adds 1 to the number on the top of the stack and then doubles the result.

2-35. Write a FORTH word that prints out the smallest of the top four numbers on the stack.

2-36. Repeat Problem 2-35 leaving the stack undisturbed.

2-37. Repeat Problem 2-35 finding the largest number.

2-38. Repeat Problem 2-36 finding the largest number.

2-39. Repeat Problem 2-35 finding the largest magnitude.

2-40. Repeat Problem 2-36 finding the largest magnitude.

2-41. Repeat Problem 2-35 finding the smallest magnitude.

2-42. Repeat Problem 2-36 finding the smallest magnitude.

2-43. Compare the FORTH commands **NEGATE** and **ABS**.

2-44. What is a random number?

2-45. What is a seed?

2-46. Write a FORTH word that generates a random number between 1 and 55.

2-47. Write a FORTH command that converts a decimal number to hexadecimal.

2-48. Repeat Problem 2-46 converting the number to octal.

2-49. Write a FORTH word that takes five numbers in hexadecimal and prints their sum in both hexadecimal and decimal.

Chapter 3

Basic Input and Output

So far only the FORTH word . has been used to output numeric data to the screen of our terminal. In this chapter we shall extend our ideas of data input and output. We shall consider FORTH commands that allow us to print text (words). Such text can be used to explain the numeric data and to make it more readable. In addition, text can be used to prompt the user to supply the needed input data. This is a great help when the person running the program is not an experienced programmer. Procedures that will make numeric output more readable will also be discussed.

3-1. PRINTING OF TEXT

We shall now consider some FORTH words that will allow us to output text to the video screen of the terminal. For instance, suppose that we run a program that takes the sum of four numbers, the output could contain the text SUM IS to explain it. If we had a program that printed a table of values, it would be desirable to print text to provide the headings for the table.

." and "—The FORTH word ." (pronounced dot-quote) and the symbol " (pronounced quote) are used to print text. For instance if we enter

   ." LET US PRINT TEXT" (RETURN)   (3-1)

then the following will appear on your screen.

   LET US PRINT TEXT ok   (3-2)

Note that there is a *space* following the word ."', just as a space
follows every FORTH word. All of the text following the space after
the word ."' will be printed on the screen. These words do not affect
the stack. Before considering a more involved example, we shall
discuss some additional FORTH words.

#IN—The FORTH command **#IN** which is pronounced number-in,
results in the following operation. When **#IN** is executed,
computation ceases and a ? is printed on the screen of your terminal.
You then enter an integer in the range −32768 to 32767 followed
by RETURN. The integer that you entered is pushed onto the stack
and then computation proceeds. The word **#IN** is not part of
FORTH-79, but it is provided by MMSFORTH and similar words may
be provided by other FORTH systems.

CR—The FORTH word **CR** causes a carriage return and a line feed
to occur. That is, any additional material will be printed at the
beginning of the *next* line. If there are two **CR** words, then an
additional line will be skipped, and so forth. The word **CR** does not
affect the stack.

QUIT—There are times when, for appearance's sake, we do not
want the word ok to be printed on the screen. This will be
accomplished if the last FORTH word in your program is **QUIT**. The
program will terminate and the FORTH system will be ready to
accept new input, but ok will not be printed. The word **QUIT** clears
the return stack, but does not alter the stack.

PAGE—Often, when running a program, we want to clear all the
material from the screen. In this way your program can run on a
"clean page." The FORTH word **PAGE** clears the screen. It does not
affect the stack. (**PAGE** is not part of FORTH-79. It is part of
MMSFORTH.)

To illustrate the use of the words that we have introduced here
let us write a program that obtains the sum of four numbers. This
will differ from the other programs in one important respect. We
shall assume that the program is to be run by a person who is not
familiar with FORTH. Thus, instead of expecting him or her to put
data on the stack, the program will ask for the data and, after the
results have been computed, explain the information that is printed.

The program is shown in Figure 3-1. The screen for a typical run is shown in Figure 3-2.

```
0  ( AN ILLUSTRATION OF TEXT WITH INPUT AND OUTPUT)
1  : ADD4      PAGE
2             ." ENTER FOUR NUMBERS TO BE ADDED WHEN PROMPTED BY ? "
3             CR    ." FOLLOW EACH NUMBER BY RETURN "      CR
4             #IN  #IN  #IN  #IN       CR
5             + + +
6             ." THE SUM OF THE FOUR NUMBERS IS "       CR
7             .    QUIT    ;
8
9
10
11
12
13
14
15
```

Figure 3-1. A program that prints prompting text to request input and also prints text with the output.

```
ENTER FOUR NUMBERS TO BE ADDED WHEN PROMPTED BY ?
FOLLOW EACH NUMBER BY RETURN
 ? 4 ? 5 ? 6 ? 7
THE SUM OF THE FOUR NUMBERS IS
22
```

Figure 3-2. A sample of the screen after **ADD4** of Figure 3-1 is run.

Consider this program. In line 1 we establish the name of the word we are defining. It is **ADD4**. **PAGE** then clears the screen. Line 2 uses the word ." and the symbol " to cause "ENTER FOUR NUMBERS TO BE ADDED WHEN PROMPTED BY ?" to appear on your screen. The first word in line 3 is **CR**. This causes the subsequent material to be printed on the next line. Then the ." and " cause "FOLLOW EACH NUMBER BY RETURN" to appear on your screen. The next **CR** causes any subsequent material to appear on the next line. Each **#IN** of line 4 causes a ? to be output on the screen. Computation then pauses after each ? until the required data is entered. In response to each prompt the user of the program types in an integer followed by RETURN. These four numbers are pushed onto the stack in the order in which they are entered. That is, the number that is entered last will be on the top of the stack. The three

+ words, in line 5, result in the four numbers being removed from the stack and their sum being pushed onto the stack. Line 6 results in "THE SUM OF THE FOUR NUMBERS IS" being printed. The **CR** causes the subsequent output to appear on the next line. The word . in line 7 causes the sum to be printed. **QUIT** terminates the operation.

SPACE—Sometimes we want to insert a space in text. The FORTH word **SPACE** accomplishes this. That is, the word **SPACE** is equivalent to ." ". **SPACE** can be used to position data on the screen as well as in text. We shall consider other ways of positioning data subsequently. **SPACE** does not alter the stack.

SPACES—The FORTH word **SPACES** pops the top number off the stack and outputs that number of spaces. The stack relation is

$$n \rightarrow \tag{3-3}$$

For example

$$6 \ 10 \ 5 \ . \ \text{SPACES} \ . \ (\text{RETURN}) \tag{3-4}$$

would result in the output

$$5 \qquad\qquad 6 \ \text{ok} \tag{3-5}$$

Note that there are 10 spaces between the 5 and 6.

PTC—There are times when we want to print information at a particular point on the screen. There is a mark or *cursor* that indicates this point when you are putting in data. When you output data, the cursor, which may not actually be printed, indicates the point on the screen where the printing is to take place. The word **PTC** (pronounced put-cursor) allows you to position the cursor. The screen is divided into rows and columns. **PTC** pops the top two numbers off the stack; the number that was on the top of the stack specifies the column, the number that was second on the stack specifies the row. Consult your operating manual to determine how many rows and columns your screen has. Do not exceed these numbers. The stack relation is

$$n_1 \ n_2 \rightarrow \tag{3-6}$$

For example if we input the following

$$10 \ 6 \ \text{PTC} \ ." \ \text{WELCOME} \ " \tag{3-7}$$

then WELCOME will be printed on line 10 starting in column 6. The word **PTC** is not part of FORTH-79; however, it is provided in MMSFORTH.

Printed Output

We have, thus far, assumed that the output was to the screen of your terminal. If you have a printer, the output can be directed to it. There are no FORTH-79 words that accomplish this, but most FORTH systems have words that allow you to have the output printed by your printer. We shall introduce some words here that are provided in the MMSFORTH system. These words, or similar ones, may be made part of the FORTH-79 language.

PRINT—The word **PRINT** causes the output that normally would be sent to the screen to be sent to the printer. **PRINT** does not alter the stack. When you enter data it is normally printed on the screen. Depending on your system, **PRINT** may not affect such input. It will still appear on the screen and not be output on the printer. However, the result of the program will be sent to the printer and will not appear on the screen.

PCRT—The FORTH word **PCRT** functions in the same way as **PRINT** except that the output *also* appears on the screen. **PCRT** does not alter the stack. Note that **PCRT** does not alter the screen of your terminal, but in addition, it causes output to be sent to the printer.

You should not use the words **PRINT** or **PCRT** if there is no printer in your system. If you do this, your system will probably "hang up" and you will be forced to reboot it.

CRT—The MMSFORTH command **CRT** cancels the effect of **PCRT** or **PRINT**. After **CRT** is executed, the printer is deactivated and all the output is to the terminal.

Most of the commands that we have discussed in this section produce a corresponding output if a printer is used. For instance, **PAGE** will cause the printer to advance the paper to the start of the next page. There will be variation from system to system and some words may not work with all systems. You should experiment with the instructions in this section to see how they function with your printer.

3-2. THE ASCII CODE

All information that the computer uses is in the form of binary numbers. However, letters and other symbols are also used. For instance, we enter FORTH words, and text information is output to the video screen or printer. The computer is able to work with symbols becuase each one is given a numerical code. The input and output devices can generate or receive these codes. For instance, suppose that the code for a letter A is 65. When you press the key for the letter A on your keyboard, 65, in a binary form, is sent to the computer. Similarly, if the computer is to output an A, it actually outputs a 65, in binary form. The terminal or printer then decodes that number and prints the letter A.

If computers are to function with terminals and printers from various manufacturers, then they all must use the same code for characters. Although there are several codes in use, the most popular one is called the ASCII code. ASCII (pronounced ask-key) stands for American Standard Code for Information Interchange. The ASCII code is given in Table 3-1.

Table 3-1. ASCII CODE					
Decimal Value	Character	Decimal Value	Character	Decimal Value	Character
0	NUL	47	/	94	△
1	SOH	48	0	95	—
2	STX	49	1	96	[
3	ETX	50	2	97	a
4	EOT	51	3	98	b
5	ENQ	52	4	99	c
6	ACK	52	5	100	d
7	BEL	54	6	101	e
8	BS	55	7	102	f
9	HT	56	8	103	g
10	LF	57	9	104	h
11	VT	58	:	105	i
12	FF	59	;	106	j
13	CR	60	<	107	k
14	SO	61	=	108	l
15	SI	62	>	109	m
16	DLE	63	?	110	n
17	DC1	64	@	111	o

18	DC2	65	A	112	p
19	DC3	66	B	113	q
20	DC4	67	C	114	r
21	NAK	68	D	115	s
22	SYN	69	E	116	t
23	ETB	70	F	117	u
24	CAN	71	G	118	v
25	EM	72	H	119	w
26	SUB	73	I	120	x
27	ESC	74	J	121	y
28	FS	75	K	122	z
29	GS	76	L	123	{
30	RS	77	M	124	|
31	US	78	N	125	}
32	space	79	O	126	~
33	!	80	P	127	DEL
34	"	81	Q		
35	#	82	R		
36	$	83	S		
37	%	84	T		
38	&	85	U		
39	'	86	V		
40	(	87	W		
41	)	88	X		
42	*	89	Y		
43	+	90	Z		
44	,	91	[		
45	–	92	\		
46	.	93	]		

There are ASCII codes for items that are not symbols. The first 26 ASCII codes are also the codes for the *control characters*. These can be generated from most terminals by pressing the control key and the key for a letter at the same time. Control A has an ASCII code of 1, control B has an ASCII code of 2, etc. The first 26 ASCII codes have other meanings also. For instance ASCII 8 represents a backspace. (Thus control H also represents backspace.) ASCII 10 represents a line feed. ASCII 13 represents a carriage return. ASCII 12 represents a form feed; it will advance the printer to the start of the next page. (This assumes that your printer can respond to such signals.) ASCII 27 represents escape. Sequences of ASCII codes that begin with 27 are called *escape codes*. These are often used to control sophisticated printers. The ASCII codes for the digits 0 to 9 are not the numbers 0 to 9 but are 48 through 57.

ASCII codes were originally used for teletypewriter communication. Many of the control codes were used to control this communication. The next section shows how these codes can be used in conjunction with computer output.

3-3. FORMATTED NUMBERS

In this section we shall discuss how we can control the appearance of the numerical data that is output by the computer to make it more understandable. This process is called *formatting* the numerical output.

Numbers in Fields

A specific number of spaces can be allocated to a number when it is printed. These spaces constitute a *field*. FORTH *right justifies* or *right adjusts* numbers in fields. That means that they are printed all the way over to the right. If we specify a field to be 10 spaces wide, and we print a 3 digit positive number in that field, then 7 blanks will appear to the left of the number.

.R—The FORTH command that allows us to specify a numeric field for printing is **.R** (pronounced dot-r). This word uses the top two numbers on the stack. They are popped off—the number that was on top specifies the field width, while the number that was second on the stack is the number that is actually printed. The stack relation is

$$n_1 \ n_2 \ \rightarrow \qquad\qquad\qquad\qquad (3\text{-}8)$$

For instance, if we enter

$$23 \ 10 \ 7 \ 10 \ .R \ .R \ (\text{RETURN}) \qquad\qquad (3\text{-}9)$$

the output will be as shown in Figure 3-3 where the empty boxes represent blank spaces. Both 23 and 7 are printed right justified in fields whose width is 10. We could specify different field widths for each number.

By specifying field widths we can space the numbers as necessary to make the output more readable. Usually we compute the output number. Thus, when we begin, we may not know how many digits

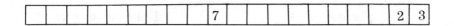

Figure 3-3. An illustration of two integers, each printed in a field 10 spaces wide.

it has. It is possible that the number has more digits than the specified field width. In this case FORTH automatically increases the field width to accommodate the number. Note that **.R** is not, at present, a part of FORTH-79. It is provided on MMSFORTH and other FORTH systems.

As an example we will write our own word that outputs numbers in fields that are 15 spaces wide.

    : .15 15 .R ;   (3-10)

The name of our word is **.15**. It starts by pushing 15 onto the stack; then **.R** is executed. Thus, the number that was originally on the top of the stack is printed in a field 15 spaces wide.

Pictured Numeric Output

Often, when we print numeric data, we would like to include symbols within the number. For instance, we might print a decimal point, or commas. FORTH has a provisiion for doing this; it is called *pictured numeric output*. We must use several words to utilize this feature. These will be presented in this section.

Before starting the discussion of pictured numeric output we shall digress and discuss double-length numbers. These numbers were introduced in Section 2-5. Manipulations using these numbers will be introduced in a subsequent chapter. Here we shall discuss some facts that are necessary for pictured numeric output. The basic pictured numeric output instructions only work with double-length numbers. (For the time being assume that the numbers are positive.) We would, at this time, like to use these manipulations with single-length numbers. Let us see how this can be done. A single-length number is stored in a single stack location while a double-length number is stored in two consecutive stack locations. This is illustrated in Figure 3-4. Note that we have labeled the top stack position of Figure 3-4b as MSB, which stands for *most significant bits*. Similarly the second stack position is labeled LSB, which stands for *least significant bits*. If we were working with a decimal number

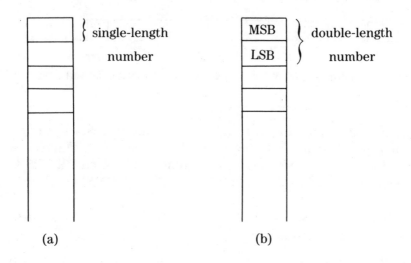

Figure 3-4. The stack. (a) with a single-length integer; (b) with a double-length integer.

we would speak of most significant digits and least significant digits. For instance, consider the decimal integer 356789. Its three most significant digits are 356 and its three least significant digits are 789. Now suppose that we have the 3-digit integer 789 and we want to write it as a 6-digit integer whose value is still equal to 789. We can do this by writing the number as 000789. That is, we make the three most significant digits 0. Now suppose that we have a single-length positive integer on the top of the stack and we want to convert it to a double-length integer. We can accomplish this simply by pushing 0 onto the stack. Now we have a double-length integer whose most significant bits are all 0. Thus it is numerically equal to the single-length integer. This applies only if the number is positive.

Most computers use the binary number system where the most significant bit (each digit of a binary number is called a bit) of a number is used to signify if it is positive or negative. If we have a negative number, then simply pushing a 0 onto the stack will give us the *wrong* double-length integer. To work with numbers that might be either positive or negative the following procedure could be implemented. Use **DUP** to duplicate the single-length number on the stack. Then execute **ABS** so that the top number on the stack is replaced by its magnitude. If we push 0 onto the stack, the correct magnitude double-length number will be stored in the top two stack positions. The single-length number that is in the third stack position can then be used to determine the proper sign. We shall illustrate this procedure later in this section. Let us now consider some FORTH commands that allow us to utilize pictured numeric output.

<# and #>—The FORTH commands <# (pronounced less-number or less-sharp) and #> (pronounced number-greater or sharp-greater) are used for pictured numeric output. Some other words must be introduced before we can provide an example of their use. However, here are some general ideas. The form for the use of these words is

$$<\# \text{ formatting instructions } \#> \qquad (3\text{-}11)$$

When an instruction in the form of (3-11) is executed, the double-length number that is on top of the stack is popped off. The formatting instructions produce a sequence, or *string,* of ASCII codes. Each one represents a single digit of the number or other desired output, such as a decimal point. After the entire instruction in the form of (3-11) is executed, the ASCII codes would not be stored on the stack but would be stored in consecutive memory locations in the main memory. Two single-length integers are then pushed onto the stack when (3-11) is executed. One gives the starting memory address where the ASCII codes are stored; the second integer will equal the number of ASCII codes that were stored (i.e., the number of characters that are to be printed). This number will be on the top of the stack. The stack relation is

$$n_1 \ n_2 \ \rightarrow \ n_{addr} \ n_{length} \qquad (3\text{-}12a)$$

in terms of single-length integers, where n_1 was the original single-length integer and n_2 was zero. For double-length integers this relation is

$$d \rightarrow n_{addr} \ n_{length} \qquad (3\text{-}12b)$$

Now consider (3-11). The instructions are scanned from left to right. The first instruction will apply to the rightmost digit of the number. The second instruction will apply to second digit from the right, etc. (The instructions do not necessarily have to apply to digits of the number. We can add other symbols such as decimal points.) Now let us consider FORTH commands that can be used as instructions.

#—The word # (Pronounced number sign or sharp) is used to manipulate *single* digits. For instance, in an instruction in the form of (3-11) the double-length integer that is on the top of the stack will eventually be converted into a sequence of ASCII codes, one for each digit. (If the output is decimal then these digits will be decimal digits. If **HEX** has been executed, then these are hexadecimal digits, etc.) For this discussion assume that the digits are decimal digits. The word # (which can only be used between <# and #>) takes the least significant decimal digit and removes it from the number. (The fact that the numbers are stored in binary form need not concern us here.) The ASCII code for this digit will be stored in the appropriate memory location The word # can only be used with a positive number. (See the discussion about negative numbers earlier in the section.) Remember that each time that # is executed, one decimal digit is removed from the number.

#S—The FORTH word #S converts a double-length number into a sequence of ASCII codes. Each one represents one decimal digit of the number. #S should only be used with positive double-length integers. If the double-length integer is zero, then a single ASCII 0 will be output. As in the case of #, #S should only be used between <# and #>. Note that the word # only converts a single digit to an ASCII code while #S converts the entire remaining number to a string of ASCII codes.

   HOLD—The FORTH command **HOLD** allows us to insert the ASCII code for a symbol into the string of ASCII codes that are used to represent a number. **HOLD** pops the top single-length number off the stack and puts it into the string of ASCII codes. The stack relation is

n →   (3-13)

Note that **HOLD** can only be used between <# and >#.
   To illustrate the words that have been discussed here let us write a FORTH word that will take a single-length positive integer and write it with a decimal point two digits from the right. The inclusion of a decimal point can come about in a number of ways. Suppose that you are adding a number of cash receipts in dollars and cents. If we only know how to work in integers then the data would be entered without decimal points. For instance, $34.50 would be entered as 3450. However, we want the decimal point to appear in

the output. The word that we shall write will cause the data to be output with a decimal point to indicate cents. The word is

: WRD 0 <# # # 46 HOLD #S #> ;   (3-14)

Consider the operation of **WRD**. We assume that there is a positive single-length integer on the top of the stack. We start by pushing a 0 onto the top of the stack. This forms a double-length integer of the same magnitude, as we discussed earlier. Now enter the instructions that lie between <# and #>. The first # removes the least significant decimal digit from the double-length number on the top of the stack. The ASCII code for this digit is generated and stored. The second # does the same to the least significant decimal digit of the *remaining* number. Next 46 is pushed onto the stack. **HOLD** removes the 46 from the top of the stack and causes a 46 to be put into the string of ASCII characters that is being stored. Note that 46 is the ASCII code for the period, or decimal point. Next the #**S** is executed. This converts the entire *remaining* double-length number to a string of ASCII codes, one for each decimal digit. After the #> is executed, the complete string of ASCII codes that we have generated will be stored in the memory. We have inserted a decimal point between the two rightmost digits and the remainder of the number. The original number has been removed from the stack. Two numbers are pushed onto the stack. They represent the starting location in the main memory where the string of ASCII codes are stored and the total number of ASCII codes that have been stored. No printing will take place at this time. We need an additional FORTH command to accomplish this.

TYPE—The FORTH word **TYPE** is used to print ASCII codes that are stored in the computer's memory. It causes the transmission of the ASCII codes to the output device (the terminal or the printer). **TYPE** pops the top two numbers off the stack. The number that was on the top of the stack indicates how many characters are to be transmitted to the output device. The number that was second on the stack indicates the starting address in memory for the string of ASCII codes. The stack relation is

naddr nlength   (3-15)

Now let us modify (3-14) so that we have a new word that causes the number to be output to the screen. To do this we simply change the name and add the word **TYPE**.

: WRTT 0 <# # # 46 HOLD #S #> TYPE ;   (3-16)

(It is not necessary to change the name.) For example if, after (3-16) is compiled, we enter

15756 WRTT (RETURN)   (3-17)

The following will appear on your video screen.

157.56 ok

SIGN—The procedures that we have been using will only work with positive integers. Now let us see how to print a number that is either positive *or* negative. The FORTH word **SIGN**, which can only be used between <# and #>, generates the ASCII code for a minus sign and inserts it into the string of ASCII codes *if* the number on the top of the stack is negative. If the number on the top of the stack is positive then *SIGN* does nothing. Now let's write a word that prints a number with two digits following the decimal point and precedes it with a minus sign, (if the number is negative).

: WRTTN DUP ABS 0 <# # # 46 HOLD #S

ROT SIGN #> TYPE ;   (3-18)

Consider the operation of this word. **DUP** duplicates the single-length integer that we want to print. Next **ABS** pops the top number off the stack and pushes its absolute value onto the stack. Thus, the number on the top of the stack is the magnitude of the original number and is positive. Then we push a 0 onto the stack. There are now double-length positive numbers stored in the top two storage locations. Next we encounter the <#. This initiates the processing of the double-length number on the top of the stack. The # # **46 HOLD #S** converts this number to a string of ASCII codes just as in the case of word (3-16). The 0 and the absolute value of the modified number are still on the stack. Now the **ROT** is executed. We can include ordinary FORTH words between <# and #>.) This brings the third number to the top of the stack. This is the original number that we seek to output. **SIGN** pops this number from the stack. If that number is negative then **SIGN** inserts the ASCII code for a minus sign in the string of ASCII codes. If the number in question is positive then SIGN does nothing. The #> causes the string of ASCII codes to be stored in memory. The starting memory address and length of the string are pushed onto the stack. **TYPE** causes

the number to be output. The instructions between the <# and #>
are executed from left to right, which is the usual procedure. The
first word executed within the <# and <# is # and the last word
executed is **SIGN**. The ASCII codes are output in the reverse of the
order in which they were generated. For instance, the instruction
executed last is the one that is printed first. Thus **SIGN** which is
the rightmost command between <# and #> causes a minus sign
to be printed to the left of the number (if it is negative).

As a final example let us modify word (3-18) so that the number
is printed with a dollar sign ($) between the minus sign and the
number. The modified word is

  : WRT$ DUP ABS 0 <# # # 46 HOLD #S
    36 HOLD ROT SIGN #> TYPE ;   (3-19)

This is essentially the same as word (3-18) except that 36 **HOLD** has
been added. 36 is the ASCII code for the dollar sign. Hence, this
will be inserted in the string of ASCII codes before the code for the
minus sign.

EXERCISES

In the following exercises check all programs and user-written
FORTH words by running them on your printer.

3-1. What does text mean?

3-2. Write a FORTH word that prints your letterhead on the
screen.

3-3. Write a FORTH word that averages four numbers. The
command should prompt the user for the input data and
computation should pause until the requested data is
entered. The quotient and remainder should be output
with suitable explanatory comments.

3-4. Modify the FORTH word in Problem 3-3 so that the word
ok is not printed on the screen.

3-5. Modify the FORTH word in Problem 3-4 so that the
quotient and remainder are printed on separate lines.

3-6. Use the FORTH word **SPACES** to modify the word in Problem 3-5 so that the results are appropriately spaced.

3-7. Repeat Problem 3-2, having the output directed to your printer.

3-8. Repeat Problem 3-3, having the output directed to your printer.

3-9. Repeat Problem 3-4, having the output directed to your printer.

3-10. Repeat Problem 3-5, having the output directed to your printer.

3-11. Repeat Problem 3-6, having the output directed to your printer.

3-12. What is an ASCII code?

3-13. Write a table giving the ASCII codes for the control characters.

3-14. Assume that an ASCII code for an uppercase letter is stored on the top of the stack. Write a FORTH command that converts that number to the ASCII code for the corresponding lowercase letter.

3-15. Repeat Problem 3-14 converting a lowercase letter to an uppercase letter instead.

3-16. What is meant by a field?

3-17. Write a FORTH word that will print the top two numbers on the stack. The number on the top of the stack should be right-justified in a field 15 characters wide. The second number should be right-justified in a field 25 characters wide.

3-18. Discuss the basic ideas of pictured numeric output.

3-19. Discuss how a positive single-length integer can be converted into an equal double-length integer.

3-20. Write a FORTH word that prints a 5-digit number with a comma after the first two digits. Assume that the number is positive.

3-21. Write a FORTH word that prints a 5-digit number with the word cents after the last two digits and the word dollars after the first three digits. Assume that the number is positive.

3-22. Will pushing a 0 onto the top of the stack to convert a single-length number to a double-length number work if the number is negative?

3-23. Repeat Problem 3-20, but do not assume that the number is positive. If the number is negative, print a minus sign before the number.

3-24. Repeat Problem 3-21, but do not assume tht the number is positive. If the number is negative, print a minus sign before any other output.

3-25. Repeat Problem 3-20, having the output directed to your printer.

3-26. Repeat Problem 3-21, having the output directed to your printer.

Chapter 4

Control Statements—
Basic Ideas of
Structured Programming

The FORTH programs that we have considered so far have executed each statement in order. Far more powerful programs can be written if there are several possible *branches* or *paths* available. The computer chooses which path to take based upon some decision-making process that you have written into your program. For instance, the choice of branches might depend upon whether a number were positive or negative. We shall consider procedures for such branching in this chapter.

There are other times when it is desirable for a program to loop back over a set of statements a number of times. We shall also consider how this can be done.

There are procedures for writing these programs that make them less prone to error and easier to debug. We shall discuss the basic elements of structured programming in this chapter. Such procedures are called *structured programming*.

4-1. LOGICAL CONDITIONS

In FORTH and in other programming languages, decisions are made which depend upon whether some value is true or false. For instance, we can check if the number on the top of the stack is positive. When the check is made, the number is popped off the stack and a 1 is pushed onto the stack if the number is positive. If the number that was popped off the stack was not positive, then a 0 will be pushed onto the stack. This 1 or 0 is called a *flag*. The 1 represents true while the 0 represents false. The flag values 0 and 1 are ordinary single-length integers. For instance, there is no way to distinguish the flag value 1 and a 1 that you push onto the stack. In subsequent sections of this chapter we shall discuss how we can cause the program to branch depending upon whether the flag on the top of the stack represents true or false. In this section we shall discuss the FORTH words, called *comparison* words, that are used to push a flag onto the stack.

0 = —The FORTH word **0 =** ; which is promounced zero equals, pops the top number off the stack and pushes a flag onto the stack. The flag is 1 if the original number popped off the stack was 0. The flag is 0 if the stack number was not zero. The stack relation is

$$n \rightarrow n_{flag} \tag{4-1}$$

The flag will be true if $n = 0$. Remember that the flag is just a single-length integer. It is 0 if it represents false and 1 if it represents true. In the remainder of this book we shall speak of the flag as being either true or false. Figure 4-1 illustrates a stack before and after **0 =** has been executed. Note that the top number, which is not a 0, has been popped off the stack and a 0 has been pushed onto the stack.

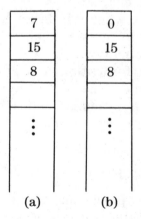

Figure 4-1. (a) A typical stack; (b) the stack after **0 =** has been executed.

0<—The FORTH word **0<**; which is pronounced zero less, pops the top number off the stack and pushes a flag onto the stack. The flag is true if the original number that was popped off the stack was less than zero. If the original number was equal to or greater than zero then the flag is false. The stack relation is

$$n \rightarrow n_{flag} \qquad\qquad (4\text{-}2)$$

The flag will be true if n is less than 0. **0<** functions in essentially the same way as **0 =** except that the flag is true if the number in question is less than 0.

0>—The word **0>**; which is pronounced zero greater, pops the top number off the stack and pushes a flag onto the stack. The flag is true if the original number that was popped off the stack was positive. The flag will be false if the original number was equal to or less than zero. The stack relation is

$$n \rightarrow n_{flag} \qquad\qquad (4\text{-}3)$$

The flag will be true if n is greater than zero and false otherwise. As an example let us write our own FORTH command that pops the top number off the stack and pushes a flag onto the stack. The flag should be true if the original number was *equal to or less* than zero and the flag should be false if the original number was greater than zero. A word that accomplishes this is

```
: LEZ DUP 0< SWAP 0= + 0> ;                     (4-4)
```

The word is called **LEZ**. Two comparison words are to be used here. We start by duplicating the number in question. Next the word **0<** is executed. A 1 will be on the top of the stack if the original number was less than zero, otherwise a 0 will be on the top of the stack. next we execute a **SWAP**. This brings the original number to the top of the stack. Then **0 =** is executed. Now a 1 will be on the top of the stack if the original number was a 0, otherwise a 0 will be on the top of the stack. The second number on the stack will be the flag from the **0<** operation. If *either or both* of the top two numbers on the stack are 1, then we want to push a true flag onto the stack (after removing the top two numbers from the stack). To accomplish this we next execute **+ .** The top two numbers are popped off the stack and their sum is pushed onto the stack. If the top number is greater than or equal to 1 then we want the resulting flag to be true. If the top number on the stack is 0 then we want

the flag to be 0. Thus, the **0>** word is executed next. Now the top
number is popped off the stack and a flag is pushed onto the stack.
The flag will be true if the popped number is positive and 0
otherwise. Thus, we have achieved the desired result.

We shall now consider some FORTH comparison words that make
a logical decision based upon the comparison of two numbers. In
these cases the two numbers will be the top two numbers on the
stack. They will be popped off the stack and a flag will be pushed
onto the stack.

= —The FORTH word = pops the top two numbers off the stack and
pushes a flag onto the stack. The flag will be positive if the original
two numbers that were popped off the stack were equal. If the
original two numbers were unequal, then the flag will be false. The
stack relation is

$$n_1 \quad n_2 \quad \rightarrow \quad n_{flag} \tag{4-5}$$

The flag will be true if $n_1 = n_2$ and zero otherwise. A typical stack,
before and after the execution of the word = , is shown in Figure 4-2.

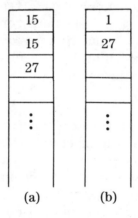

Figure 4-2. (a) A typical stack; (b) the stack after = has been executed.

< —The FORTH word < pops the top two numbers off the stack and
pushes a flag onto the stack. The flag will be true if the number
that was second on the stack is less than the number that was on
the top of the stack. The flag will be false if the number that was

second on the stack was greater than or equal to the number that was on the top of the stack. The stack relation is

$$n_1 \; n_2 \; \rightarrow \; n_{flag} \qquad\qquad\qquad\qquad (4\text{-}6)$$

Note that the flag will be true if n_1 is less than n_2. The flag will be false otherwise.

$>$—The FORTH word $>$ pops the top two numbers off the stack ans pushes a flag onto the stack. The flag will be true if the number that was second on the stack is greater than the number that was on the top of the stack. The flag will be false if the second number on the stack was equal to or less than the top number. The stack relation is

$$n_1 \; n_2 \; \rightarrow \; n_{flag} \qquad\qquad\qquad\qquad (4\text{-}7)$$

Now the flag will be true if n_1 is greater than n_2. The flag will be false otherwise.

As an example, let us write our own FORTH word that pops two numbers off the stack and pushes a flag onto the stack. The flag should be true if the second number is *equal to or less than* the number that was on the top of the stack. The flag should be false if the number that was second on the stack is greater than the number that was on the top of the stack. A word that accomplishes this is

```
: LE 2DUP < ROT ROT = + 0> ;          (4-8)
```

Consider this word. We want to perform two logical comparisons. We have to duplicate a pair of single-length integers. We can accomplish this by using the **2DUP** command. Next we use < to compare the top two numbers. They are popped off the stack and a flag is pushed onto the stack. The flag will be true if the number that was second on the stack is less than the number that was on the top of the stack. Otherwise the flag will be false. Next **ROT** is executed twice. Now the original pair of numbers is brought to the top of the stack. The next comparison is to be the = word. Thus it does not matter in which order the two numbers are brought to the top of the stack. Now when the word = is executed the top two numbers will be popped off the stack and a flag will be pushed onto the stack. The flag will only be true if the two numbers that were popped off the stack were equal. At this point we have the

two flags in the top two stack positions. Now we proceed as in word
(4-4). + and then **0>**are executed. The desired flag will be pushed
onto the stack.

Some Additional Words

There are some additional comparison words that are not as yet
part of FORTH-79. They are found in MMSFORTH and other FORTH
systems we shall present them here.

The FORTH word **<>**(pronounced not equals) functions in the
same way as = except that the flag is true if the top two numbers
on the stack are not equal and the flag is false if the two numbers
are equal.

The word **< =** functions in the same way as < except that now
the flag is true if the second number on the stack is less than or
equal to the number on the top of the stack.

The FORTH word **> =** functions in the same way as > except that
now the flag is true if the second number on the stack is greater
than or *equal* to the number on the top of the stack.

4-2. Conditional Branching

We shall now discuss how the conditional words that were
introduced in the last section can be used to cause a program to
take on of two branches. This will greatly increase our computing
ability.

IF and THEN—There are two FORTH commands that are basic to
the branching we have discussed. They are **IF** and **THEN**. These
two words are always paired. Their general form is

IF statements a THEN statements b   (4-9)

The operation is as follows. When **IF** word is executed the top
number is popped off the stack and considered as a flag. IF the flag
is true, then statements a that follow the **IF** word will be executed.
Next statements b will be executed. If the flag that was popped off
the stack was false, then statements a will be *ignored* and only
statements b will be executed. Note that the flag precedes the **IF**;
it does not follow it. This is consistent with reverse notation (but
not with English). When an **IF** is executed, the flag on the top of
the stack is popped off. If the flag is true, then the statements

between the **IF** and **THEN** words will be executed. If the flag is false, then the statements between the **IF** and **THEN** words will be ignored. In either case the statements following the **THEN** word will always be executed.

Consider an example of a FORTH word that has two branches. We shall write a word that compares two numbers on the stack. If the numbers are equal, then the words "NUMBERS ARE EQUAL" are output. If the numbers are unequal then the words "DIFFERENCE IS" followed by the difference between the two numbers is printed. A word that accomplishes this is shown in Figure 4-3. In line 1 we

```
0 ( EXAMPLE OF BASIC BRANCHING )
1 : CHECKEQ   2DUP    =
2              IF    ." NUMBERS ARE EQUAL "    2DROP      QUIT
3              THEN     -         ." DIFFERENCE IS "    .      ;
4
5
6
7
8
9
10
11
12
13
14
15
```

Figure 4-3. A simple illustration of branching.

define the name of the word, **CHECKEQ**. Since two operations may have to be performed on the integers in question we duplicate both of them using **2 DUP**. Next the top pair of numbers is popped off the stack and compared using the FORTH word = . If the numbers are equal then the flag that is pushed onto the stack will be true; otherwise it will be false. Now **IF** is executed. The flag is popped off the stack. If it is true then the words between **IF** and **THEN** will be executed. Thus, "NUMBERS ARE EQUAL" will be printed. Since no further use is to be made of the stack, **2DROP** is executed to clear it. Then, **QUIT** is executed. This causes operation to cease and control is returned to your terminal. Note that the word **QUIT** can be included as part of a branch. If the branch containing **QUIT** is executed, the statements following **THEN** are not. Note that if

CHECKEQ were called by another FORTH word then the execution of **QUIT** would terminate all computation, not only the computation of **CHECKEQ**. Thus, you must be careful when **QUIT** is used.

Now suppose that the flag is false. The words between the **IF** and the **THEN** are ignored. In this case - will be executed. Two numbers will be popped off the stack and their difference will be pushed onto the stack. The ." will then be executed and "DIFFERENCE IS" will be printed. Finally the . will be executed and the numerical difference will be printed. Since − and . each pop a number off the stack, we need not use any **DROP** words here.

ELSE—Branching can be more versatile than we have thus far indicated. The FORTH command **ELSE** can be incorporated in the **IF-THEN** sequence in the following way.

IF statements a ELSE statements b THEN statements c

(4-10)

The operation in this case is as follows. The top integer on the stack is a flag. If the flag is true, then statements a will be executed, but statements b will not. Next statements c will be executed. If the flag is false then statements a will be ignored, but statements b will be executed. Next statements c will be executed. The general form of the operation is: if the flag is true then the statements between **IF** and **ELSE** will be executed while those between **ELSE** and **THEN** will be ignored. If the flag is false then the statements between **IF** and **ELSE** will be ignored while those between **ELSE** and **THEN** will be executed. In general, the stack relation whenever the **IF** word is executed is

n_{flag} (4-11)

Let us illustrate the use of the **ELSE** word with the program in Figure 4-4. This is a simple program that a teacher might use to print a grade based upon a student's average. The average is an integer that is put on the top of the stack. When the word **GRADES** is executed the following is to occur. If the average is less than 60 then "GRADE IS FAILING" will be printed. If the average is equal to or greater than 60 then "GRADE IS PASSING" will be printed. In either case the difference between the average and the perfect average of 100 will be printed with a suitable explanatory statement.

Let us consider the operation of **GRADES** (see Figure 4-4). In line 1 we start by having the words "GRADE IS" output. Next 60 is

```
0 ( SIMPLE GRADING )
1 : GRADES      ," GRADE IS "  60   -    DUP     0<
2                IF  ," FAILING"   ELSE ," PASSING"
3                THEN  40 - NEGATE  ."  YOU NEED " .
4                ," MORE POINTS TO DO PERFECT WORK"    ;
5
6
7
8
9
10
11
12
13
14
15
```

Figure 4-4. A simple grading program.

pushed onto the stack. Then − is executed. The number on the top of the stack is now the average minus 60. If this number is negative then the average is failing. Since this number is to be used twice, it is duplicated using the word **DUP**. Then the **0<** command is executed. The top number on the stack, which is the average minus 60, will be popped off the stack and a flag will be pushed onto the stack. The flag will be true if the number that was popped off the stack was less than 0 or, equivalently, if the average was less than 60. Now the **IF** word is encountered. The flag is popped off the stack. If its is true the word "FAILING" will be output and the words between **ELSE** and **THEN** will be ignored. On the other hand, if the flag is false, then the words between **IF** and **ELSE** will be ignored and the word "PASSING" will be output. At this point the number on the top of the stack will be the original average minus 60. This is there because of the **DUP** statement in line 1. Now 40 is pushed onto the stack and the word − is executed. Both numbers are popped off the stack and their difference is pushed onto the stack. Now the number on the top of the stack is the original average minus 100. Since this is a negative number, the next word executed is **NEGATE**. Now the number on the top of the stack is positive. This is the number that must be added to the original average to make it 100. Suppose that this number is 15. The remainder of the program causes "YOU NEED 15 MORE POINTS TO DO PERFECT WORK" to be output.

Nested Control Structures

The **IF-ELSE-THEN** construction can be said to have two branches, one between **IF** and **ELSE** and the other between **ELSE** and **THEN**. There can be branches within one or more branches. Such a program structure is called a *nested control structure*. Let us illustrate the use of nested control structures by writing a FORTH word that can be used to assign letter grades to a student on the basis of average. The program is to function in the following way. The average is to be on the top of the stack. Then the word **LETTERGRADES** that we will write is executed. If the average is less than 60 then the words "GRADE IS F" will be printed. If the average is less than 70, but greater than or equal to 60 then the words "GRADE IS D" are to be printed. If the average is less than 80, but equal to or greater than 70 then the words "GRADE IS C" are to be output. If the average is less than 90, but equal to or greater than 80 then the words "GRADE IS B" are to be output. Finally if the average is 90 or greater, the words "GRADE IS A" are to be output.

The program is illustrated in Figure 4-5. The name of the word is **LETTERGRADES**. In line 1 we start by outputting "GRADE IS".

```
0  ( A NESTED CONTROL STRUCTURE )
1  : LETTERGRADES    ." GRADE IS  " 60 -     DUP      0<
2          IF   ." F"  DROP
3              ELSE    10 - DUP    0<      IF
4                  ." D"  DROP
5                      ELSE  10 -  DUP     0<    IF    ." C" DROP
6                          ELSE    10 -       0<   IF ." B"
7                              ELSE   ." A "      THEN
8                          THEN
9              THEN
10          THEN    ;
11
12
13
14
15
```

Figure 4-5. A FORTH word with nested control structures.

Next 60 is pushed onto the stack and the - command is executed. Since it is assumed that the average was originally on the stack the top of the stack now contains the average minus 60. **DUP** causes this number to be duplicated. Next 0< is executed. The top number is popped off the stack and a flag is pushed on. If the flag is true then the original average was less than 60. In this case "F" will be output. Now all words between **ELSE** and **THEN** will be ignored. We must exercise care here. The branch between **ELSE** and **THEN** contains an **IF** word. Thus, a set of branches is said to be *nested* within this branch. Every **IF** word is related to a *particular* **ELSE** and **THEN** word. We must be careful to group together the proper **IF**, **ELSE**, and **THEN** words. The following procedure can be used. Find the *innermost* **IF** word. The *next* **ELSE** and **THEN** words are grouped with the **IF** word in question. Next find the preceding **IF** word. The *next* **ELSE** and **THEN** (ignoring the ones that were previously found) are grouped with this **IF** word. Proceeding in this way we work our way out and can group each **IF**, **ELSE**, and **THEN**. We can use an alternative procedure. The first **IF** is grouped with the next **ELSE** and the last **THEN** in the nested structure (not necessarily the last **THEN** in the word). Then we repeat this procedure with the remaining **IF**, **ELSE**, and **THEN** words, in turn. For instance, in Figure 4-5, the **IF** on line 2 is grouped with the **ELSE** on line 3 and the **THEN** on line 10. Note that the first **IF** is grouped with the next **ELSE** and with the last **THEN**. Hence, if the original flag was true after "F" was printed and **DROP** was executed to clear the stack, then execution would terminate. On the other hand, if the flag was false, then the words between **IF** on line 2 and **ELSE** on line 3 would be ignored. Now the words between **ELSE** on line 3 and THEN On line 10 will be executed. The number that is on the top of the stack at this point in the execution is the duplicated average that has been reduced by 60. Now (see line 3) 10 is pushed on the stack and -is executed. The number that is on the top of the stack will be equal to or greater than 0 if the original average was equal to or greater than 70. This number is now duplicated when **DUP**, on line 3, is executed. Then **0<** is executed and a flag is pushed onto the stack. The next **IF** word is executed and the flag is popped off. If the flag is true, then "D" will be output. Group the **IF** word that was just executed with its **ELSE** and **THEN**. Proceeding as before, the **IF** word on line 3 is grouped with the **ELSE** word on line 5 and the **THEN** word on line 9. Thus if the flag was true, then "D" would be output. Then the **DROP** would be executed to clear the stack. Control of the program would proceed to line 9 and then to line 10. Thus, operation would terminate. If the flag was false then the statements between the **IF** on line 3 and the **ELSE** on line 5 would be ignored. Now the statements between the **ELSE** on line 5 and the **THEN** on line 9 would be executed. The basic ideas here follow the previous ones and the letters "C" and "B" are printed when appropriate. Note that if the word **IF** on line 6 is executed, the grade must be either "B" or "A." Then if the flag which resulted from the execution of the **0<** on line 6 is true, a "B" should be output. If that flag is false then an "A" is output.

The FORTH system uses the return stack to keep track of nested control structures such as the one in Figure 4-5. You must use great care if the **>R** and **R>** words are used. There must be an *equal* number of **>R** and **R>***executed* in each branch. Note that it is *not* sufficient simply to have an equal number of **>R** and **R>** words. An equal number must be executed. This applies to *every* possible branch of the program. Note that even if there is only one pair of branches and no nested branches, the number of **R>** and **>R** words that are executed in each branch must be equal. If you do not observe these precautions, you may "crash your system." You will have to reboot it and may lose much data if it had not been saved on disk.

4-3. UNCONDITIONAL LOOPING

There are times when we want a program to repeat a sequence of instructions many times. This is called *looping*. We could write a FORTH word that consists of a set of instructions and then write another word that executes this first word many times. However, that could be very cumbersome. FORTH has words that provide for looping without having to repeat words in this way. FORTH looping affords some other very versatile features that we shall also discuss.

DO and LOOP—The FORTH words **DO** and **LOOP** are used to perform basic looping. The general structure of such a loop is the following:

$$n_1 \ n_2 \ \text{DO statements a LOOP} \tag{4-12}$$

Let us discuss the details of the operation. When (4-12) is executed, n_1 and n_2 are popped off the stack and are stored on the return stack, with n_2 on the top of the stack. (You need not concern yourself with the details of restoring the return stack as far as n_1 and n_2 are concerned. When the looping is completed the return stack will automatically be cleared of n_1 and n_2.) Next, statements a will be executed. When **LOOP** is encountered the value of n_2, which is stored on the return stack, will be increased by one and the new value compared with n_1. If n_2 is less than n_1 then statements a will be executed again. Every time that **LOOP** is reached n_2 will be increased and tested. When it becomes *equal to or greater* than n_1 then the looping will be terminated, that is, the statements after **LOOP** will be executed. On the other hand, if n_2 is still less than n_1, then statements a will be repeated again. For instance the statement

$$\text{7 4 DO .'' PRINT'' LOOP} \qquad\qquad (4\text{-}13)$$

will result in PRINT appearing three times.

The stack relation when **DO** is executed is

$$n_1\ n_2\ \rightarrow \qquad\qquad (4\text{-}14)$$

The number n_1 is called the *loop test value*: it remains constant. The number n_2 is called the *loop index*. It is increased on each "pass" through the loop. Note that there will always be at least one pass through a loop since the index is not compared to the test value until the word **LOOP** has been reached.

The loop index can be copied from the return stack to the stack using the FORTH word **I**. The loop test value can be copied from the return stack to the stack using the word **I'**. Note that neither of these operations alter the return stack. These words were discussed in Section 2-6.

Let us illustrate looping by writing a FORTH command that calculates the factorial of the integer on the top of the stack. In mathematical literature, the factorial is written using an exclamation point **!**. To illustrate,

$5! = 5(4)\ (3)\ (2)\ (1). = 120$. Similarly $3! = 3(2)\ (1) = 6$. The FORTH word **FACT** is shown in Figure 4-6. Let us consider its operation. If we want to calculate 5! we would write

$$\text{5 FACT (RETURN)} \qquad\qquad (4\text{-}15)$$

That is, 5 would be on the top of the stack when **FACT** is executed. **FACT** will set up the structure that will loop and perform one multiplication with each pass. The initial value of the index is 1. If we are to compute factorial 5, then we should loop five times. Thus, the test value should be 6. Remember that looping terminates when the increased index equals the test value. Now consider Figure 4-6. We start by pushing 1 onto the stack and executing + . This results in the original value on the stack being increased by 1. Alternatively, we could have used the single **1 +** word to accomplish this. Next 1 is pushed onto the stack. At this point in the execution

```
0  ( CALCULATION OF FACTORIAL )
1  : FACT   1   +   1     1     ROT     ROT
2            DO   I   *     LOOP     .        ;
3
4
5
6
7
8
9
10
11
12
13
14
15
```

Figure 4-6. A FORTH word that calculates the factorial.

the number on the top of the stack is 1 and the second number on the stack is one more than the number whose factorial we wish to compute. Now we push another 1 onto the stack. We shall use this in our calculations. However, we want to set up the initial value of the loop index and the loop test value as the first and second items on the stack. The two **ROT** words accomplish this. For example if we had entered (4-15), after the two **ROT** words had been executed the stack would be in the form 1 6 1. Remember that the rightmost value represents the top of the stack. Now the **DO** word is executed. The top two values are popped from the stack and stored in the return stack. There is now a 1 on the top of the stack. Consider the statements between **DO** and **LOOP**. The first one is **I**. This duplicates the index onto the top of the stack. Then * is executed. This pops the top two numbers from the stack and replaces them by their product. The first time through the loop we have 1*1. On the second pass through the loop, the index is two. Hence, the product 1*2 = 2 is taken. On the third pass through the loop the product 2*3 = 6 is taken. When the looping is complete the desired factorial will be computed. After the looping is completed the word . causes the answer to be output.

Variable Increment +LOOP

We have assumed that the loop index is increased by one each time that the loop is cycled. There are times when we want the loop index to vary by a number other than one. We can replace **LOOP** with a FORTH word that accomplishes this. The word is **+LOOP**. when **LOOP** is executed the loop index is increased by 1 and then tested to see if it is less than the loop test value. When **+LOOP** is executed, the number that is on the top of the stack, which is now called the *loop increment*, is popped off the stack and added to the index. This value is then tested to see if it is less than the test value. (This assumes that the loop increment is positive.) The stack relation for **+LOOP** is

$$n \rightarrow \qquad\qquad\qquad\qquad (4\text{-}16)$$

As an example, we shall write a FORTH command that obtains the sum of the odd integers that lie in the range specified by the top two numbers on the stack. We shall call the word **ODDSUM**. Then

$$17 \; 3 \; \text{ODDSUM (RETURN)} \qquad\qquad\qquad (4\text{-}17)$$

will output the sum of the odd numbers from 3 to 17 inclusive. The word is

$$: \text{ODDSUM SWAP } 1+ \; 0 \; \text{SWAP ROT DO I } + \; 2 \; +\text{LOOP . ;}$$
$$(4\text{-}18)$$

The first operation is a **SWAP**. For the example of (4-17) this brings the 17 to the top of the stack. Then it is increased by one. Next a 0 is pushed on the stack and a **SWAP** is executed again. Next **ROT** is executed. In example (4-18), the stack is 0 18 3. Thus when **DO** is executed, its initial index value (for the example of (4-17) is 3 and its loop test value is 18. These two numbers are popped off the stack so that a 0 is now on the top of the stack. When the statements of the loop are executed **I** pushes the loop index onto the stack. Thus, for the example, the first time through the loop, 3 is added to 0. Both these values are popped off the stack and replaced by their sum. Then 2 is pushed onto the stack. Next **+LOOP** is executed, increasing the index by 2. Hence, the next time that the loop is executed, 5 will be added to the sum. Finally when the increased index is greater than the loop test value, execution of the loop is terminated. The desired sum will then be output.

We have used positive values for the initial value of the loop index, the loop test value, and the loop increment. This need not be the case, negative integers can be used. If the loop increment is positive, then looping terminates when the loop index is equal to or greater than the loop test value. On the other hand, if the increment is negative, then the looping terminates when the loop index is less than the test value. For example consider the word **NEGTEST**

: NEGTEST -5 2 DO I . -2 +LOOP ;   (4-19)

When this is executed the following will be printed

2 0 -2 -4 ok

LEAVE—The FORTH word **LEAVE** is used to force termination of a loop. When **LEAVE** is executed the test value is set equal to the current value of the index. Thus the looping will terminate the next time that **LOOP** is encountered. **LEAVE** is almost always used in conjunction with a branching instruction. We shall demonstrate its use later in this section.

Nested Loops

A loop can be nested within another loop. We shall illustrate this with a single example.

: NEST 10 1 DO 5 3 DO I . LOOP LOOP ;   (4-20)

When the word **NEST** is executed, the numbers 3 and 4 will be printed nine times. There are two loops—an outer one whose index starts at 1 and whose test value is 10 and an innter loop which has an index that starts at 3 and a test value of 5. When **NEST** is executed, the outer loop cycles. This results in the numbers 5 and 3 being pushed onto the stack. Then the **DO** from the inner loop is executed. The 5 and 3 are popped off the stack and pushed onto the return stack. The 10 and 1 which were pushed onto the return stack when the first **DO** was executed are now pushed farther down the return stack. Now the FORTH word **I** is executed. This duplicates the current number onto the top of the stack. Note that **I** pushes the loop index of the loop that is *currently* being circled onto the stack. The inner loop is being executed. On the first pass through the loop, the index has a value of 3, and this value is pushed onto the stack. Then the word . pops this value from the stack and causes a 3 to be printed. On the next pass through the inner loop the index is 4. This value is printed. The operation of the inner loop terminates and its parameters are dropped from the return stack. Remember that we are still cycling through the outer loop. Since the parameters of the inner loop were dropped from the return stack, the parameters of the outer loop are back at the top of the return stack. Now the outer loop goes through its second cycle. Thus, 5 and 3 are again pushed onto the stack. The inner **DO** is executed again. Hence, 3 and 5 are popped from the stack and are pushed onto the return stack, as before. 3 and 4 are printed again and the operation of the inner loop terminates. This procedure is repeated until the outer loop has cycled 9 times.

Consider the use of the word **I**. It takes the index of the loop that is being executed and pushes it onto the stack. If the inner loop is being executed then **I** will push the index onto the stack. On the other hand, if the exection of the inner loop is *complete*, then the execution of **I** will cause the index of the outer loop to be duplicated onto the stack. In a similar way the execution of **I'** will cause the test value of the loop that is being executed to be pushed onto the stack. There are times when an inner loop is being executed, but we want the index of the outer loop to be pushed onto the stack. The FORTH word **J** (see Section 2-6) accomplishes this. Note that **I, I'**, and **J** do not change the return stack. When the execution of a loop is completed the return stack's parameters will be dropped. You do not have to concern yourself with this.

An inner loop must *lie completely within an outer loop*. Note that each **DO** is paired with a **LOOP**, or a **+LOOP**. You can determine the pairing in essentially the same way as the **IF** and **THEN** were paired in a nested control structure. Find the innermost **DO**. It is paired with the next **LOOP**, or **+LOOP**. Next find the preceding **DO**. It is paired with the next **LOOP**, or **+LOOP**, omitting the previously paired **LOOP**. Proceeding in this way we can find the *range* of each loop.

As an example of nested loops we shall write a program that computes Pythagorean triples. (These are three integers that can be equal to the lengths of the sides of a right triangle. Consider that a, b, and c are *integers*. They constitute a Pythagorean triple if we can write

$$a^2 + b^2 = c^2 \qquad\qquad (4\text{-}21)$$

For instance if $a = 3$ and $b = 4$ then $c = 5$ and 3, 4, 5 is a Pythagorean triple. There are only certain integers that will satisfy (4-21). We shall write a FORTH program that computes these triples for a and b between 1 and 100. The program is listed in Figure 4-7. We start by defining two words that we will use. **SQUARE** pops the top

```
0 ( PYTHAGOREAN TRIPLE   )
1 : SQUARE  DUP    *      ;
2 : PT 15 .R   ;
3 : PYTHTRIP   100      1       DO     I   DUP   SQUARE
4                    100    I       DO    DUP   I    SQUARE   +
5                 142    I       DO    DUP  I   SQUARE     -      DUP
6                   0= IF  I   J    6 PICK   CR   PT   PT   PT       THEN
7                   0<  IF  LEAVE    THEN
8                   LOOP             DROP
9                LOOP         DROP       DROP
10            LOOP    CR       ;
11
12
13
14
15                                                                      )
```

Figure 4-7. A FORTH word that calculates the integers that satisfy.
$a^2 + b^2 = c^2$ for a and b in the range 1 to 100.

number off the stack and replaces it by its square. This word was discussed in Section 2-3. The second word is **PT**. This prints a number in a field 15 spaces wide.

PYTHTRIP the word that actually computes the triples starts on line 3. This word has three loops: an outer one that has two loops nested within it, a middle loop nested within the outer loops and the inner loop that is nested within the two other loops.

Now let us consider the actual operation of the word **PYTHTRIP**. In line 3 we start by pushing 100 and 1 onto the stack. **DO** pops these numbers from the stack and pushes them onto the return stack. Thus, we have set up the outer loop. Next **I** is executed; this duplicates the index of the outer loop onto the top of the stack. **DUP** and **SQUARE** are executed next. Hence the top two numbers on the stack are the index of the outer loop and its square. (The square is on the top of the stack.) In the next line we set up the middle **DO** loop. It is important to note that after the middle loop completes a cycle, the top of the stack must be unchanged. that is, it must contain the index of the outer loop and its square. In line 4 we start by pushing 100 onto the stack. Next **I** is executed. Thus, the top number on the stack will be the index of the outer loop. (This is done to avoid duplicating triples and thus, speed up the operation of the program. For instance if we find 3, 4, and 5 we do not also want to find 4, 3, and 5.) Next the **DO** on line 4 cause the top two numbers to be popped off the stack and pushed onto the return stack. Then **DUP** is executed. When this occurs, the square of the index of the outer loop is duplicated. Now **I** is executed. Remember that **I** duplicates the index of the loop that is currently being executed. Thus, the index of the middle loop is duplicated on the top of the stack. Next **SQUARE** and + are executed. The number that is on the top of the stack now is the sum of the squares of the indices of the inner and middle loops. This represents $a^2 + b^2$. In the next line we start by setting up the inner loop. It is important to note that the stack should be undisturbed after each cycle of this loop. In line 5 we start by pushing 142 onto the stack. Next **I** is executed so that the index of the middle loop is duplicated onto the top of the stack. These numbers will be the test value and the starting index of the inner loop. Note that if a and b are 100 or less, then c, which is the index of the inner loop, can be no greater than 142. Also c cannot be smaller than either a or b. The inner loop will test all possible values of c and we do not want it to test impossible values. This is the reason that these indices are used. The **DO** on line 5 then pops these two numbers off the stack and pushes them onto the return stack. Next **DUP** is executed. Thus $a^2 + b^2$ is duplicated. Now **I** is executed. The index of the inner loop is then pushed onto the stack and **SQUARE** and - are then executed so that the number on the top of the stack is $a^2 + b^2 - c^2$. If this number is zero then we have found a Pythagorean triple.

In line 6 we test to see if the number on the top of the stack is 0. First **0 =** is executed then **IF** is executed. If the flag is true, then we want to print the indices of the three loops. The **I** and **J** following the **IF** causes the indices of the inner and middle loops to be duplicated onto the stack. Then 6 is pushed onto the stack and **PICK** is executed. This duplicates the index of the outer loop onto the stack. The top three stack values are output using the **PT** word discussed earlier. If the flag was false then the statements between **IF** and **THEN** are ignored.

If the square of the index of the inner loop becomes greater than the sum of the squares of the indices of the other two loops then there is no reason to cycle the inner loop any further. In line 6 we test for this. If **0<** results in a true flag, then **LEAVE** is executed. Now the test value of the loop currently being executed, the inner loop in this case, is made equal to the index. Thus, the inner loop terminates when **LOOP** is reached. Next we will cycle the middle loop again. Before doing this, the stack must be returned to the condition it was in *before* the inner loop cycled. The **DUP** on line

4 left a value of $a^2 + b^2$ on the stack. The **DROP** on line 8 drops this. When the **LOOP** in line 9 is encountered the middle loop cycles again. This procedure repeats until the middle loop has cycled 100 times. Its cycling is complete. To remove the index of the outer loop and its square from the top of the stack the two **DROP** words on line 10 are used. The outer loop then cycles and the procedure is repeated.

We have typed the program so that each loop is indented to a different level. This is done to make the program more readable; this lets you pick out each loop by eye. This is important because it helps you keep track of the operation of the program and avoid bugs.

When you do any looping, you should be careful that data does not "pile up" on the stack. This can overwrite your operating system and make it necessary to reboot. You should also be careful that you do not set up loops that cycle indefinitely. For instance, if the increment of a loop were zero it would cycle an indefinite number of times. Infinite cycling can occur at other times, for instance if the initial value and test value are positive but the increment is negative.

4-4. CONDITIONAL LOOPING

In the last section we discussed what was called unconditional looping. The loop test value and the initial value of the index were pushed onto the stack. The loop cycled until the index was equal to or greater than the test value (for positive incrments). This is called unconditional looping since the **DO** and **LOOP** words do not provide any means for terminating the loop based upon calculated conditions. That is, the number of loop cycles is determined by the initial value of the index, the test value, and the loop increment. Of course, **IF** and **THEN** could be used in conjunction with **LEAVE** to terminate the loop prematurely. In this section we shall consider words which result in looping, but they also can be set up to terminate the looping.

BEGIN and UNTIL—The FORTH words **BEGIN** and **UNTIL** can be used to set up conditional looping. They are used in the following way.

BEGIN statements a (flag) UNTIL   (4-22)

The operation is as follows. When **BEGIN** is encountered for the first time statements a are executed. When **UNTIL** is encountered it pops the top value off the stack and treats it as a flag. (The flag will usually have been put on the stack as a result of statements a.) If the flag is false then statements a are repeated. This continues until the flag becomes true. Then the looping terminates and the statements after the word **UNTIL** are executed. The stack relation for the word **UNTIL** is

$$n \rightarrow \qquad\qquad (4\text{-}23)$$

As an example let us write a FORTH command that adds an arbitrary number of integers. When the word, which we call **ADDER** is executed, it calls for an integer to be entered with the prompt ?. After the integer is entered and RETURN is pressed the prompt reappears. You keep entering numbers in this way until a 0 is entered. Then, the sum of all the numbers is output and execution terminates. The program is shown in Figure 4-8.

```
0  ( SUM OF AN ARBITRARY NUMBER OF NUMBERS)
1  : ADDER   0     BEGIN     #IN      DUP         ROT     + SWAP
2              0=    UNTIL    CR    .      ;
3
4
5
6
7
8
9
10
11
12
13
14
15
```

Figure 4-8. A program that adds an arbitrary number of numbers.

Let us consider the operation of this program. We start by pushing 0 onto the stack. Next the **BEGIN** word is encountered. This defines that start of the loop. The next word **#IN** causes the ? prompt to appear on the screen and computation pauses until an integer is entered and RETURN is pushed. The number is duplicated. Next **ROT** is executed to bring the third number, which at the start is 0 but after subsequent loopings will be the last computed sum, to the top of the stack. Now + is executed. The number just entered is added to the sum. The next **SWAP** causes the entered number to be at the top of the stack. Next **0 =** is executed. The top number is popped off the stack and a flag is pushed onto the stack. The flag will only be true if the last entered number is 0. Next **UNTIL** is executed. The flag is popped off the stack. If it is true, looping terminates and the words after the **UNTIL** are executed. If the flag is false then looping continues and the words between **BEGIN** and **UNTIL** are again executed. The first of these is #IN. Note that the number on top of the stack at the end of each loop is the sum. If a 0 is entered when line 2 is executed the flag will be true. Looping will terminate, a **CR** will be executed, and the desired sum will be popped off the stack and output.

BEGIN, WHILE, and REPEAT—There is another conditional looping structure that is used in FORTH. It uses the words **BEGIN, WHILE, and REPEAT**.

BEGIN statements a (flag) WHILE statements b REPEAT(4-24)

The operation is as follows. The **BEGIN** marks the start of the loop. Statements a are executed. The **WHILE** causes the number on the top of the stack to be treated as a flag and it is popped off the stack. If the flag is true, then **WHILE** causes no other operation and statements b are executed. The operation then loops back to the statement following **BEGIN**. Thus, statements a are executed again. If the flag is true when the **WHILE** is executed, then statements b are executed and looping continues. On the other hand, if the flag was false, then looping would terminate and statements b would *not* be executed. The statements after the **REPEAT** would then be executed. Note that with the **BEGIN-WHILE-REPEAT** form looping continues as long as a condition is true and the condition can terminate looping from any part of the loop. On the other hand the **BEGIN-UNTIL** form continues looping as long as a condition is false and operation will only terminate at the end of the loop.

As an example let us rewrite the word that computes the factorial, (see Section 4-3). The alternative factorial is shown in Figure 4-9. The word **FACT** will be used as illustrated in (4-15). Let us consider its operation. A number, whose factorial is desired, will be on the top of the stack when **FACT** is executed. Then this number is duplicated (see line 1). Now the loop begins. The number on the

```
0 ( ALTERNATE FACTORIAL )
1 : FACT   DUP       BEGIN    1-     DUP 1-      0>        WHILE
2          DUP       ROT   *     SWAP      REPEAT
3          SWAP      .      DROP    ;
4
5
6
7
8
9
10
11
12
13
14
15
```

Figure 4-9. An alternative program that computes the factorial.

top of the stack is decreased by 1. This decreased number is duplicated when **DUP** is executed. Now **1 –** is executed again. This number is tested using *0>*. Thus, the flag on the stack will be true if the number that was popped off the stack when *0>* was executed was greater than zero. **WHILE** causes the flag to be popped off the stack. If it is true, **WHILE** does not affect the further operation of the loop. Then **DUP** is executed. The stack now contains the original number, which we call n, and in each of the two spaces above it, the original number diminished by 1. The ROT brings the origianl number to the top of the stack. When the FORTH word * is executed, the product n(n-1) will be on the top of the stack. After the **SWAP** is executed, n-1 will be on the top of the stack and n(n-1) will be in the second position. The looping then repeats. The number on the top of the stack is diminished by one. Thus, at the end of the second loop we will have computed n(n-1)(n-2). The looping will continue in this way until the second 1- in line 1 reduces the number to 0. Now the flag will be false. When **WHILE** is executed it will cause the remainder of the loop, between **WHILE** and **REPEAT**, to be skipped. Thus looping has terminated. The **SWAP** in line 3 will then bring the desired factorial to the top of the stack. The word . will result in its being printed. Finally the **DROP** will drop the remaining word from the stack and operation will terminate.

Conditional loops only terminate when some condition is satisfied. If your program has a bug, then the condition may never be met and the program will loop indefinitely. If your program appears to hang up, such infinitely long loops may be responsible. Check your programs carefully to see that this does not occur.

4-5. SOME ADDITIONAL COMPARISON WORDS

There are other comparison words in the FORTH language. We shall discuss them in this section. Since the underlying ideas have already been covered we shall only briefly discuss these words.

?DUP—The FORTH command **?DUP** (pronounced query dupe or question dupe) duplicates the top number on the stack provided that it is *not* zero. If the top number on the stack is zero then **?DUP** takes *no* action.

ABORT—The FORTH command **ABORT** clears both the stack and the return stack, terminates the program, and returns control to the terminal. Thus, this word can be used to "clean up" the stacks as well as to terminate operation. In some FORTH systems there is a different, but similar word **ABORT"**. It is used in the form

ABORT" text "   (4-25)

ABORT" functions in the same way as **ABORT** except that the operation takes place on the basis of a flag. If the flag on the top of the stack is true when **ABORT"** is executed, then the stacks are cleared, the program is terminated and control is returned to the terminal. In addition, the text material between the quotes is printed. **ABORT"** can be used to terminate execution so as to prevent some undesirable operation from taking place. Note that if the flag is false, **ABORT"** causes the flag to be dropped from the stack and proceeds as if ABORT" were *not* present.

As an example of the use of **ABORT"**, consider the following. Suppose that you were looping with a variable increment where the increment was either computed by the program or entered by the user. A loop increment of zero would result in indefinite looping. You could use **ABORT"** to prevent this from happening. For instance, consider the following segment of a FORTH word.

DUP 0= ABORT" PROGRAM TERMINATED " +LOOP

DUP duplicates the top number on the stack. Next **0=** is executed. The top number is popped off the stack and replaced by a flag. When **ABORT"** is executed, the flag is popped from the stack. If the flag is false, the **ABORT"** will cause no further action. On the other hand, if the flag is true then the operation of the program will be terminated and the words PROGRAM TERMINATED will be printed.

Y/N—The word **Y/N** is not part of FORTH-79. It is implemented in MMSFORTH. When **Y/N** is executed computation pauses and (Y/N) ? is printed on your terminal. The user then must respond with a Y or an N (yes or no). No RETURN need be typed and no other input will be accepted. A flag is then put onto the stack. It is false if a Y was entered and true if an N was entered. This is the opposite of what most people would assume, so be careful. The stack relation is

$$\rightarrow \quad n_{flag} \tag{4-26}$$

The word **Y/N** allows you to question the person using the program.

As an illustration of the use of the word Y/N consider Figure 4-10. There we write a word called **PWR2**. It prints out the first power of 2 (i.e., 2) and then asks the user if the program should continue. A response of Y causes the next power of two (4) to be printed. The program continues in this way until N is input in response to the ? prompt. Now consider Figure 4-10. The **BEGIN-UNTIL** loop computes and prints the powers of two. **Y/N** is executed before the word **UNTIL**. A response of Y puts a false flag onto the stack and looping continues. A response of N puts a true flag onto the stack and looping ceases.

```
0 ( AN ILLUSTRATION OF Y/N )
1 : PWR2    1 BEGIN    2  *    DUP   .    CR
2             ." DO YOU WISH TO CONTINUE"    CR
3             Y/N    CR      UNTIL          ;
4
5
6
7
8
9
10
11
12
13
14
15
```

Figure 4-10. A program that is terminated by the user.

NOT—The FORTH command **NOT** pops the top word off the stack and treats it as a flag. If the flag is true then a false flag is pushed onto the stack. If the original flag is false then a true is pushed onto the stack. The stack relation is

$$n_{flag1} \rightarrow n_{flag2} \tag{4-27}$$

For instance if we follow the **Y/N** word with **NOT** then the resulting flag will be true if Y were input. The resulting flag would be false if N were input.

4-6. BRANCHING THROUGH THE USE OF CASE WORDS

In this section we shall discuss another procedure for branching. Although it is not part of FORTH-79, it is found in MMSFORTH. It would be very convenient if we could branch to different FORTH words in a program. For instance, under one condition we might execute one FORTH word while under another condition we might execute a different FORTH word. This is called a branching by *case*. The word that provides this branching is **NCASE**.

The general form for the use of NCASE is

NCASE n_1 n_2 n_3 " WORDA WORDB WORDC
    OTHERWISE statements q CASEND statements x   (4-28)

Here n_1, n_2, and n_3 constitute a list of integers in the range -128 to 127. This is followed by a *single* " mark and a list of FORTH names. We have illustrated this using three numbers and three names; there could be more or less. However, there must be an equal number of numbers and names. The word **OTHERWISE** follows the list of names. Any valid FORTH statements may follow. Then the word **CASEND** is entered. The operation of the **NCASE** word is as follows. The list of numbers corresponds to the list of names. When NCASE is executed the top number is popped off the stack. If it is equal to n_1 then **WORDA** will be executed. If the number is equal to n_2 then **WORDB** will be executed. Only one word in the list will be executed; the statements q will *not* be executed. The statements x after **CASEND**, if any, will be executed next. If the number that was on the top of the stack does not equal *any* of the numbers in the list then *none* of the words in the list will be executed. Now statements q will be executed. Then, statements x following **CASEND** will be executed. The stack relation for **NCASE** is

$$n \rightarrow \tag{4-29}$$

In Figure 4-11 we consider an example of the use of **NCASE**. This is a program that will add, subtract, or multiply two numbers that are in the second and third positions on the stack. The top number on the stack determines if addition, subtraction, or multiplication is to take place. If the number that is on the top of the stack is 1 then addition will take place. If the number that is on the top of the stack is 4 then subtraction will take place. Similarly a 7 on the top of the stack results in multiplication. (The numbers need not be sequential.) Now let us consider the program. In lines 1,2, and 3, we define the words **ADD**, **SUBTRACT**, and **MULTIPLY** that pop the top two numbers off the stack and either add, subtract, or multiply them, respectively. Starting in line 4 we define a word **CHOICE**. When **NCASE** is executed it pops the top number from the stack. If it is 1 then **ADD** will be executed and the operation will then proceed to the words following **CASEND**. If the number that was popped off the stack was 7 then **MULTIPLY** would be executed. On the other hand, if the number that was popped off the stack was not a 1, 4, or 7, then the words between the '' and **OTHERWISE** would *not* be executed; in this case the statements between **OTHERWISE** and **CASEND** *would* be executed. Thus, **WRONG CHOICE** would be printed. The statements following **CASEND** would always be executed. Thus, the program always terminates with the words PROGRAM FINISHED.

```
0 ( AN ILLUSTRATION OF CASE )
1 : ADD  +      .     ;
2 : SUBTRACT    -      .    ;
3 : MULTIPLY    *      .    ;
4 : CHOICE   NCASE   1 4 7   " ADD SUBTRACT MULTIPLY
5        OTHERWISE ." WRONG CHOICE    "     CASEND
6           ." PROGRAM FINISHED"      ;
7
8
9
10
11
12
13       .
14
15
```

Figure 4-11. An illustration of the use of the word **NCASE**.

4-7. STRUCTURED PROGRAMMING

Programs that are written in a modularized form that is easy to debug are called *structured programs*. The FORTH language is such that most programs are easily, almost automatically, written in a structured form. In this section we shall discuss procedures for writing structured programs.

MODULARIZATION—A FORTH program usually consists of many commands. For instance consider Figure 4-7. The word **PYTHTRIP**, which is the main program, calls upon the words **SQUARE** and **PT**. In a very complex program the main word might call upon many words. These words could, in turn, call upon other words. In general, you should try to keep your words short. The maximum length should typically be one screen. (For instance, the 16 lines of Figure 4-7 constitute a screen.) In this way each word is simple and can be tested and debugged easily. More complex words are then built up from simple words that have already been tested. This procedure also lends itself to team programming; for instance, different people can work on different words. Of course, you cannot start writing the simple words until you know the overall structure of the program. This *must be done first*.

Algorithms—Top-Down Design

When you write a complex program, or any program for that matter, you must conceive of a general plan for it. Such a plan is called an *algorithm*. You should determine the algorithm before starting to write the program. If the program is simple, it may seem as though the first step could be skipped and the program written immediately. In such cases, the algorithm is already in the programmer's mind. If the program is complex then it is a good idea to sketch the ideas before starting to program. For instance, for the program Figure 4-7 we could conceive of the idea of having three nested loops. The two outer loops generate the values of a^2 and b^2. The inner loop generates the value of c^2 and compares it with the sum $a^2 + b^2$, see Section 4-3. If these two quantities are equal, then we have found a Pythagorean triple. This is the basic algorithm for the program in Figure 4-7. The algorithm is not complete. We must fill in the details. In a more complex program the first step in obtaining the algorithm would be to prepare a general procedure such as the one just outlined. This would ultimately take the form of a FORTH word. This word would have many subwords. At the start their functions would be defined, but the details of these words would not be considered at this time. After the main word is written and debugged, the procedure would be repeated with each of the subwords. That is, we would obtain an algorithm for each subword and then write and debug the program. The subwords themselves would then define their own subwords. We can represent this with a *hierarchical diagram*. Such a diagram is shown in Figure 4-12. In this figure the main FORTH word calls on two subwords, a and c. These subwords, in turn, call upon subwords b, d, and e. Subword a and subword c both call upon subword d. At some point we must actually write the program. Before writing all the subwords it would be advisable to see if the original algorithm is correct.

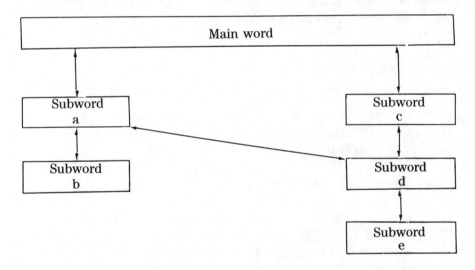

Figure 4-12. A simple hierarchical diagram.

A procedure that can be used very easily with modular programs is called *top-down design*. We start by drawing the hierarchical diagram. In general, when we plan the algorithm we must consider that the program will be broken up in this way. We write the main word first. This should be tested *before* the subwords are written. To do this we replace the actual subwords with simple ones called *stubs*. The stubs do not perform any real computation. They simply enter test data into the main word. They also test that the main word properly supplies data to the stub.

After the main program is checked and running properly, we test the stubs. The same top-down type of design is used here. The subwords should be checked on their own, without the main program, and then checked to see that they run properly with the main program. Consider Figure 4-12. The main word would be checked first with stubs representing subwords a and c. Next subword a would be written and checked using stubs for subwords b and b. Then subword a would be checked to see that it runs properly with the main program. Subword b would then be written and checked. Proceeding in this way, the entire program would be written and checked. If there were several teams working on this program, one would work on subwrod a and the other on subword c. The top-down procedure may seem tedious, but it is a great help when complex programs are written.

EXERCISES

The following exercises call for writing FORTH words or programs. Check the programs by running them on your computer. Do not make any single FORTH command too long. Instead, write one FORTH word that calls shorter words that you write.

4-1.   What is meant by a flag?

4-2.   Write a FORTH word that will subtract two integers and out put their difference if they are unequal or print the words NUMBERS EQUAL if they are equal.

4-3.   Write a FORTH word that will print the smallest of three numbers on the stack. Use the comparison words that were introduced in Section 4-1.

4-4.   Repeat Problem 4-3 finding the largest of the three numbers.

4-5.   Repeat Problem 4-4 but now find the largest absolute value.

4-6.   Discuss what is meant by conditional branching.

4-7. Write a FORTH word that adds three numbers and multiplies them by 4 if their sum is less than 50. If the sum is between 50 and 70 multiply the numbers by 6 and if the sum is greater than 70 multiply by 8.

4-8. Write a FORTH command that computers the following polynomial for different values of x:

$$4x^3 + gx^2 + 5x + 3$$

where $g = 4$ if x is equal to or less than 15, and $g = 9$ if x is greater than 15.

4-9. Write a FORTH word that computes the sum of all the numbers that lie between two integers on the stack. The smallest integer of the pair should be on the top of the stack.

4-10. Write a FORTH word that evaluates the polynomial

$$x^3 - 2x^2 + 2x - 15$$

for all values of x between 1 and 20.

4-11. Write a FORTH command that evaluates the following function for all values of x between -2 and 5, and all values of y between -6 and 4.

$$3xy^3 - 2x^2 + 5xy - 3x - 5y + 18$$

4-12. Repeat Problem 4-9 using a **LEAVE** word to terminate the FORTH word if the sum becomes greater than 10,000.

4-13. Write a FORTH word that computes the product of all the odd numbers between 1 and an odd number that is on the top of the stack. The program should terminate if the product becomes greater than 20,000. A suitable error message should be printed.

4-14. Repeat Problems 4-12 using the **BEGIN-UNTIL** form.

4-15. Repeat Problems 4-13 using the **BEGIN-WHILE-REPEAT** form.

4-16. The students in a class each take four tests. Write a FORTH word that uses other FORTH words (that you must write) to perform the following computations. The grades in the four tests are placed on the stack. Then the student's average for the four tests should be evaluated and a grade based on this average obtained. If the average is 90 or more the grade will be an A. If the average is between 89 and 80 then the grade will be a B. If the average is between 79 and 70 then the grade will be a C. If the average is between 69 and 60 then the grade will be a D. If the average is less than 59 the grade will be an F. The average must be an integer. When the division is performed, increase the quotient by 1 if the remainder is 2 or more.

4-17. Discuss the use of the FORTH word **ABORT**.

4-18. Compare the FORTH words **ABORT** and **ABORT"**.

4-19. Repeat Problem 4-16 but now, after the grade is evaluated, ask the user if the program is to be run again. Also change the form of entering the data. Prompt the user for the four grades.

4-20. Repeat Problem 4-19 using the FORTH word **NOT**.

4-21. Write a FORTH word that calls upon other FORTH words that you have written to print out a different message for each day of the week. (Make up the message yourself.)

4-22. What is meant by structured programming?

4-23. What is meant by top-down programming?

4-24. Repeat Problem 4-19, using ideas from top-down programming.

Chapter 5

A General Discussion
of Numbers

We have discussed single-length or single-precision integers in
several parts of this book. In this chapter we shall discuss arithmetic
operations with double-length integers. This will allow us to work
with much larger numbers. However, that is not the only reason for
using double-length integers. We shall introduce a topic called
scaling that will allow us to use integer arithmetic in some
applciations where decimals are used. There are other forms of
integer arithmetic that will also be discussed.

There are times when we must work with extremely large or small
numbers. In such cases, even double-length integer arithmetic does
not suffice so we must work with *floating point* numbers. We shall
introduce them in this chapter. Floating point arithmetic is not part
of FORTH-79, but it is included in many FORTH systems so it will
be discussed here. Actually floating point arithmetic takes more
computer time and memory space than either single-length or
double-length integer arithmetic does, but there are times when it
is desirable to use it. Double-length integer arithmetic takes more
computer time, and memory storage, than single-length integer
arithemetic does. Various forms of floating point arithmetic will be
discussed in this chapter.

5-1. DOUBLE-LENGTH INTEGERS

Single-length integers use one stack word. As we have discussed,
these integers can be used to represent numbers that lie in the range

$-\overline{3}2678$ to 32767. Double-length integers use two stack words and can be used to represent numbers that lie in the range $-2,147,483,648$ to $2,147,483,647$. In Section 2-5 we discussed some details of stack manipulation using double-length integers. We shall now consider some details of their arithmetic. Double-length integers should only be used when their large range is required. They occupy twice as much memory as single-length integers and computation takes longer when they are used. Your FORTH system may not automatically have double-length integer capability when it boots up. You may have to load the blocks that contain the double-length FORTH words.

In the FORTH language most of the single-length arithmetic and comparison words have corresponding double-length arithmetic words. We shall consider them in this section. Many of the details of operation are similar to those for single-length integers so we will not consider double-length integer operation in as much detail.

D + —The FORTH word **D +** pops two double-length integers off the stack and then pushes their sum (also a double-length integer) onto the stack. Four stack positions stored the original two words. There is no way of studying the stack to determine if the numbers stored there were single length or double length. For instance, suppose that you pushed four single-length integers onto the stack. When you executed **D +**, the top two stack positions would be treated as if they contained double-length integers. Similarly the third and fourth stack positions would also be treated as if they contained a double-length integer. Thus, double-length addition would proceed. The stack relation is

$$d_1 \; d_2 \; \rightarrow \; d_{sum} \tag{5-1}$$

We use d to represent a double-length word, while n represents a single-length word. That is, d represents *two* stack positions while n represents *one* stack position.

Entering Double-length Integers

In order to do arithmetic using double-length integers, we must have a way of pushing them onto the stack. Actually FORTH will do this automatically, we need only indicate that the numbers are double length. To do this we include a decimal point anywhere in the number. For instance we could write 34.56. This would be treated as the double-length integer 3456. These are integers so the decimal point does not indicate a fractional part. In fact we could write 3.456, 3456., 345.6 and achieve the same result as far as the numbers stored on the stack are concerned. In every case the double-length integer 3456 would be stored. In the next section we shall see how we can use double-length integers in calculations involving numbers with fractional parts. In Section 3-3 we discussed the storage of double-length integers. Remember that the most significant bits of a double-length integer are stored on the top of the stack so that a positive single-length integer on the top of the stack can be made into a double-length integer by pushing a zero onto the stack (see Section 3-3). For instance if we want to store the number 35 as a double-length integer we could use either of the following.

    35. (RETURN)   (5-2a)
    35 0 (RETURN)   (5-2b)

These ideas are discussed in greater detail in Section 3-3.

D.—The FORTH word **D.** (pronounced d-dot) pops the top double-length integer from the stack and causes it to be output. **D.** functions in the same way for double-length integers as . does for single-length integers. The stack relation for **D.** is

    d →   (5-3)

As an example let us write a FORTH word that pops the top two double-length integers from the stack and prints their sum.

    : DOUBADD D+ D. ;   (5-4)

Note that this uses essentially the same ideas as the single-length integer add.

    D −—The FORTH word **D −** pops the top two double-length integers off the stack and pushes their difference onto the stack. The top number on the stack is subtracted from the second number. The answer is a double-length integer. The stack relation is

    d_1 d_2 → d_{diff} (5-5)

where d_{diff} is equal to $d_1 - d_2$. Again we see that **D-** functions in essentially the same way as − , except that double-length integers are now used.

Multiplication and Division

The FORTH words for multiplication and division of double-length integers are not part of FORTH-79. However, they are implemented in MMSFORTH and other FORTH SYSTEMS. These words correspond to their single-length counterparts. For example the FORTH word **D*** pops the top two double-length integers from the stack and replaces them by their product. The result is a double-length integer.

The FORTH commands for division using double-length integers are **D/** and **D/MOD** (pronounced d-divide and d-slash-mod). These FORTH words function in a manner that is analogous to their single-length integer counterparts / and **/MOD**.

In most applications *both* single-length and double-length integers are used. For instance calculated quantities may be double-length integers, but loop parameters will, in general, be single-length integers. As an example we shall rewrite the factorial program of Figure 4-6 using double-length integers. Note that 8! + 40320. This number is too large to be expressed as an ordinary single-length integer. The program is given in Figure 5-1. Consider its operation.

```
0 ( CALCULATION OF FACTORIAL USING DOUBLE-LENGTH INTEGERS)
1 : FACT  1  +   1  0   1   4 ROLL    SWAP
2         DO  I 0   D*    LOOP  D,            ;
3
4
5
6
7
8
9
10
11
12
13
14
15
```

Figure 5-1. A FORTH word that uses double-length integers in the calculation of the factorial.

We assume that you are familiar with the original factorial program of Figure 4-6. Now consider Figure 5-1. Assume that the number whose factorial we wish to compute is pushed onto the stack as a single-length integer. Add 1 to it. Next, set up a double-length 1 on the stack. This is accomplished by pushing 1 and then 0 onto the stack. Alternatively, we could have indicaated that the 1 was double length by writing 1. in place of the 1 and 0. After the 4 **ROLL** and **SWAP** are executed the stack will consist of (reading from top down) 1, the number whose factorial is desired increased by 1, and the double-length integer 1. Next **DO** is executed. The top two numbers are popped off the stack and pushed onto the return stack. Now the looping is started. First, **I** pushes the index of the loop onto the stack. This is made into a double-length integer by pushing a 0 onto the stack. The operation of the remainder of the program follows that of Figure 4-6 except that double-length operations are used.

Double-length Integer Stack Manipulations

The FORTH words that are used for stack manipulation have already been discussed in Section 2-5.

Comparison Words

Some of the comparison words that were discussed in Section 4-1 have analogous double-length integer words. The FORTH word **D =** corresponds to **=**. When **D =** is executed the top two double-length integers are popped off the stack and are replaced by a flag. The flag will be true if the two integers are equal. The flag will be false otherwise. Note that the flag is a single-length integer. The stack relation is

$$d_1 \; d_2 \; \rightarrow \; n_{flag} \qquad\qquad (5\text{-}6)$$

The FORTH word **D<** is analagous to the single-length word **<**. When **D<** is executed the top two double-length integers are popped off the stack and a flag is pushed onto the stack. The flag will be true if the double-length integer that was second on the stack was less than the double-length integer that was in the top two positions on the stack. The stack relation is also given by (5-6).

There are not as many double-length comparison words as there are single-length FORTH comparison words. However, we can write our own FORTH words to make up the deficiency. For instance, suppose that we want a double-length word that corresponds to **>**. The word, which we shall call **DD>**, will pop the top two double-length integers off the stack and push a flag onto the stack. The flag will be true if the double-length integer that was second on the stack was greater than the double-length integer that was in the top two stack positions. The word is shown in Figure 5-2. We start by duplicating the top double-length integer. Next we bring

```
0  ( DOUBLE LENGTH COMPARISON )
1  : DD>   2DUP   2ROT   2DUP   2ROT
2          D<   0    2ROT   2ROT   D=   ROT
3          +    0=    .        DROP            ;
4
5
6
7
8
9
10
11
12
13
14
15
```

Figure 5-2. The FORTH word **DD>** that compares two double-length integers.

the original, second double-length integer to the top of the stack by executing **2ROT**. This double-length integer is then duplicated. Now we execute **2ROT**. The stack is now in the form of d_2 d_1 d_1 d_2. The original stack configuration was d_1 d_2. Now **D<** is executed. Thus, the resulting flag on the top of the stack will be true if d_1 is less than d_2. Next we push a 0 onto the stack. Now the flag can be considered as a double-length integer. Next **2ROT** is executed twice. This brings the original two double-length integers to the top of the stack. Since we will be using the **D =** comparison next, we need not concern ourselves about the order of these two double-length integers. Now **D =** is executed. The top three stack positions contain a flag, 0, and another flag. **ROT** is executed so that the two flags are on the top of the stack. If either of these flags is true then **DD>** should result in a false flag. Next + is executed. We only need to use a single-length add in this case. If this results in 1 or 2 then a false flag should be obrained. Now **0 =** is executed. A true flag will only be obtained if *both* flags were originally false. Thus, we have obtained the desired result.

Some Additional FORTH Words for Double-Length Integers

There are additional FORTH words that are used with double-length integers. These are analogous to words that were used with single-length integers. Let us consider some of these.

DNEGATE—The FORTH word **DENEGATE** is equivalent to the word **NEGATE** (see Section 2-7). That is, **DNEGATE** changes the sign of the double-length integer that is stored on the top of the stack.

DMIN, DMAX and DABS—The FORTH words **DMIN, DMAX**, and **DABS** are equivalent to **MIN, MAX,** and **ABS** that were discussed in Section 2-7. For instance **DMIN** pops the top double-length integers off the stack and pushes the lesser one back onto the stack. The FORTH word **DABS** pops off the double-length integer that is on the top of the stack and replaces it with a double-length integer that is equal to the absolute value of the original integer.

D#IN—The FORTH word **D#IN** is analagous to the **#IN** command (see Section 3-1). This word is not a part of FORTH-79 but it is implemented in MMSFORTH. when **D#IN** is executed, computation pauses and a ? appears on the screen. A double-length integer is entered followed by RETURN. Even if the integer that was entered did not contain a decimal point, it would be treated as a double-length integer. The stack relation is

$$\rightarrow \text{ d} \qquad\qquad\qquad (5\text{-}7)$$

Number Formatting

Double-length integers can be printed using the formatting procedures that were discussed in Section 3-3. Some of these procedures use different words for double-length integers, but others do not.

Numbers in Fields

The FORTH word **D.R** is analogous to **.R** which was discussed in Section 3-3. When **D.R** is executed there should be at least two integers on the stack, a single-length integer on the top of the stack and a double-length integer below it. When **D.R** is executed, both numbers are popped off the stack. The single-length integer specifies the width of the field which the double-length integer is output. The stack relation is

$$\text{d n} \rightarrow \qquad\qquad\qquad (5\text{-}8)$$

In general, all the discussions from Section 3-3 in regard to the printing of numbers in fields applies here.

Pictured Numeric Output

Pictured numeric output was discussed in Section 3-3. All of that discussion applies to double-length integers. Pictured numeric output is really used exclusively with double-length integers. In Section 3-3 we were concerned with the output of single-length integers. In order to use pictured numeric output we had to convert the single-length integers to double-length integers by pushing a 0 onto the stack. Thus, all the techniques discussed in Section 3-3 can be used to print double-length integers using pictured numeric output. (Of course, now it is not necessary to push the 0 onto the stack.)

Change of Number Base

The discussion of change of number base that was presented in Section 2-7 applies also to double-length integers. For instance, if you type **HEX** (RETURN) then the output of any single-length or double-length integer will be in hexadecimal.

5-2. SCALING OF NUMBERS

We have thus far concerned ourselves with integers and have assumed that all calculations are completely accurate. However, this is not always the case and inaccuracies do occur. Suppose that we want to compute the following

$$(2/4)*6 \tag{5-9}$$

The fraction 2/4 is equal to 1/2, and 1/2 times 6 is equal to 3. Now let us see how this would be calculated in FORTH. Suppose that we entered the following

$$6 \ 2 \ 4 \ / \ * \ (\text{RETURN}) \tag{5-10}$$

Now, when the / is executed we divide 2 by 4. This results in **zero** (see Section 2-1). When 0 is multiplied by 6 the result will be zero. The FORTH system has not failed. In fact, the FORTH calculations are exact. The loss of the remainder accounts for the error. This is just a rather extreme case of what is called **roundoff error**. Let us consider another example. Suppose that when (5-10) was executed the stack was 6 21 4. The exact result should be $(5.25)6 = 31.5$. On the other hand the FORTH calculation would result in $(5)6 = 30$. Remember that any fractional part of division is dropped. Thus, when 21 is divided by 4 the fractional part is dropped and the answer 5 is obtained.

We can improve the accuracy of the previous calculation by performing the multiplication *before* we perform the division. For instance, suppose that we rewrite (5-10) as

4 6 2 * SWAP / (RETURN)   (5-11)

In this case, when we perform the calculations we start by taking the product $2(6) = 12$. When we divide by 4 the result 3 is obtained. In this case we have obtained the correct answer. Now let us consider the second example where the stack would be 4 6 21. We take the product $21(6) = 126$; $126/4 = 31.5$. When the fractional part is dropped we obtain the answer 31. Previously we obtained 30 as the answer. Of course, 31 is more accurate than 30.

The previous calculations demonstrated that we can improve accuracy by multiplying *before* dividing. However this is not the complete answer. Even if we deal with numbers that are only moderately large the intermediate product may become too large for the system. For instance, when we work with single-length integers all numbers must lie in the range -32768 to 32767. Now suppose that we want to calculate $(459)(734)/915$. The product 336906 is too large to be represented by a single-length integer and an error would result if we attempted to take this product. (Note that the system might not indicate that an error had occurred.) On the other hand, the final answer is 368.2 which is not too large. We could eliminate the difficulty by working with double-length integers. However these integers require more computer time and take up more memory. Fortunately FORTH provides us with a word that allows us to work with large intermediate products, such as the one in the previous example, without having to use double-length integers throughout all the calculations.

*/—The FORTH word */ (pronounced times-divide) operates on three single-length integers on the stack. The stack relation is

n_1 n_2 n_3 $\rightarrow$ n_{ans} (5-12)

The following operations are performed. First the product $n_1 n_2$ is figured. The product is stored as a double-length integer. Next that double-length product is divided by n_3. The final answer is stored as a single-length integer. The intermediate product is stored as a double-length integer so that the overflow problem (i.e., the number becoming too large) is solved. However, we do not have to work with double-length integers throughout the program. As an example let us now write the input the calculations of (5-10) but now using */.

6 2 4 */ (RETURN)   (5-13)

/MOD—The FORTH word **/MOD** functions in the same way as */ except tht two single-length integers result. One is the quotient and the other is the remainder of the final division. The stack relation is

$n_1 \ n_2 \ n_3 \rightarrow n_{rem} \ n_{quot}$ (5-14)

The number on the top of the stack is the quotient of the division while the second integer on the stack is the remainder.

D*/ and D*/MOD—The FORTH words **D*/** and **D*/MOD** function in the same way as */ and */MOD except that they work with double-length integers. The intermediate product is two double-length words. This is called a *quadruple-length* word. Thus, we can obtain the advantages of the previously discussed words when double-length integers are used. The words **D*/** and **D*/MOD** are not part of FORTH-79. They are found in MMSFORTH.

Scaling of Calculations

There are times when we want to perform computations using integers but the numbers that we are using contain fractional parts. We can use a procedure called *scaling* in these situations. For instance, suppose that we were computing a salesman's commission. We would have to work in terms of dollars and cents. In addition, we would have to take a percentage of his sales. All of this involves the use of decimal fractions. However, we can use integers in our computations. Suppose that we have the quantity $56.42. If we multiply it by 100 then it can be represented by the integer 5642. If all the dollars and cents are multiplied by 100 then they can all be represented by integers. These numbers have been said to be scaled by a factor of 100. Note that the FORTH words */ and */MOD can be said to use a special form of scaling. In a way, FORTH will automatically scale double-length integers. That is, if they are entered with a decimal point *anywhere* in the number they will automatically be treated as double-length integers. You must be very careful here. The scaling of all numbers must be the same. For

instance if you enter 45.78 and 4.578 they will be treated as the
same integer, whereas one number is actually ten times the other
one. As an example of scaling let us compute the commission of a
salesman. We will write a FORTH word to add his sales and then
take 15 percent of the total as his commission. We shall consider
two different words. One will use single-length integers while the
other will use double-length integers. Both words are shown in
Figure 5-3.

```
0  ( EXAMPLES OF SCALING )
1  : TOTAL          1   DO      +      LOOP    ;
2  : COMMISSION     TOTAL    15  100          */
3         CR    0    <#   #   #    46 HOLD    #S     #>     TYPE ;
4
5
6  ( SECOND EXAMPLE USING DOUBLE LENGTH INTEGERS )
7  : DTOTAL         1   DO     D+     LOOP    ;
8  : DCOMMISSION    DTOTAL   15.  100.         D*/
9         CR        <#   #   #    46 HOLD    #S     #>     TYPE ;
10
11
12
13
14
15
```

Figure 5-3. An illustration of scaling using single-length and double-length
integers.

Let us start by considering the program that uses single-length
integers. The word **COMMISSION** calls upon the word **TOTAL**.
Consider **TOTAL** first. It obtains the sum of all the sales. The amount
of each sale is pushed onto the stack and finally the number of the
individual sales is pushed onto the stack. The numbers that represent
the amount of each sale should be entered in dollars and cents
without a decimal point (i.e., in cents). For instance, if there were
three sales of $45.09, $56.02, and $103.45, then the following would
be entered

4509 5632 10345 3   (5-15)

Note that by entering the data in this way we have scaled it. When
TOTAL is executed a 1 is pushed onto the stack. Next **DO** is executed
and the top two integers are popped off the stack and pushed onto
the return stack as parameters of the loop. For the data entered,

+ will be executed twice. Thus, the sum of the sales will be on the top of the stack. Now let us consider the word **COMMISSION**. It starts by calling **TOTAL**. Thus, the total sales will be on the top of the stack. Next 15 and 100 are pushed onto the stack and */ is executed. Hence, the total sales are multiplied by 15 and divided by 100. Therefore, 15 percent of the sales has been obtained. We want to print this with the decimal point in the proper place. This is done in line 3, where we use pictured numeric output (see Section 3-3). A zero is pushed onto the stack to make the number that is to be output a double-length integer. The pictured numeric output is written so that the two least significant decimal digits of the number are printed to the right of the decimal point. This follows the examples in Section 3-3.

Now let us consider the second example in Figure 5-3 which uses double-length integers. Now the data should be entered with the decimal point included. The usual dollars and cents format *must* be used. For instance, in this case the data of (5-15) would be entered as

    45.09 56.32 103.45 3   (5-16)

Note that the 3 is a single-length integer. The word **DTOTAL** functions in essentially the same way as **TOTAL** except that **D +** is used instead of **+** . Similarly the word **DCOMMISSION** functions the same way as **COMMISSION**. There are some differences. The periods in 15. and 100. that are added so that these numbers are treated as double-length integers. Of course, **D */** is used rather than */. We do not have to push a zero onto the stack prior to using the pictured numeric output since the number that we wish to output is actually a double-length integer.

Not all FORTH systems have the word **D */**. The double-length integer program of Figure 5-3 can still be used if your FORTH system allows the use of the words **D*** and **D/**. This does not allow us to use a quadruple-length integer for an intermediate product.

5-3. Mixed-length Calculations

There are times when it would be convenient to work with both single-length and double-length integers in the same calculation. For instance the product of two single-length integers is, at times, too large to be represented by a single-length integer. If they were positive we could convert both single-length integers to double-length integers by pushing zeros onto the stack at appropriate times and then using double-length multiplication, but some FORTH systems provide words that will take care of these circumstances with a minimum of effort. These words are not part of FORTH-79 but they are provided by MMSFORTH and other FORTH systems. Calculations involving both single-length integers and double-length integers are called *mixed-length* or *mixed-precision* operations. We shall discuss them in this section.

M*—The FORTH word M* pops the top two single-length integers off the stack, computes their product as a double-length integer, and pushes this number back onto the stack. The stack relation is

$$n_1 \ n_2 \ \rightarrow \ d_{prod} \tag{5-17}$$

For instance the following word will take the product of two single-length integers and print the resulting double-length integer.

$$: \ MIXMULT \ M* \ D. \ ; \tag{5-18}$$

M/ and M/MOD—We have just discussed the convenience of expressing the product of two single-length integers as a double-length integer. Conversely, it may be convenient to express both the quotient and the remainder of the division of a double-length integer by a single-length integer as single-length integers. The FORTH word **M/** obtains the quotient in such a calculation. The stack relation is

$$d \ n \ \rightarrow \ n_{quot} \tag{5-19}$$

Note that the double-length integer that is in the second and third stack positions is divided by the single-length integer that is on the top of the stack. Both of these numbers are popped off the stack and are replaced by the single-length quotient.

The word **M/MOD** functions in a manner similar to **M/** except that two single-length integers are pushed onto the stack. One is the quotient and the other is the remainder. The stack relation is

$$d \ n \ \rightarrow \ n_{rem} \ n_{quot} \tag{5-20}$$

Note that the quotient is on the top of the stack.

M + and M – —Sometimes we want to add a double-length integer and a single-length integer. The word that accomplishes this is **M +** . The result of this operation is a double-length integer. The stack relation is

$$d \ n \ \rightarrow \ d_{sum} \tag{5-21}$$

Note that the single-length integer is on the top of the stack.

We can subtract a single-length integer from a double-length integer using the word **M −**. This word is not present in many FORTH systems. The stack relation is

$$d \quad n \quad \rightarrow \quad d_{dif} \qquad\qquad (5\text{-}22)$$

The single-length integer that is on the top of the stack is subtracted from the double-length integer that is in the second and third stack positions. Of course, both of these integers are popped from the stack and are replaced by their difference which is a double-length integer.

As an example let us write our own word for positive numbers that replaces **M-**. It is

$$: \text{ MIX- } 0 \text{ D- } ; \qquad\qquad (5\text{-}23)$$

We simply push a 0 onto the stack so that the single-length integer that is on the top of the stack can now be treated as a double-length integer.

M*/—The word **M*/** functions in a manner similar to ***/** or **D*/** except that the product of a double-length integer and a single-length integer is taken and the result is stored in a triple-length word (i.e., it occupies three stack positions). This product is divided by a single-length integer and the resulting quotient is a single-length integer. The stack relation is

$$d \quad n_1 \quad n_2 \quad \rightarrow \quad n_{quot} \qquad\qquad (5\text{-}24)$$

Here the product dn_1 is computed and the result is divided by n_2.

5-4. UNSIGNED NUMBERS

We have, thus far, assumed that we were dealing with *signed* integers. This means that the numbers could be either positive or negative, they have a + or − sign preceding them. Numbers are stored in your computer as a sequence of 0's and 1's called binary bits (see Section 1-2). One of these bits represents the sign of the number. (A negative number is not formed from a positive one simply by changing one bit.) If we were going to work with positive numbers all the time, we would not have to make provisions for negative numbers and there would be an extra bit available to represent the number's magnitude. For instance, in a typical FORTH system, 16 bits are used to represent signed single-length integers. As we have discussed, such integers should lie in the range − 32768 to 32767.

If we used 16 bits to represent only numbers that were positive, then these numbers could lie in the range 0 to 65535. FORTH provides words that allow us to treat single-length integers as though they were unsigned. It should be emphasized that you cannot tell simply by inspecting the stack if the number stored there is signed or unsigned. It is determined only by the way in which the number is interpreted.

U.—The FORTH word **U.** (pronounced u-dot) functions in the same way as the FORTH word . except that the output number is treated as an unsigned number. The stack relation is

$$u \rightarrow \tag{5-25}$$

We have used the letter u to represent an unsigned single-length number. Actually u and n both represent one stack position. Thus U. pops the top single-length integer off the stack and outputs it as an unsigned integer. As an example consider the word

; CHECK DUP U. . ;   (5-26)

CHECK duplicates the single-length integer that is on the top of the stack and then outputs it both as an unsigned integer and as a signed integer. For instance, if we enter

3 CHECK

The resulting output will be

3 3

That is, if an integer is positive, then its signed and unsigned values will be the same. Very different results are obtained for a negative number. For instance,

−1 CHECK

will produce the output

65535 −1

The binary representation for a signed number equal to −1 is the same as that for an unsigned number equal to 65535.

U.R—The FORTH word U.R. is equivalent to .R (see Section 3-3), except that it interprets the integer that is output as an unsigned integer. The stack relation is

$$u \; n \rightarrow \tag{5-27}$$

The top two numbers are popped off the stack. The number that is on the top of the stack specifies the field within which the unsigned integer, that was second on the stack, is to be printed. If the field width is not large enough, the FORTH system will override the field specification so that the entire number can be printed.

U*—The FORTH command **U*** pops the top two numbers off the stack and treats them as unsigned integers. Their product is taken and pushed onto the stack as a *double-length-unsigned* integer. The double-length word is treated as an unsigned integer. In general, double-length unsigned integers can lie in the range 0 to 4,294,967,295. The stack relation is

$$u_1 \quad u_2 \quad \rightarrow u_d \qquad\qquad\qquad (5\text{-}28)$$

A u with a subscript d will represent an unsigned double-length integer. There are no FORTH words for printing unsigned double-length integers. However they are usually used for storing intermediate products. We shall now discuss how unsigned double-length integers can be manipulated to obtain an unsigned single-length integer.

U/MOD—The FORTH command **U/MOD** results in the unsigned double-length integer that is in the second and third stack position being divided by the unsigned single-length integer that is in the top stack position. Both of these numbers are popped off the stack and replaced by the resulting quotient and remainder. The stack relation is

$$u_d \quad u \quad \rightarrow \quad u_{rem} \quad u_{quot} \qquad\qquad (5\text{-}29)$$

The quotient and remainder are both unsigned single-length integers. Remember that **U.** rather than **.** is used to output unsigned single-length integers.

U<—The FORTH command **U<** pops the top two numbers off the stack and pushes a flag onto the stack. The flag will be true if the number that was second on the stack is less than the number that was on the top of the stack. Both numbers are treated as unsigned single-length integers. The stack relation is

$$u_1 \quad u_2 \quad \rightarrow \quad n_{flag} \qquad\qquad\qquad (5\text{-}30)$$

The flag will be true if u_1 is less than u_2.

DO and /LOOP—The parameters of a loop can be unsigned integers. The FORTH words that are used to establish the loop are **DO** and **/LOOP**. These function exactly as **DO** and **+ LOOP** except that all the loop parameters are treated as unsigned integers. Thus, the discussion in Section 4-3 applies here. Since unsigned integers are used, the loop parameters can be larger than those used with signed integers.

5-5. INDIVIDUAL BIT OPERATIONS

The numbers that are stored in the memory of your computer are all in binary form. They consist of a sequence of 0's and 1's. Each 0 and 1 is called a *bit*. There are times when it is convenient to manipulate the individual bits of the binary numbers. We shall discuss FORTH words that allow us to do this in this section.

The AND, OR, and XOR Operations—There are certain logical operations that are performed often. These operations will be applied to only two bits. The AND operation compares two bits. If they are both 1, then the result of the AND operation is a 1. If either or both of the original bits are 0 then the result of the AND operation will be 0. The OR operation compares two bits. If either or both are 1 then the result will be 1. The OR operation results in a 0 only if *both* the original bits are 0. If we call the original bits b_1 and b_2 then the AND operation results in a 1 if b_1 *and* b_2 are both 1. The OR operation will result in a 1 if either b_1 *or* b_2 are 1. The XOR operation is similar to the OR operation except that it yields a 0 if *both* b_1 and b_2 are 1. The FORTH words that we discuss here are not standard FORTH. They are found in MMSFORTH and other FORTH systems.

AND—The FORTH word **AND** pops the top two single-length integers off the stack and compares them on a bit-by-bit basis using the AND operation. The first bit of the first number is compared with the first bit of the second number using the AND operation. If both of these bits are 1's, then the first bit in the resulting number will be a 1 if either of these bits is a zero then the first bit in the resulting number is a 0. Next, the second bit of the first number is compared with the second bit of the second number and the process is repeated. This is done with each bit in turn. After the process is completed the resulting number is pushed onto the stack. The stack relation is

$$n_1 \ n_2 \ \rightarrow \ n \tag{5-31}$$

Let us illustrate the use of **AND**. To provide clarity, we shall write the numbers in their binary form in this section. Remember that many FORTH systems can output numbers in various bases (see Section 2-7). Suppose that we are working in base 2 and we write the following FORTH word

  : ANDTEST AND . ;   (5-32)

Now if we type

  10011001 01110001 ANDTEST (RETURN)

the resulting output will be

  00010001

Only the first and fifth bit positions (from the right) are 1's in both numbers. Thus, after **AND** is executed, only those bit positions contain 1's . (The leftmost 0's may not be output by your FORTH system.) If the input and output were in decimal form instead of binary, the results would be the same, except the numbers would be the decimal equivalents of the binary numbers.

OR—The FORTH word **OR** functions in a manner similar to the **AND** command except that the bit-by-bit comparisons use the OR operation. The stack relation is given by (5-31). For example suppose that we write the word

  : ORTEST OR . ;   (5-33)

Now if we type

  10011001 01110001 ORTEST (RETURN)

the resulting output will be

  1111101

XOR—The FORTH command **XOR** functions in essentially the same way as the FORTH WORD **OR** except that the XOR operations is used in the bit-by-bit comparison.

5-6. Floating Point ARITHMETIC

We have thus far considered FORTH operations that manipulated integers only. Even when we worked with numbers that had fractional parts we scaled them so that the computation could be done with integers. In general, when working with computing languages, a distinction is made between operations using integers (i.e., whole numbers) and operations using floating point numbers. A *floating point* number in a computer usually consists of two parts, the *fractional part* and the *exponent*. The exponent is usually represented in the output as a power of ten. For instance we could write

$$.567 \ x10^2 \ = \ 56.7 \qquad\qquad (5\text{-}34a)$$

In most computers powers of 10 are indicated by an E. Thus we can write

$$56.7 \ = \ .567 \ E \ 2 \qquad\qquad (5\text{-}34b)$$

Let us consider some other numbers:

$E2 = 100$
$E6 = 1000000$
$E-2 = .01$
$E-4 = .0001$

In general, the use of floating point numbers allows us to represent very large and very small numbers in addition to representing fractions. In small computers the range of the exponent is typically from -38 to $+37$. This encompasses an enormous range of numbers. The computer operations using integer arithmetic are usually much simpler than those using floating point arithmetic. Since floating point manipulations must keep track of both the fractional part and the exponent, more storage space is required and more computer time is used. Although integer operations are precise, floating point operations are subject to roundoff error at every step. Thus, integer arithmetic should be used in FORTH whenever possible. However, there are times when floating point arithmetic must be used. FORTH-79 does not include floating point arithmetic. However, MMSFORTH and other FORTH systems do make provisions for it. We shall discuss the FORTH words used by the MMSFORTH system in this section. There is no FORTH standard for floating point. The words used may differ from system to system, but the basic ideas will be the same. Many of the detail of FORTH operations using floating point numbers are similar to those applied to integers. We shall not stress these details here.

Floating Point FORTH Arithmetic Words

If a floating point number is to be entered, there must be some way of indicating to the computer that the number is a floating point number. To do this we precede the number by a percent sign and a space. For instance,

% 6 % y (RETURN)   (5-35)

will put 6 and 7 onto the stack as floating point numbers. A number on the stack cannot be distinguished by type. If you were to look at the stack you would not be able to tell what type of numbers were stored there. Each floating point number occupies two stack positions. Thus it takes up as much room as a double-length integer.

The word **F#IN** can be used to prompt for the input of a floating point number. It functions in the same way as **#IN** except that a floating point number is pushed onto the stack.

F. and F.R—To print a floating point number we use the FORTH word **F.** (pronounced f-point). This pops the top floating point number off the stack and outputs it. The stack relation is

f →   (5-36)

Note that we use an f to indicate a floating point number. Remember that each f occupies two stack positions.

Floating point numbers can be printed in fields (see Section 3-3). The FORTH word that we use is **F.R**. The stack relation is

f n →   (5-37)

There is a single-length integer on the top of the stack that specifies the field width. When **F.R** is executed both the floating point number and the integer are popped off the stack. The floating point number is output in the field specified by the integer.

Addition, Subtraction, Multiplication, and Division

The FORTH words for addition, subtraction, multiplication and division of floating point numbers are **F +** , **F −** , **F***, and **F/**. These correspond to the single-length integer words + , -, *, and /. The stack relation for these floating point words is

$$f_1 \quad f_2 \quad \rightarrow \quad f_{ans} \qquad\qquad (5\text{-}38)$$

In each case the top two floating point numbers are popped off the stack and the desired operation is performed. The resulting floating point answer is pushed onto the stack. Note that there is no need for a **MOD** in the floating point division since the quotient can now be a fraction. For instance if we type

% 50 % 3 F/ (RETURN)

the number that is pushed onto the stack will represent the floating point number .166667 E 10.

We can mix integers and floating point numbers on the stack. (Remember that there is no way of looking at a stack location and telling what type of number it represents.) For instance if we were using floating point numbers in a computation that involved looping, then the parameters of the loop would be integers. .

Stack Manipulations

Floating point numbers occupy two stack positions. Double-length integers also occupy two stack positions. If we wish to manipulate floating point numbers on the stack, we can use the same FORTH words that were used for the stack manipulations of double-length integers. In particular we can use **2DUP**, **2DROP**, **2SWAP**, and **2ROLL**. As an example we will write a FORTH word that computes the factorial, only in this case we will use floating point numbers. The program is shown in Figure 5-4. This program is very similar

```
0 ( CALCULATION OF FACTORIAL USING FLOATING-POINT NUMBERS)
1 : FFACT  1  +  %  1       1    4 ROLL    SWAP
2          DO   I   I-F   F*    LOOP  F,         ;
3
4
5
6
7
8
9
10
11
12
13
14
15
```

Figure 5-4. A FORTH word that calculates the factorial using floating point numbers.

to the program of Figure 5-1. The only difference is that floating point numbers are used in place of double-length integers. The FORTH word **I-F** (pronounced i-to-f or int-to-float) pops off the top single-length integer and pushes an equivalent floating point number onto the stack. The stack relation is

$$n \rightarrow f \qquad\qquad\qquad (5\text{-}39)$$

This operation replaces an integer that occupies one stack position by a floating point number that occupies two stack positions. Let us now compare Figures 5-1 and 5-4. In line 2 of Figure 5-1 we push the double-length integer 1 onto the stack by pushing both 1 and 0 onto the stack. Similarly, in line 2 of Figure 5-4 we use % 1 to push the floating point number 1 onto the stack. In line 2 of Figure 5-1 we use **I** and 0 to push a double-length integer equal to the loop index onto the stack. In line 3 of Figure 5-4 we use **I** and **I-F** to push a floating point number that is equal to the loop index onto the stack. In line 3 of Figure 5-1 we use **D.** to print the double-length integer that is equal to the factorial. Similarly in line 3 of Figure 5-4 we use **F.** to print a floating point number that is equal to the factorial. The stack manipulation words in Figures 5-1 and 5-4 are identical. This is because in both cases we are dealing with numbers that occupy two stack positions. Thus, the operation of the FORTH words in Figures 5-1 and 5-4 is essentially the same.

Floating Point Functions

There are various FORTH words that can be used to perform operations on floating point numbers. We will start by considering operations that are similar to those that have been performed on integers.

FABS and FMINUS—The FORTH command **FABS** is similar to the FORTH word **ABS**. **FABS** pops a floating point number off the top fo the stack and pushes its absolute value onto the stack.

The FORTH word **FMINUS** is similar to the word **NEGATE** in that **FMINUS** pops the top floating point number from the stack and pushes its negative onto the stack. The stack relation for both **FABS** and **FMINUS** is

$$f_1 \rightarrow f_2 \qquad\qquad\qquad (5\text{-}40)$$

One floating point number is replaced by another.

Comparison Words SGN and FCOMP

There are several FORTH words that are used for comparison of floating point numbers. These will be discussed next. The FORTH word **SGN** which is a pronounced sign pops the floating point number that is on the top of the stack off and replaces it by a single-length integer that can be used as a flag. The single-length integer will be -1, 0, or 1 if the original floating point number was less than 0, 0, or greater than 0 respectively. The stack relation is

$$f \rightarrow n \qquad\qquad (5\text{-}41)$$

The FORTH command **FCOMP** pops the top two floating point numbers from the stack and pushes a single-length integer onto the stack. The single-length integer is either -1, 0, or 1. The stack relation is

$$f_1 \; f_2 \rightarrow n \qquad\qquad (5\text{-}42)$$

Now n will be -1 if f_1 is less than f_2, it will be zero if $f_1 = f_2$, and it will be 1 if f_1 is greater than f_2.

Floating Point Integer Converstion I-F and CINT

There are times when we want to mix floating point numbers and integers in the same calculation. There are no FORTH words that provide for such mixed calculations. However, as we saw in Figure 5-4, there are words that convert integers to floating point numbers. We shall now consider these.

We have already discussed the FORTH word **I-F**. This pops off the single-length integer that is on the top of the stack and pushes a floating point number, that is equal to the popped integer, onto the stack. The stack relation is

$$n \rightarrow f \qquad\qquad (5\text{-}43)$$

The FORTH word **CINT** pops off the top floating point number on the stack and pushes on an integer. The integer is the largest number that is not greater than the original floating point number. The stack relation is

$$f \rightarrow n \qquad\qquad (5\text{-}44)$$

Floating Point Number Adjustment: FIX and INT

There are times when we want to make a floating point number equal to an integer but maintain it as a floating point number. There are two FORTH words that can be used here. One is **FIX**. This pops the floating point number from the top of the stack and truncates (i.e., drops) the fractional part. The resulting floating point number is pushed onto the stack.

The FORTH word **INT** pops the floating point number from the top of the stack and replaces it with another floating point number that is equal to the largest integer that is not greater than the original number. If the numbers are positive, then **FIX** and **INT** produce the same result. However, when the numbers are negative they may yield different values. Note that -8 is the largest integer that is not greater than -7.3

Mathematical Functions

There are FORTH words that perform mathematical operations using floating point numbers. We shall now consider them. In general these words pop a floating point number from the stack and push another one on.

The FORTH words **LOG** and **LOG10** each pop a floating point number off the top of the stack and push a floating point number equal to its natural logarithm or to its base 10 logarithm onto the stack. For instance

% 100 LOG10 (RETURN)

will result in the floating point number 2 being in the top two stack positions.

The FORTH words **EXP** and **10↑** each pop the floating point number from the top of the stack and push a floating point number equal to e or 10, respectively, raised to the power of the original number that was on the stack. Check to see how ↑ can be generated on your computer.

The FORTH words **1/X** and **SQR** each pop a floating point number from the top of the stack and push a floating point number equal to the reciprocal or to the square root of the original number, respectively, onto the stack.

The FORTH words **SIN**, **COS**, **TAN**, and **ATAN** each pop a floating point number from the stack and push a floating point number equal to the sine, cosine, tangent, or arctangent, respectively, of the original number onto the stack. The appropriate number may be expressed in either radians or degrees because of two very helpful FORTH words, **RADIANS** and **DEGREES**. These words do not affect the stack. If we execute **DEGREES**, then the angles of all the trigonometric functions will be interpreted, or output, in degrees. If we execute **RADIANS** then the corresponding angles will be in radians.

The FORTH word **RND** pops the top floating point number from the stack and pushes a pseudorandom number onto the stack. The pseudorandom number will be less than or equal to the original number, provided that the original number was equal to or greater than 1. The pseudorandom number will be equal to an integer but will be represented by a floating point number. If the original number on the stack was between 0 and 1, but less than 1, then the pseudorandom number will be a fraction in the range 0 to 1. Be careful because **RND** in this case is not the same as the integer **RND** (see Section 2-7).

We have thus far considered mathematical operations that used only one number from the stack. We shall now consider FORTH words that pop two floating point numbers from the stack and then push a single floating point number onto the stack. The FORTH word **X↑Y** replaces the two popped floating point numbers by a floating point number that is equal to the number that was second on the stack raised to the power of the number that was on the top of the stack. The stack relation is

$$f_1 \ f_2 \ \rightarrow \ f_1{}^{f_2} \tag{5-45}$$

The FORTH word **ATN2** pops the top two floating point numbers from the stack, divides the second number by the number that was first on the stack and pushes the arctangent of this number onto the stack. This is a four-quadrant arctangent function.

The FORTH words that have been discussed in this section are used in the MMSFORTH system. Remember that these words are not FORTH-79 and may differ from system to system.

5-7. DOUBLE-PRECISION AND COMPLEX NUMBERS

In this section we shall discuss numbers that occupy four stack words. We shall start with a discussion of *double-precision* numbers. The floating point numbers that we discussed in the last section typically have a precision of six significant figures. Precision is not related to the size of the number. For instance, 1.23456, 123.456, and .123456 E 15 all have significant figures but they differ greatly in numerical size. When floating point calculations are performed there are often small errors, called *roundoff errors*, that occur. In

some computer programs many calculations are performed and even
small errors can become significant. There is often a provision made
for performing calculations with numbers that have more significant
figures than the six of ordinary floating point numbers. This will
greatly reduce the roundoff error. Such high-precision calculations
are said to be done with *double-precision floating point* numbers.
Ordinary floating point numbers are called *single-precision* numbers
or *single-precision floating point* numbers. When double-precision
numbers are printed using exponential notation the letter D is used
instead of E. This serves to indicate that double precision is being
used. Double-precision numbers use four stack words, which is twice
as much as ordinary floating point numbers. Thus, double-precision
calculations will be considerably slower and use more memory than
ordinary floating point calculations. For this reason double precision
calculations should be avoided unless the extra acuracy is needed.
Similarly, single-precision floating point calculations should be
avoided if integers can be used. Double-precision words are not part
of FORTH-79. They are found in MMSFORTH. We shall discuss these
words here.

If a double-precision floating point number is to be entered it is
preceded by a **D%**. Remember that for single-precision floating point
numbers we used a % (see Section 5-6). In general the FORTH words
that manipulate double-precision floating point numbers are formed
by adding a D to the FORTH words that manipulate single-precision
integers. For instance **DF#IN** is analogous to **F#IN**. The stack relation
for **DF#IN** is

$$\rightarrow d_f \tag{5-46}$$

We used d_f to represent the four stack positions occupied by
double-precision floating point numbers.

Stack Manipulations

Double-precision numbers occupy four stack positions. There are
special stack manipulating words that are used for them. These are
4DUP, **4DROP**, **4SWAP**, and **4ROLL**. These correspond to those
floating point words where the 4 is replaced by a 2. For instance
4DUP causes the double-precision word that is on the top of the
stack to be duplicated. The stack relation is

$$d_f \rightarrow d_f d_f \tag{5-47}$$

This causes the group of the top four stack positions to be duplicated.

The FORTH word **4DROP** causes the top double-precision word to be dropped from the stack. This is equivalent to dropping four single-length integers from the stack. The stack relation is

$$d_f \rightarrow \tag{5-48}$$

The FORTH word **4SWAP** interchanges the top two double-length words. The stack relation is

$$d_{f1} \ d_{f2} \rightarrow d_{f2} \ d_{f1} \tag{5-49}$$

The FORTH word **4OVER** duplicates the double-precision floating point number that is second on the stack onto the top of the stack. This means that the fifth through eighth stack positions are duplicated onto the top of the stack. The stack relation is

$$d_{f1} \ d_{f2} \rightarrow d_{f1} \ d_{f2} \ d_{f1} \tag{5-50}$$

DF. and DF.R—The FORTH commands **DF.** and **DF.R** are analagous to **F.** and **F.R**. For instance when **DF.** is executed, the double-precision floating point number on the top of the stack is popped off and output. The FORTH command **DF.R** pops both a single-length integer and a double-precision floating point number off the top of the stack. The integer specifies a field width. Then the double-precision floating point number is output within that field. Note that the integer was originally on the top of the stack.

```
0 ( CALCULATION OF FACTORIAL USING DOUBLE-PRECISION NUMBERS)
1 : DFFACT 1 +      D% 1      1     6 ROLL    SWAP
2        DO  I   I-F  FDF   DF*    LOOP  DF.           ;
3
4
5
6
7
8
9
10
11
12
13
14
15
```

Figure 5-5. A FORTH word that calculates the factorial using double-precision floating point numbers.

Addition, Subtraction, Multiplication, and Division

The FORTH words for addition, subtraction, multiplication, and division of double-precision floating point numbers are **DF +**, **DF −**, **DF***, and **DF/** respectively. These correspond to **F +**, **F**, **F***, and **F/** except that four stack positions, rather than two, are involved. The general form of the stack relation is

$$d_{f1} \quad d_{f2} \;\rightarrow\; d_{fans} \tag{5-51}$$

Single-Precision/Double Precision Conversion FDF DFF

There are two FORTH words that convert a double-precision floating point number to a single-precision floating point number and vice versa. **FDF** causes the single-precision floating point number on the top of the stack to be popped off. It is replaced by an equal double-precision floating point number. The stack relation is

$$f \;\rightarrow\; d_f \tag{5-52}$$

The FORTH command **DFF** pops a double-precision floating point number off the top of the stack and pushes on an equal single-precision floating point number. The extra significant figures are rounded off. The stack relation is

$$d_f \;\rightarrow\; f \tag{5-53}$$

As an example of the use of double-precision floating point numbers we will rewrite the factorial program in Figure 5-4 using double-precision floating point numbers. The program is shown in Figure 5-5. The two programs are very similar. Let us consider their differences. In line 2 we use **D%** rather than **%**. In this way 1 is placed on the stack as a double-precision floating point number. In addition 6 **ROLL** is used rather than 4 **ROLL**. This accounts for the two additional stack words used by the double-precision floating point numbers. The word **SWAP** is used in both Figures 5-4 and 5-5. This is because, in each case, we are swapping single-length integers. In line 2 we want to push the index of the loop into the stack as a double-precision floating point number. To do this convert the single-length integer to a floating point number using the FORTH word **I-F**. Next the floating point number is converted to a double-precision floating point number using **FDF**. The remainder of the program follows that of Figure 5-4 except that the words **DF*** and **DF.** are used rather than **F*** and **F.**.

Double-Precision Functions

There are some double-precision functions that correspond to the floating point functions. These are **DFABS, DFMINUS, DFSIGN,** and **DFCOMP.** They correspond to **FABS, FMINUS, FSIGN,** and **FCOMP,** respectively. There are many more single-precision floating point functions than double-precision floating point functions.

Complex Numbers

Complex numbers are numbers that consist of a real and an imaginary part. MMSFORTH provides words that allow you to manipulate these numbers. Each complex number consists of a pair of single-precision floating point numbers. Thus, each complex number occupies four stack positions. For this reason the stack manipulating words **4DUP, 4DROP, 4SWAP,** and **4OVER** that were used to manipulate double-precision floating point numbers can also be used to manipulate complex numbers.

Complex numbers are pushed onto the stack using **CP%.** The FORTH word **CP.** is used to pop the complex number from the stack and print it. The rectangular form is assumed here with the imaginary part of the complex number being on the top of the stack. For instance

CP% 5 7 CP. (RETURN)

will result in

(5,7)

being printed.

The words **CP +, CP −, CP*,** and **CP/** result in the top two complex numbers being popped off the stack and the appropriate answer (sum, difference, product, or quotient) being pushed onto the stack. The stack relation is

$$C_{p1} \quad C_{p2} \;\rightarrow\; C_{pans} \tag{5-54}$$

We use the symbol c_p to represent a complex number. Remember that it represents four stack positions.

The words **MAG** and **PHASE** pop the complex number from the top of the stack and replace it with a single-precision floating point number that is equal to either the magnitude or the phase (i.e., angles) of the complex number, respectively. The angle can be expressed in either degrees or radians. You can pick the desired form by executing either **DEGREES** or **RADIANS** (see Section 5-6).

The words **R-P** and **P-R** pop a complex number off the stack and replace it with another form of complex number. When **R-P** is executed, the number that was on the top of the stack should be in rectangular coordinate form with the imaginary part on the top of the stack. The number that is pushed onto the stack is in the polar coordinate form (i.e., magnitude, angle). The angle is on the top of the stack. The real part, imaginary part, magnitude, and angle are each single-precision floating point numbers. Care should be exercised here. Remember that there is no way of looking at the stack and telling what type of numbers are stored there. For instance a single complex number cannot be distinguished from four single-length integers. The mathematical operations **CP +** , **CP –** , **CP***, and **CP/** assume that the complex numbers are in rectangular form. In general, **P-R** and **R-P** should only be used on in put and/or output to convert the complex numbers between polar and rectangular coordinates.

There are two other words that are available: **CPMINUS** and **CONJ**. These pop a complex number from the top of the stack and replace it by its negative or conjugate, respectively.

EXERCISES

The following exercises ask you to write FORTH words or programs. Check the words or programs by running them on your computer. Do not make any FORTH word that you write too long. Instead write one FORTH word that calls upon shorter FORTH words.

5-1. Discuss the difference between single-length integers and double-length integers.

5-2. Repeat Problem 4-8 using double-length integers.

5-3. Repeat Problem 4-9 using double-length integers.

5-4. Repeat Problem 5-3 but now have the FORTH word terminate execution if the sum becomes greater than 200,000.

5-5. Repeat Problem 4-13 using double-length integers and have the program terminate and flash an error message if the product becomes greater than 1,000,000.

5-6. Repeat Problem 4-11 using double-length integers and print the output in a field that is 20 characters wide.

5-7. Write a FORTH word that computes the function

ab/(c + d)

in the most accurate way. The variables a, b, c, and d are to be supplied on the stack.

5-8. Repeat Problem 5-7 using double-length integers.

5-9. Write a FORTH word that uses double-length integers to compute a student's average in five tests. The average is to be printed, with a suitable decimal point. There are to be three digits printed after the decimal point.

5-10. Write a FORTH word that computes a salesman's commission according to the following procedure: The commission should be 10 percent on all sales up to $10,000,00. the commission on sales equal to or greater than $10,000.00 but less than $50,000.00 should be 15 percent. The commission on sales of $50,000.00 or above is to be 18 percent. The FORTH word is to computer the sum of the sales and then compute the commission. The output must be printed with a dollar sign and decimal point and a suitable explanatory statement. Insert commas into the number if there are more than 999 dollars. Assume that the maximum commission will be less than $100,000.00. Use double-length integers. There can be more than one FORTH word in your program.

5-11. Write a program that computes the Pythagorean triples using double-length integers.

5-12. Write a FORTH word that computes the following:

ab/(c + d) + e

where a, b, c, d, and e are integers. Use mixed-length integers in your calculation.

5-13. Discuss the advantages of using mixed-length calculations.

5-14. What is meant by an unsigned integer?

5-15. Can an unsigned integer be a double-length integer?

5-16. Write a FORTH word that computes the Pythagorean triples using unsigned single-length integers.

5-17. Repeat Problem 5-16 but now use unsigned double-length integers. Consider carefully how to output the data.

5-18. Discuss the use of the FORTH words **AND**, **OR**, and **XOR**. Write FORTH words that illustrate your discussion.

5-19. Discuss the differences between floating point numbers and integers.

5-20. Repeat Problem 5-10 using floating point numbers and integers.

5-21. Repeat Problem 5-11 using floating point numbers.

5-22. Repeat Problem 5-20 using double-precision numbers.

5-23. Repeat Problem 5-21 using double-precision numbers.

5-24. Write a FORTH word that computes the function

(a + b)c/d

where a, b, c, and d are complex numbers.

Chapter 6
Constants, Variables, and Arrays

We have, thus far, stored all our numeric data on the stack. This is good FORTH programming since it saves memory locations and results in programs that run rapidly. However, there are times when other procedures are much more convenient for the programmer. For instance, suppose that you use one constant many times in a single program. If there were many digits in the constant it would be tedious to keep typing it in every time you wanted to use it. FORTH provides a procedure that allows constants to be given names and stored in the main memory of the computer. We can simply use the name of the constant in place of the constant itself. Often there are quantities called *variables* whose values are computed in the program. These variables are frequently used in the calculation of other quantities. If there are meny variables it is extremely tedious to keep track of them on the stack. FORTH provides procedures to allow variables to be named and stored in the main memory of the computer. There is a simple procedure for using the names of these variables which allows us to get them from the main memory and push them onto the stack. The value of the stored variable can be changed easily. Thus, we can compute a variable, store it in the memory, use that variable in a subsequent calculation, and then change the stored value of the variable and repeat the process. We will discuss and illustrate this procedure in the next chapter.

Often we do repetitive calculations on different variables. For instance, we might write a program that computes a student's grades.

Since there are generally many students in a class, it would be tedious to run the program for each of them. We shall demonstrate how sets of variables such as the students' grades can be worked with easily. To do this we shall introduce the topic of *arrays* later in this chapter. We will start by discussing constants.

6-1. CONSTANTS

We will now discuss a procedure whereby *constants* can be stored under names of your own choosing, in the main memory of the computer. The constant can then be pushed onto the stack simply by entering its name. Constants are values that do not change during the execution of the program. There are procedures for changing the values of constants during the execution of a program. However, they are relatively cumbersome, and shall usually not be used. If there is a quantity whose value is changed by the computation and you want to store it under a name, then variables should be used. The value of a constant can be changed before execution by editing the program. This will be illustrated later in the section.

CONSTANT—To define a constant we use the FORTH word **CONSTANT**. The form that we use is

3600 CONSTANT H/S (RETURN)   (6-1)

We have set the constant called **H/S** equal to 3600. We can now use **H/S** just as we would use the number 3600. When the word **CONSTANT** is executed, the single-length integer that is on top of the stack, 3600 in this case, is popped off the stack and stored in the dictionary in the main memory of the computer. The name of the constant is the word that immediately follows **CONSTANT**. The stack relation is

$$n \rightarrow$$ (6-2)

As an example, in Figure 6-1 we write a FORTH word that converts hours to seconds. In line 1 we define the constant **H/S** just as we did in (6-1). In line 2 the FORTH word **HRS/SEC** is defined. With this simple word we wish to multiply the integer that is on the top of the stack by 3600. Thus we want to push 3600 onto the stack. We could simply write 3600. Instead we use the constant **H/S**. Although this is a simplified illustration of the use of a constant it presents the general ideas. The constant is not defined as part of a word. A constant must be defined before it can be used in a word.

```
0 ( AN ILLUSTRATION OF THE USE OF CONSTANTS )
1 3600 CONSTANT H/S
2 : HRS/SEC  H/S  *       .   ;
3
4
5
6
7
8
9
10
11
12
13
14
15
```

Figure 6-1. An illustration of the use of constants.

Constants are used for several reasons. One is that the constant may be easier (shorter) to write than the number. Another reason is that the constant may be easier to remember than the number. A third reason is that the constant may easily be changed before the program is run. For instance suppose that a certain value such as an interest rate is used many times in a program and you want to change this value each time that interest rates change. If the numerical interest value were actually written many times throughout the program it would be a tedious job to edit the program and change all occurences. On the other hand if a constant name were used to represent the interest rate throughout the program, you would only have to update the line where the constant was defined. The use of constants can also speed execution and reduce memory requirements.

2CONSTANT—We have considered constants that represented single-length integers. We can also define constants that represent double-length integers. To do this we use the FORTH word **2CONSTANT**. **2CONSTANT** is used in exactly the same way as **CONSTANT** except that now a double-length integer is defined. For istance, if we type

65535. 2CONSTANT MEMSIZE (RETURN)   (6-3)

then MEMSIZE can be used in place of the double-length integer 65535. The stack relation for **2CONSTANT** is

d →   (6-4)

Remember the double-length integer blocks must be loaded to use any double-length integer operations.

FLOATING POINT CONSTANTS

If your FORTH system has a floating point arithmetic package then, in all probability, it has the ability to define floating point constants. We shall discuss the words used by the MMSFORTH system. In order to use these words your floating point package must be loaded. Remember that there is no FORTH standard for floating point numbers so the words may differ from system to system. The FORTH commands that apply here are **2CONSTANT** and **4CONSTANT**. These pop the single-precision or double-precision floating point number from the top of the stack and store it in the dictionary in the main memory under the specified name. The general form of the use of these words is the same as that of (6-1) or (6-3). The word used to define a floating point constant is the same as the one used to define a double-length integer. The discussion in Section 2-4 applies here.

6-2. VARIABLES

A value that is computed during the execution of a program is called a *variable*. Often, that variable may be used at various times in the FORTH word that is being executed, or in other FORTH words that are part of the same program. In such cases it is very tedious to keep track of the location of the variable on the stack. FORTH provides a method of naming variables and storing them on the stack. Variables are similar to the constants that were discussed in the last section, but there is one major difference. The FORTH variable is optimized for most efficient changing. The FORTH constant is optimized for most efficient reading. To obtain this versatility there are several FORTH words that must be used with variables.

VARIABLE—The FORTH word **VARIABLE** is used to set aside a memory location for a single-length integer variable. This is different than **CONSTANT** which not only sets aside a memory location but also pops the top single-length integer from the stack and stores it. A sample execution of **VARIABLE** is

VARIABLE KEE (RETURN)   (6-5)

This sets aside a memory location in the dictionary called **KEE** which can store a single-length integer. When **KEE** is executed the *address* of that memory location will be pushed onto the stack.

! and **@**—The FORTH word **!** (referred to as store) is used to store a value in a memory location. Often that memory location has been assigned a name by executing the FORTH word **VARIABLE**. For instance, if we had previously named a variable **KEE** (see 6-5) we could now store the value 234 in the memory location named **KEE** in the following way.

$$234 \quad KEE \quad ! \qquad\qquad (6\text{-}6)$$

When **KEE** is executed its address is pushed onto the top of the stack. When **!** is executed the address of **KEE** and 234 are popped off the top of the stack. The single-length integer 234 is stored in the memory address that was popped off the stack. The stack relation for **!** is

$$n \quad a \quad \rightarrow \qquad\qquad (6\text{-}7)$$

Note that a is a single-length unsigned integer that represents the address. If there had been a value previously stored in the location called **KEE**, its value would be lost. When (6-6) is executed the value stored in the memory location designated by **KEE** will be 234, regardless of the number that was stored there previously.

The FORTH command **@** (fetch) is used to recover an integer from a memory location and push it onto the stack. Suppose that we had previously stored 234 in the memory location called **KEE** and now we want to retrieve that number and push it onto the stack. This next operation would accomplish that.

$$KEE \quad @ \qquad\qquad (6\text{-}8)$$

The stack relation for **@** is

$$a \quad \rightarrow n \qquad\qquad (6\text{-}9)$$

@ pops the top number from the stack and treats it as a memory address. The single-length integer that is stored in this address is then pushed onto the stack. The value of **KEE** stored in memory is unchanged by this operation. As an example of the use of variables we shall again compute the Pythagorean triples, now using variables (see Figure 6-2). We shall compare this program to the one in Figure 4-7, which used stack manipulations. In lines 1 and 2 of Figure 6-2

```
0 ( PYTHAGOREAN TRIPLE USING VARIABLES )
1 VARIABLE A VARIABLE B VARIABLE C
2 VARIABLE A1   VARIABLE B1   VARIABLE C1
3 : PT 15 .R  ;
4 : SQUARE    DUP    *  ;
5 : VPYTHTRIP   CR   100    1 DO I DUP SQUARE   A !    A1 !
6           100   I    DO  I   DUP   SQUARE   B !   B1 !
7             142   I    DO I DUP   SQUARE   C !   C1 !
8              A @ B @   + C @   -   DUP        0= IF
9               A1 @ PT   B1 @ PT   C1 @ PT    CR
10                  THEN    0< IF LEAVE THEN
11                LOOP
12          LOOP
13      LOOP ;
14
15
```

Figure 6-2. A FORTH word that calculates the integers that satisfy.
$a^2 + b^2 = c^2$ using variables.

we designate six variables **A**, **B**, **C**, **A1**, **B1**, and **C1**. In lines 3 and
4 we define the FORTH words **PT** and **SQUARE**. These are the same
words that were defined in Figure 4-7. Now let us consider the word
VPYTHTRIP that starts in line 5. The first **CR** is included to improve
the appearance of the output. There are three nested loops. The
outer one loops 100 times. The loop index is pushed onto the stack
and duplicated. Next **SQUARE** is executed. Now the top stack word
contains the square of the outer loop index and the second stack
word contains the outer loop index. After **A** and ! are executed,
the single-length integer that is stored in the top stack position is
popped off and stored in the memory location designated by **A**. Thus,
that memory location stores the square of the index of the outer
loop. Similarly, after **A1** and ! are executed, the memory location
designated by **A1** will store the value of the index of the outer loop.
After line 5 is executed, the stack will be empty. In lines 6 and 7
we essentially repeat the above procedure. Thus, after the execution
of these lines the memory locations designated by **B** and **B1** will
store the square of the index and the index of the middle loop. **C**
and **C1** will store the corresponding quantities for the inner loop.
In line 8 the values stored in the memory locations designated by
A and **B** are pushed onto the stack. Then + is executed. Next the
value stored in the memory location designated by **C** is pushed onto
the stack and − is executed. The value stored in the top stack
position is now $a^2 + b^2 - c^2$. This number is duplicated and **0**= is

executed. If the flag on the top of the stack is true then the values stored in the memory locations designated by **A1**, **B1**, and **C1** will be taken from memory and printed. Next the value of $a^2 + b^2 - c^2$ is checked to see if it is less than 0. If it is, then the looping of the inner loop is terminated. This follows the operation of the program in Figure 4-7. Note that the variables were not defined as part of a word. Variables must be defined before they are used in words.

The use of variables simplifies the programmer's job considerably. For instance the program in Figure 6-2 requires considerably less attention to detail than does the program in Figure 4-7. However, programs using variables usually take longer to run. This is because of the additional operations involved. Let us consider them. When a variable is defined, it is included in the dictionary. A dictionary entry for a variable will be different than one for a word (see Section 2-4). For instance the dictionary entry for a word contains the instructions for that word while the dictionary entry for a variable has storage space set aside for that variable. Dictionary entries contain other items such as the name of the word or variable. When the variable name is executed, the address of the dictionary entry for the variable is pushed onto the stack. For instance, in (6-6), when **KEE** is executed, its address is pushed onto the stack. When ! is executed the address and the next number are popped off the stack and the second number is stored in the memory location specified by the number that was originally on the top of the stack. Most numbers occupy more than one memory location and are stored in a sequence of consecutive memory locations. In this case the numerical value that was on the top of the stack indicates the first memory location in the sequence. In a similar way, when @ is executed, the number that is on the top of the stack is popped off. This is used as the memory location for the fetch. Memory locations are treated as single-length unsigned integers. When ! or @ is executed, it need not be preceded by a variable name. If the appropriate memory locations were known, then that number could be pushed onto the stack.

These procedures slow the operation of the program. The dictionary searches take time. The fetching or storing of addresses and numbers also takes a lot of time. Thus, all other things being equal, a FORTH program that does not use variables will run faster than one that does. For instance, the program in Figure 4-7 runs about 1.35 times as fast as the program in Figure 6-2. The word

FORGET (see Section 2-4) applies to variables and constants as well as to other dictionary entries.

+!—At times we want to add an integer to a variable that is stored in memory. We could fetch the variable, add the two numbers, and then store the sum, but there is a single FORTH word that can be used here. The word is +! (referred to as plus-store). When +! is executed, the single-length integer that is second on the stack is popped off and added to the data whose address is on the top of the stack.

Use of Variables with Double-Length Integers

Variables can be used with double-length integers. The details follow those for single-length integers. We shall now consider the actual words.

2VARIABLE—The FORTH word **2VARIABLE** functions in the same way as **VARIABLE** except that memory space for a double-length integer is allocated in the dictionary. For instance

2VARIABLE KEY   (6-10)

would set up a dictionary entry called **KEY** that would store a double-length integer.

2! and 2@—The FORTH commands for the storing and fetching of double-length integers are **2!** and **2@**. The stack relation for **2!** is

d a →   (6-11)

The stack relation for **2@** is

a → d   (6-12)

Remember that a is an unsigned single-length integer and d is a double-length integer.

Use of Variables with Floating Point Numbers

The MMSFORTH system and other FORTH systems provide words that allow you to use variables with floating point numbers. We will now look at these. Remember that these words are not standard. The words for single-precision floating point numbers are the same as those for double-length integers, that is **2VARIABLE**, **2!** and **2@**.

The stack relations for **2!** and **2@** are,

$$f \quad a \rightarrow \qquad\qquad (6\text{-}13a)$$

and

$$a \rightarrow f \qquad\qquad (6\text{-}13b)$$

The words for double-precision floating point numbers correspond to those for single-precision floating point numbers except that the 2's are replaced by 4's. Thus, the words are **4VARIABLE**, **4!**, and **4@**. The stack relations for **4!** and **4@** are

$$d_f \quad a \rightarrow \qquad\qquad (6\text{-}14a)$$

and

$$a \rightarrow d_f \qquad\qquad (6\text{-}14b)$$

6-3. ARRAYS

Sometimes we have to write programs that perform repetitive calculations on lists of variables. We have seen that looping can be a great help when such repetitive calculations are performed. We will now consider a procedure that further simplifies programs which contain lists of variables. Such lists of variables are called *arrays*.

In the last section we discussed that the declaration of a variable caused a set of memory locations to be set aside for the storage of that variable. Now we will be more specific. In a typical small computer, single-length integers are stored using sixteen bits. A single *byte* is equivalent to eight bits. This, single-length integers are stored using two bytes. Double-length integers are stored using four bytes. In a small computer, memory words are usually one byte so we will assume that to be the case here. Even if your computer uses larger words, the basic ideas discussed here will apply. Let us assume that we are working with single-length integers. When we declare a variable (see (6-5)) two bytes are set aside for the numerical value of that variable in its dictionary entry. Then we would have room to store two single-length integers under the name of that variable. Similarly, if we could allocate 100 bytes for the storage of a variable, we could store fifty single-length integers under the name of that one variable. We will now discuss how storage space can be extended in the dictionary entry for a single variable and how a large number of variables can be stored in and fetched from this allocated memory space.

ALLOT—The FORTH word **ALLOT** pops the top single-length integer from the stack and adds that number of bytes to the storage area of the most recently defined word. The number of added bytes is equal to the single-length integer that was popped from the stack. For instance consider the following sequence.

VARIABLE KEE   (6-15a)

40 ALLOT   (6-15b)

When (6-15a) is executed the dictionary entry for the variable **KEE** will contain two bytes that are allocated for the storage of the variable **KEE**. After (6-15b) is executed there will be forty-two bytes allocated for variable storage in the dictionary entry for **KEE**. Two bytes were allocated when the variable was declared in (6-15a) and forty more were added when **ALLOT** was executed in (6-15b). The stack relation for **ALLOT** is

n →   (6-16)

Now let us see how we can store and fetch single-length integers from the memory locations that we have allocated. Remember that a single-length integer is stored in two bytes or two memory words. When we execute **KEE**, its address is pushed onto the stack. Actually the address of the first of the two bytes that store **KEE** is pushed onto the stack. When ! or @ is executed the FORTH system "knows" that the address is for the first byte of the pair that stores the variable. Now suppose that we want to store a single-length integer in the third and fourth memory locations that have been allocated to **KEE** for the storage of variables. The following will accomplish this.

98 KEE 2 + ! (RETURN)   (6-17)

The single-length integer 98 will be stored in the third and fourth memory locations of **KEE**. When (6-17) is executed, 98 is pushed onto the stack. Next **KEE** is executed, which causes the address of the first byte of **KEE** to be pushed onto the stack. Next 2 is pushed onto the stack and + is executed. Thus, the single-length integer that is on the top of the stack is 2 greater than the address of the first byte of **KEE**. Thus, it is the address of the second and third memory locations of **KEE**. Hence, after ! is executed, 98 will be stored in these locations. A similar procedure is used to fetch the variable. For instance

KEE 2 + @   (6-18)

will result in 98 being pushed onto the stack. Remember that a fetch does not change the value of the stored variable. In the example that we have just discussed, **KEE** is called an *array*. That is, it stores a list of variables.

Now let us consider an example using an array. We shall write a program that assigns grades to students based on their averages. Let us assume that we have stored the averages of the students' grades in an array called **AVERAGE**. The first item stored in this array is a single-length integer that is equal to the number of students that are in the class. All the other single-length integers that are stored there are the students' averages. We assume that the position in the array indicates the student's ID number. When we work with single-length integers, we usually define the first two bytes in an array as position 0. The next two bytes are position 1, etc. The FORTH word that we write (see Figure 6-3) will print out each student's

```
0 ( AN ILLUSTRATION OF ARRAYS USING ALLOT )
1 VARIABLE  AVERAGE    200 ALLOT
2 : PASS/FAIL    AVERAGE @   1 +    1
3        DO CR 2  I *  AVERAGE  +  @    59       -        0>      IF
4          ." STUDENT NO.  "   I  .    ." PASSES"
5          ELSE  ." STUDENT NO.  "   I  .    ." FAILS"
6          THEN
7      LOOP  ;
8
9 ( ILLUSTRATION OF INPUT TO ARRAY )
10 : INPAVE   CR    ." ENTER NUMBER OF STUDENTS"
11        #IN    DUP   AVERAGE !    1 + 1     CR     DO
12          ." ENTER AVERAGE FOR STUDENT NO.  "  I  .    #IN
13          CR   AVERAGE  I  2  *  +      !
14        LOOP  CR    ;
15
```

Figure 6-3. An illustration of the use of the FORTH word **ALLOT** to set up an array.

ID number and the word PASSES or the word FAILS. If the average is 60 or more, then the student will pass. Now let us consider the program in Figure 6-3. In line 1 we define a variable called **AVERAGE**. Thus, a dictionary entry is set up with storage space for one single-length integer. Next 200 is pushed onto the stack and **ALLOT** is executed. This adds 200 bytes to the storage space of **AVERAGE**. Hence an additional 100 single-length integers can be stored there. The array is said to have 101 *elements*. There are two words defined in Figure 6-3. **PASS/FAIL** calculates and prints the desired output. **INPAVE** is used to enter data into the **AVERAGE** array. Let us assume that the data is in the array and consider **PASS/FAIL**. The first number in the **AVERAGE** array gives the number of students in the class. We assume that this is less than 100, since we only added memory space for 100 single-length integers when **ALLOT** was executed. You must be careful not to use more memory space than is allotted. For instance, in this example, if you attempt to write into the 102nd element, you may destroy some dictionary information.

Consider the FORTH word **PASS/FAIL**. In line 2 we execute **AVERAGE**. This causes the first address of the data in **AVERAGE** to be pushed onto the stack. Next @is executed. Thus the single-length integer that is equal to the number of students is pushed onto the stack. Next 1 is added to this number and another 1 is pushed onto the stack. We have thus established the parameters for a loop. Now look at line 3. The FORTH word **DO** pops the top two integers from the stack and sets up a loop. **CR** is included to make the output more readable. Next 2 and the index of the loop are pushed onto the stack and multiplied. **AVERAGE** is executed and then + is executed. At this point the number that is on the top of the stack is the original address of the data in **AVERAGE** plus two times the loop index. Next @ is executed. Thus, each time that the loop is executed, one of the student's averages is fetched from memory and pushed onto the stack. Remember that each single-length integer is stored in two bytes.

After the student's average is pushed onto the stack, 59 is pushed onto the stack and - is executed. If the resulting number is greater than 0 then the student passes. If the resulting number is 0 or less then the student fails. The FORTH word **0>** pushes a flag onto the stack. The flag will be true if the student is to pass and false otherwise. The **IF-ELSE-THEN** construction then causes the desired information to be output. The student's ID number and a simple explanatory statement is also printed.

We could enter the data for the **AVERAGE** array using the procedure illustrated in (6-17). It is more convenient to use the FORTH word **INPAVE** that is also illustrated in Figure 6-3. When

INPAVE is executed, the user is prompted for all data. Only the numeric data is input by the user, thus saving much tedious typing. Consider the details of the operation of **INPAVE**. Line 10 of Figure 6-3 causes the prompt ENTER NUMBER OF STUDENTS to be output. In line 11 **#IN** is executed. Thus, the prompt ? will be displayed and the program will pause until the desired data is entered. This number is then duplicated and stored in the original memory location for **AVERAGE**. When **!** is executed, the number on the top of the stack is popped and stored. The remainder of line 11 sets up the parameters of the loop. Several **CR** words are included to make the output of the program more readable. Line 12 causes the prompt ENTER AVERAGE FOR STUDENT NO. to be output. Next the index of the loop is output. This is the student ID number. When **#IN** is executed, the program pauses until the data is entered. In line 13 **AVERAGE** is executed putting the original starting address onto the stack. Next 2 is pushed onto the stack followed by the loop index. Then * and + are executed. This works in the same way as the **PASS/FAIL** word that we discussed previously. Thus, after the looping is completed the array **AVERAGE** will contain all the desired data.

ARRAY—The word **ALLOT** has been used to set up an array. There is another word that allows us to work with arrays in a somewhat more convenient fashion. That word is **ARRAY**. **ARRAY** is not part of FORTH-79, but it is found in MMSFORTH. We can use **ARRAY** to set up an array in the following way.

100 ARRAY AVERAGE   (6-19)

This is equivalent to line 1 of Figure 6-3. For instance, when (6-19) is executed, a dictionary entry for **AVERAGE** will be established containing space for 101 single-length integers. That is, it will contain 202 bytes for the storage of the integers. The numbers that are stored in the array are called the *elements* of the array. In the case of (6-19) they are numbered from 0 to 100. The stack relation for **ARRAY** is

n $\rightarrow$ (6-20)

In general, the array will store n + 1 elements numbered from 0 to n. There will be $2(n+1)$ bytes in the memory locations used to store the array. To push the address of an element of the array onto the stack we enter the number of the element and the name of the array. For instance, the execution of

3 AVERAGE   (6-21)

would cause the address of the first byte of the fourth element of
the **AVERAGE** array to be pushed onto the stack. Remember that
the first element is numbered 0. Thus, the fourth element is
numbered 3.

As examples of the use of the word **ARRAY** we have rewritten
the FORTH words of Figure 6-3. The resulting program is shown in
Figure 6-4. It is essentially the same as the program in Figure 6-3
except that the array **AVERAGE** is established using the word
ARRAY. In addition, the addresses of the variables are pushed onto
the stack using expressions of the form of (6-21). We no longer have
to multiply the loop index by 2. Look at line 2. We enter 0 **AVERAGE**
to push the address of the first element of the array onto the stack.

There is potential for considerable confusion here. Arrays
established using **ALLOT** are addressed in a different fashion than
those established using the word **ARRAY**. You must be careful to
remember which procedure you are using. Since **ARRAY** is not part
of FORTH-79, it will not be found on all systems. If your system does
use the word **ARRAY** you will have to load the block(s) that define it.

```
0 ( AN ILLUSTRATION OF ARRAYS )
1 100 ARRAY AVERAGE
2 : PASS/FAIL   0 AVERAGE @    1 +    1
3        DO CR   I AVERAGE  @    59       -        0>      IF
4           ." STUDENT NO.  "   I   .   ." PASSES"
5           ELSE  ." STUDENT NO.  "   I   .   ." FAILS"
6           THEN
7        LOOP  ;
8
9 ( ILLUSTRATION OF INPUT TO ARRAY )
10 : INPAVE    CR ." ENTER NUMBER OF STUDENTS"
11        #IN  DUP   0 AVERAGE  !    1 +   1   CR  DO
12           ." ENTER AVERAGE FOR STUDENT NO. "  I  .   #IN
13        CR  I AVERAGE    !
14        LOOP   CR ;
15
```

Figure 6-4. An illustration of the use of the word **ARRAY**.

Use of Double-Length Integers with Arrays

You can use double-length integers with arrays. We shall start our
discussion by considering how **ALLOT** is used to set up an array.
In the previous example we used **ALLOT** to add bytes to the data

portion of the dictionary entry of the array variable. Two bytes were added for each single-length integer. If we want to store double-length integers, then four bytes must be added for each one. For instance consider the following.

2VARIABLE WORK 40 ALLOT   (6-22)

We have established a double-length variable **WORK**. Next 40 is pushed onto the stack and **ALLOT** is executed. This adds 40 bytes onto the memory locations that store the data of the variable **WORK**. If we execute **WORK**, the address of the first byte will be pushed onto the stack. Similarly if we execute **WORK 4 +** the address of the second double-length integer in the **WORK** array will be pushed onto the stack. For example in the program in Figure 6-3 we multiplied the stack index by 2 and added it to the address of **AVERAGE**. If double-length integers were being used, then the stack index would be multiplied by four. When double-length integers are stored or fetched the words **2!** and **2@** are used. Note that in the program in Figure 6-3 all the data would have to be in the form of double-length integers.

The original variable need not be defined as double-length. For instance, if we had omitted the 2 in (6-22), then **WORK** would be a single-length integer. In such cases the first two bytes could be used to store a single-length integer while each of the succeeding four bytes would store double-length integers. This would make the arithmetic of obtaining the addresses more complex.

The word **DARRAY** can be used to set up arrays containing double-length integers in the same way that **ARRAY** was used to set up single-length integer arrays. **DARRAY** is not part of FORTH-79. It is found in MMSFORTH. The details and discussions concerning the use of the word **ARRAY** work here with minor differences. For instance, the stack relation for **DARRAY** is

d →   (6-23)

If we execute

100 DARRAY WORK   (6-24)

an array that stores 101 double-length integers will be set up. There will be 404 bytes of storage space allocated to this array. If we wish to push element number 4 onto the stack we would execute

4 WORK 2@   (6-25)

Use of Arrays with Floating Point Numbers

Floating point numbers are not part of standard FORTH, but they are provided as part of the MMSFORTH system as well as in other FORTH systems. We shall discuss the array words that are supplied with the MMSFORTH system. Remember that these words are not standard but may differ from system to system. The word **2ARRAY** is used to set up an array of single-precision floating point numbers. The details of its operation are essentially the same as **ARRAY** except that floating point numbers are used. In a similar way the word **4ARRAY** is used to set up an array of double-precision floating point numbers. (In order to use these arrays, your floating point blocks must be loaded.)

Arrays of Constants CREATE and ,

There are times when we want to set up an array that contains constant terms. FORTH-79 provides words that allow us to do this easily. Two words are used: one is **CREATE** and the other is ,. Although these words can be used separately, the beginner should only use them together. When **CREATE** is executed, a dictionary entry is created for the name that follows it. For instance,

    CREATE TAB   (6-26)

will create a dictionary entry for the word called **TAB**. There will be *no memory space allocated for data at this time*. The FORTH word , pops the top single-length integer from the stack and creates a storage area for it in the next available dictionary memory location. The popped number is then stored in this newly created dictionary storage area. Now suppose that we want to store six values in the **TAB** array. The execution of the following would accomplish this.

    CREATE TAB 15 , 20 , 35 , 40 , 50 , 60 ,   (6-27)

There is a space between the commas and the numbers, and there is a comma after the last number. If **CREATE** is followed by the name of the array and the relevant numbers and commas, then the values will be put into the proper dictionary memory locations. For instance in (6-27) a dictionary entry for **TAB** is set up, and 15 is then pushed onto the stack. When , is executed, a two-byte memory location is set up following the dictionary entry for **TAB** and 15 is stored there. When **TAB** is executed hereafter, the address that is pushed onto the stack will be the address for the first byte of the memory locations that store 15. Remember that **CREATE** does not result in any dictionary space being allocated for data. Thus, the first , in (6-27) results in 15 being popped off the stack and stored in the appropriate dictionary memory location. Once the **TAB** array has been established by using (6-27), it can be treated as any other array containing single-length integers. Single-length integers can be stored in or fetched from the **TAB** array using the procedures that were discussed earlier in this section. If we do not want to initialize the value of an array with constants, then the **CREATE** word is cumbersome to use. Suppose that we wanted to set up an array containing 100 elements that were to be computed during the course of the program. We would have to type in 100 dummy constants if we wanted to establish the array using **CREATE**. In such cases the use of the FORTH word **ALLOT** would be much more convenient.

6-4. TWO DIMENSIONAL ARRAYS

There are times when we wish to manipulate several corresponding lists of data. For instance, suppose that we have a list of students' grades. It would be desirable if each grade corresponded to the appropriate student's ID number. A straightforward way of working with corresponding lists is to manipulate simultaneous arrays. Let's look at an example. Suppose that for each student in a class we have an ID number and grades for two tests. We want to compute the student's average and print it next to his ID number. The FORTH program in Figure 6-5 accomplishes this. In lines 1, 2, and 3 we set up three different arrays.

```
0 ( AN ILLUSTRATION OF MULTIPLE ARRAYS USING ALLOT )
1 VARIABLE   IDNUMB   200     ALLOT
2 VARIABLE   GRADE1   200   ALLOT
3 VARIABLE   GRADE2   200   ALLOT
4 : CLASS        IDNUMB    @   1 +   1   DO
5       CR 2   I *   GRADE1 +   @   2   I *   GRADE2   +   @  +
6         ." STUDENT NO.  "    I   2  *    IDNUMB    +   @   .
7           ." HAS AVERAGE  "   2  /   .
8       LOOP   ;
9
10 ( ILLUSTRATION OF INPUT TO ARRAYS )
11 : GRADEIN   CR    ." ENTER NUMBER OF STUDENTS"
12               #IN    DUP   IDNUMB   !    1  + 1     CR      DO
13             CR   ." ENTER ID NO. AND GRADES "    #IN  #IN  #IN
14           I 2 *  GRADE2 + !   I 2 * GRADE1 + !   I 2 * IDNUMB +
15       LOOP ;
```

Figure 6-5. An illustration of multiple arrays.

IDNUMB stored the students' ID numbers, **GRADE1** stores the grades in the first test, and **GRADE2** stores the grades in the second test. In addition, the 0 position of **IDNUMB** stores a single number that is equal to the total number of students in the class. The 0 position of the other two arrays will not be used.

Let us assume that all the data has been stored and consider the operation of the FORTH word **CLASS**. In line 4 the address of **IDNUMB** is pushed onto the stack. This represents the 0 position in the array. The corresponding single-length integer is then fetched. The remainder of line 4 sets up the parameters for a loop and **DO** initiates the loop. In line 5 the loop index is multiplied by 2 and added to the address of **GRADE1**. The corresponding stored number is then fetched. This procedure is repeated with **GRADE2**. The integers are then added. We are not considering these operations in detail since they correspond to the procedures discussed in the last section. In line 6 the loop index is again doubled so that the ID number of the student, whose test grades were fetched in line 5, is also fetched. The ID number is printed and the previously determined sum is divided by two and printed. The desired output is thus obtained. That is, the averages are printed next to the ID numbers.

Lines 10 to 15 show a program for entering data. This follows the details of the corresponding program in Figure 6-3, except that now data is entered into three arrays. The data is pushed onto the stack in the following order: ID number, grade 1, grade 2. Thus, we read it off the stack in the reverse order.

The procedures that have been discussed here can be used with double-length integers. The details are very similar. Ideas from the previous section can be applied here directly.

Two-dimensional Arrays 2ARRAY

Several arrays were used in the previous example. Each one stored different data. However, corresponding elements of each array referred to one student. In cases where several corresponding lists of data are to be stored, it is often convenient to work with a *two-dimensional array*. The type of array that we have been considering is called a *one-dimensional array*. It has one column and many rows. A two-dimensional array can have many columns as well as rows. For instance in the program in Figure 6-5 we could store all the data in a two-dimensional array. Each row of the array would correspond to a particular student. Column 0 could store the ID numbers, column

```
0 ( AN ILLUSTRATION OF TWO DIMENSIONAL ARRAYS )
1 2 100 2ARRAY GRADE
2 : CLASSAV    0 0 GRADE @  1 +  1  DO
3           CR I 1 GRADE @   I 2 GRADE @ +
4           ." STUDENT NO. "  I 0 GRADE @  .
5           ." HAS AVERAGE "  2 /  .
6     LOOP  ;
7
8 ( ILLUSTRATION OF INPUT TO ARRAY )
9 : GRADEIN  CR  ." ENTER NUMBER OF STUDENTS " .
10          #IN  DUP 0 0  GRADE  !  1 +  1  DO
11          CR  ." ENTER ID NO. AND GRADES "  #IN  #IN  #IN
12          I 2 GRADE  !  I 1 GRADE  !  I 0 GRADE  !
13    LOOP  ;
14
15
```

Figure 6-6. An illustration of the use of two-dimensional arrays.

1 could store the grades in the first test, and column 2 could store the grades in the second test. (Note that we start numbering from 0.)

The word that is used to set up a two-dimensional array is not part of FORTH-79. However, it is found in MMSFORTH. The word is **2ARRAY** and is used in the following way

$$n_1 \ n_2 \ \text{2ARRAY GRADE} \tag{6-28}$$

When **2ARRAY** is executed the top two single-length integers are popped off the stack. A two-dimensional array called **GRADES** is set up with $n_1 + 1$ rows and $n_2 + 1$ columns. The first row and column are each numbered 0. The stack relation for **2ARRAY** is

$$n_1 \ n_2 \ \rightarrow \tag{6-29}$$

The values of n_1 and n_2 must lie between 1 and 254.

Now let us see how data can be stored in, or fetched from, the **GRADE** array. To push the address of the first byte of the element in row n_1 and column n_2 of the **GRADE** array onto the stack, we would enter the following.

$$n_1 \ n_2 \ \text{GRADE} \tag{6-30}$$

For instance if we want to fetch the single-length integer that is stored in row 4 column 3 of the **GRADE** array we would enter

    4 3 GRADE

As an example of the use of two-dimensional arrays we will use them to rewrite the program of Figure 6-5. The resulting program is shown in Figure 6-6. Consider the operation of this program. In line 2 we set up a two-dimensional array with 101 rows and 3 columns. We assume that the total number of students that are in the class is stored in the (0,0) element of the array. The total number of students must be equal to or less than 100. Elements of an array are referred to in the form (row, column). In line 2 we establish the parameters of the loop. This follows the details of the program in Figure 6-5, except that the procedures for fetching data from a two-dimensional array are used. In line 3 the elements of the **GRADE** array that lie in the row corresponding to the index of the loop and in columns 1 and 2 are fetched and added. The students' ID numbers are stored in column 0. The ID number that corresponds to the index of the loop is fetched in line 4. The details of the remainder of the program follow that of Figure 6-5.

Lines 8 through 13 in Figure 6-6 list the FORTH word **GRADEIN** that is used to input the data to the **GRADE** array. The details of this program also follow the one in Figure 6-5 except that the procedures for storing data in two-dimensional arrays are used. Notice that the program in Figure 6-6 is simpler than the one in Figure 6-5.

Use of Double-Length Integers with Two-Dimensional Arrays 2DARRAY

A two-dimensional array that stores double-length integers can be set up using the FORTH word **2DARRAY**. This word is not part of FORTH-79, but it is provided in MMSFORTH. The details of the use of **2DARRAY** parallel those of **ARRAY**. The stack relation is

$$n_1 \ n_2 \ \rightarrow \hspace{10em} (6\text{-}31)$$

The integers that define the number of rows and columns are single-length, not double-length. They must lie between 0 and 65535 just as with two-dimensional arrays that use single-length integers. The words **2@** and **2!** are used to fetch and store data.

Use of Two-Dimensional Arrays with Floating Point Numbers

MMSFORTH and other FORTH systems provide words to set up two-dimensional arrays using floating-point numbers. These words are not part of FORTH-79 and may vary from system to system. The word used to set up a two-dimensional array of floating point numbers is **22ARRAY**. Its use corresponds to the use of **2ARRAY** except that floating-point numbers are used for the data stored in the array rather than single-length integers. The words **2@** and **2!** are used to fetch and store data. The stack relation is the same as (6-29). The numbers that establish the array size (i.e., n_1 and n_2) are single-length integers. The numbers that are used to specify the row and column of the array must also be single-length integers.

A two-dimensional array of double-precision, floating point numbers can be set up using the word **24ARRAY**. The operations are essentially the same as for single-precision floating point numbers. **4@** and **4!** are used to fetch and store data. Here too the numbers that are used to establish the array size or specify the row and column of an element are single-length integers that lie between 0 and 65535.

EXERCISES

The following exercises ask you to write FORTH words or programs. Check the words or programs by running them on your computer. Do not write any single FORTH word that is too long. Instead, write one FORTH word that calls upon shorter FORTH words.

6-1. Discuss the difference between constants and variables.

6-2. Write a program, using a constant, that computes the circumference and area of a circle. The radius of the circle should be pushed onto the stack. The formula for the circumference of a circle is $2\pi r$ and the formula for the circumference of a circle is πr^2. The value of π to be used in this program is 3.142. Use scaling where necessary.

6-3. Discuss three advantages of using constants in FORTH words.

6-4. Repeat Problem 6-2 using 3.1415927 as the value of π.

6-5. Repeat Problem 4-8 using variables.

6-6. Repeat Problem 4-10 using variables.

6-7. Repeat Problem 4-16 using variables. The grades are not to be placed on the stack but should be entered using prompts.

6-8. Write a FORTH word, using variables, that computes the factorial.

6-9. Repeat Problem 6-8 using double-length integers.

6-10. Repeat Problem 6-2 using a floating point constant.

6-11. Repeat Problem 6-10 using floating point variables as well as a floating point constant.

6-12. Repeat Problem 6-11 using double-precision variables and constants. Use the value of π given in Problem 6-4.

6-13. Repeat Problem 6-8 using floating point variables.

6-14. Repeat Problem 6-13 using double-precision floating point variables.

6-15. What is meant by an array?

6-16. Repeat Problem 5-10 but now have the commission of many salesman computed. Identify each one by number. Use an array in your program. Assume that the company has no more than 250 salesmen. The program should include provisions for easily entering and outputting data.

6-17. Repeat Problem 6-16 using double-length integers.

6-18. Write a program that computes the Pythagorean triples. Store the data in an array. The program should include provisions for outputting the array.

6-19. Repeat Problem 6-18 using double-length integers.

6-20. Repeat Problem 6-16 using single-precision floating point numbers.

6-21. Repeat Problem 6-16 using double-precision floating point numbers.

6-22. Repeat Problem 6-18 using single-precision floating-point numbers.

6-23. Repeat Problem 6-18 using double-precision floating-point numbers.

Chapter 7

Characters and Strings

Up to this time we have only used FORTH words to manipulate numbers. We will now consider how letters can also be manipulated. This discussion will not be restricted to letters of the alphabet but will include all characters such as the digits 0 to 9 and punctuation marks. In general, all letters, numbers, and punctuation marks are referred to as alphanumeric data. Characters are grouped together to form words or sentences. Such groupings of alphanumeric characters are called *strings*. FORTH words that manipulate strings will also be considered.

Characters are usually stored in single bytes. In this chapter we will discuss the FORTH words that allow us to manipulate single bytes. These manipulations are valid for numbers as well as for characters. An 8-bit byte can store unsigned integers in the range 0 to 255.

7-1. CHARACTERS—ONE-BYTE MANIPULATIONS

In this section we will consider the input, output, and manipulation of characters. We will see how text can be stored and manipulated. Since individual characters are stored in a single byte, we shall start by considering some FORTH words that are used to manipulate single bytes. We will then consider the input, output, and manipulation of characters.

C! and C@—The FORTH word **C!** pops the two top single-length integers off the stack; the number that was on the top of the stack is used as an address, and the number that was second on the stack is treated as an unsigned integer. The eight least significant bits of that integer are stored at the memory location specified by the address. The stack relation is

n a →   (7-1)

C! functions in almost the same way as !, except that only eight bits (i.e. one byte) are stored. However, the stack operations are the same. (A single-length integer occupies two bytes when it is stored on the stack.) We use the symbol a to represent an address. It is actually equivalent to an unsigned single-length integer.

The FORTH command C@ (referred to as c-fetch) pops the top number from the stack and treats it as an address. The one-byte integer that is stored at that address is fetched and pushed onto the stack as a single-length integer. Since a single-length integer is actually stored in two bytes, the eight most significant bits of the number that is pushed onto the stack are set equal to 0. The least significant bits are equal to the fetched number. The stack relation is

a → n   (7-2)

Both C! and C@ treat the stack as though single-length integers were being stored or fetched. However, only one byte is used to store the number in the dictionary.

CMOVE AND <CMOVE—At times when we work with characters that are stored in memory, it is convenient to move blocks of memory. For instance, consider that the data stored in memory represents the text for a paragraph. Suppose that you want to insert some text into the middle of the paragraph. It would be convenient if you could move a block of the data to a higher part of the memory to make room for the inserted material. There are two FORTH commands that allow us to do this conveniently. The first word is **CMOVE**. An example of its use is

34500 38000 100 CMOVE   (7-3)

When (7-3) is executed the block of 100 bytes whose memory address starts at 34500 is moved to the memory locations whose address starts at 38000. The data that was stored in memory locations 34500 to 34599 are now duplicated into memory locations 39000 to 38099. The old memory locations are unchanged. However, they could now be used to store other data. First the byte at 34500 is moved to 38000, next the byte at 34501 is moved to 38001, etc. The order in which the data is moved may not seem important. Indeed, in the previous example it was not. However, if we change the memory locations that are involved, then the order of the move can be important. For instance, suppose that we write

34500 34550 100 CMOVE   (7-4)

Now we are moving a block of 100 memory locations but the amount that any one memory location is moved is only 50 bytes. When the first memory location is used, it will write over the data in memory location 34550, etc. Thus, the data that was originally stored in memory location 34550 will be lost and when we attempt to recover and move it the wrong data will be moved. One procedure which would avoid this problem would be to move the block of 100 characters more than 100 memory locations and then use a second **CMOVE** to bring the data back to the desired point. However, there is also a single FORTH word that can be used to overcome this difficulty. This word is **<CMOVE** (pronounced reverse-c-move). This word operates as **CMOVE** does except that the high memory locations are moved first. For instance if we execute

34500 34550 100 <CMOVE   (7-5)

the following would occur. First the contents of memory location 34599 would be duplicated into memory location 34649. Next the contents of memory location 34598 would be duplicated into memory location 34648, etc. In this way any data in the original memory locations will not be written over until after it has been duplicated into the new memory locations. Thus, the proper data will have been moved. **CMOVE** and **<CMOVE** both perform the same function, but the order in which the data is moved is different. In addition both **CMOVE** and **<CMOVE** can be used to move data to either higher or lower memory locations. Note that **<CMOVE** is not yet part of FORTH-79. However, it is found in MMSFORTH and in other FORTH systems. The stack relation for **CMOVE** and **<CMOVE** is

$$a_1 \ a_2 \ n \ \rightarrow$$ (7-6)

A block of n bytes whose starting address is a_1 is moved to a new starting address at a_2.

MOVE—**MOVE** is another word that moves memory. **MOVE** is similar to **CMOVE** except that each unit of memory is considered to be two bytes long. For instance

a_1 a_2 n MOVE

would result in 2n bytes starting at address a_1 being moved to address a_2. **MOVE** is in FORTH-79.

KEY—The FORTH command **KEY** is used to enter alphanumeric data from the keyboard. When **KEY** is executed the ASCII code (see Section 3-2) for the next character entered from the keyboard is pushed onto the stack as an unsigned single-length integer. Note that the ASCII codes are all equal to or less than 255 so they can be represented as single-byte unsigned integers. That is, the ASCII code representation for a character can be stored or fetched using **C!** or **C@**. As an example if we type

KEY Z (RETURN)   (7-7)

the top of the stack will contain the unsigned single-length integer 90 which is the ASCII code for Z. The stack relation for **KEY** is

→ u   (7-8)

Remember that u represents an unsigned single-length integer. We shall provide examples of **KEY** after we define one additional FORTH word. When **KEY** is executed, the next character that is typed is not echoed back to the screen. For instance, when (7-7) is executed nothing will appear on the screen even though you typed Z.

EMIT—The FORTH word **EMIT** pops the top unsigned single-length integer from the stack and outputs its ASCII code. Note that the character corresponding to the popped integer must have been in the range 0 to 127. For instance, the execution of

90 EMIT (RETURN)   (7-9)

will cause Z to be output. The stack relation for **EMIT** is

u →   (7-10)

Let's consider some examples using the words that we have introduced in this section. Figure 7-1 illustrates a program that can be used to input text material to an array. For instance, you could type in a paragraph that could be output at a later time, or could

```
0 ( SIMPLE CHARACTER INPUT AND OUTPUT )
1 VARIABLE WORDS      1024 ALLOT
2 ( CHARACTER INPUT )
3 : STORE   CR  1024  1  DO    KEY      DUP    EMIT   DUP
4                WORDS  I 2+  +  C!
5                35  -  0=
6                IF  LEAVE    I  1-  WORDS  !   THEN
7         LOOP     CR    ;
8
9 ( READ STORED DATA )
10 : OUTPUT  CR     WORDS  @    1      DO
11             WORDS I 1+  +    C@
12             EMIT
13        LOOP    CR     ;
14
15
```

Figure 7-1. A program that reads character data into an array.

even be processed by a word processing program. We can use arrays with one-byte numbers using the previously discussed array manipulating procedures.

Now let us consider the program in Figure 7-1. In line 2 we set up a variable called **WORDS** and use **ALLOT** to extend its storage area by 1024 bytes. We can store 1024 characters in this array. The first two bytes that were originally allocated to **WORDS** will be used to store the actual number of characters that are entered. In line 3 we start the word **STORE**. This word essentially consists of a loop that repeats itself 1024 times. After the loop is set up, we execute **KEY**. The program pauses until a single character is input from the keyboard. This is converted to its ASCII code and pushed onto the stack. Next this number is duplicated and **EMIT** is executed. The top single-length integer is popped off the stack and the character represented by the ASCII code is output to the screen. We use the word **EMIT** here so that the user of the program can see what has been typed. The number on the top of the stack is duplicated again. Next **WORDS** is executed so that its address is pushed onto the stack. This address is increased by 2 plus the loop index and **C!** is executed. Thus, the single-length integer representing the ASCII code is popped off the stack and stored in the **WORDS** array as a single-byte integer. This will be repeated for each pass through the loop. The **WORDS** array will contain the desired data. Since we may not want to enter 1024 characters, a procedure for terminating the input is included. If you enter #, then the operation will be ended. We choose #

arbitrarily. Any character could be used to terminate input. The ASCII code for # is 35. Consider line 5 where 35 is subtracted from the ASCII code of the last character entered and **0 =** is executed. If the flag on the top of the stack is true then a # has been entered and the operation should terminate. If the flag is true then **LEAVE** will be executed and the operation will terminate at the end of the cycle through the loop. The index is pushed onto the loop and reduced by 1. This integer, which is equal to the number of characters that have been entered, is stored in the original data area for **WORDS**. Operation now terminates. The **WORDS** array contains the text material. The first two bytes of the **WORDS** array contain a single-length integer that is equal to the number of characters that are stored in the **WORDS** array.

In lines 9 to 13 of Figure 7-1 we list the word **OUTPUT** which outputs the text in the **WORDS** array to the screen. In line 10 the number of characters stored is pushed onto the stack. Then the parameters of the loop are established. In line 11 the ASCII code for each character is fetched. When **EMIT** is executed in line 12 the character is printed. This procedure is repeated for each character in the **WORDS** array.

Suppose that we want to insert some text into the middle of the data stored in the **WORDS** array. (This is a basic word processing application.) The program in Figure 7-2 will accomplish this. Let us

```
0 ( STRING INSERTION ROUTINE )
1 VARIABLE INSBUF    10 ALLOT   VARIABLE POINT
2 : INSERT   CR  ," ENTER POINT OF INSERTION"  #IN   POINT !
3             CR  ," ENTER STRING OF UP TO 10 CHARACTERS"   CR
4             10  1    DO   KEY   DUP   EMIT   DUP
5             INSBUF  I 1+    +     C!
6             INSBUF   I    !    35   -    0=
7             IF   LEAVE   THEN   I 1-   INSBUF !
8        LOOP       CR
9          WORDS 2  +    POINT  @  +    DUP   INSBUF  @  +
10           WORDS  @  POINT   @   -    <CMOVE
11        INSBUF 2+   WORDS 2 +    POINT @   +
12            INSBUF    @   CMOVE
13        INSBUF  @   WORDS   +!        ;
14
15
```

Figure 7-2. A program that inserts a string into the **WORDS** array.

consider its operation. Assume that the block represented by Figure 7-1 has been loaded and that data has been entered into the **WORDS** array. In the program in Figure 7-2 we assume that the inserted string is 10 characters or less. In line 1 of Figure 7-2 we set up an array called **INSBUF**. The first two bytes store the number of characters to be inserted. The remainder of the **INSBUF** array stores the character data. We can increase the size of the insertion buffer that stores the characters to be inserted by increasing the magnitude of the integer pushed onto the stack before **ALLOT** is executed. In general, a portion of memory that temporarily stores data to be used later is called a *buffer*. In line 2 we also define a variable called **POINT**. This will store the position in the **WORDS** array where the text is to be inserted.

Consider the operation of the word **INSERT** that starts on line 2. We begin by asking the user of the program to supply the position where the text is to be inserted in the **WORDS** array. This single-length integer is stored in the memory location called **POINT**. Line 3 causes a prompt to be printed asking the operator to type in an insertion string. This string is to be terminated by a # sign. The execution of lines 4 through 8 cause the inserted string to be stored in the **INSBUF** array; this follows the details in Figure 7-1. Space is then opened up in the **WORDS** array so that the desired text can be inserted. The first address to be moved is the first address in **WORDS**, increased by both 2 and the integer stored in **POINT**. Remember that the text data's beginning address is the one in **WORDS**, plus 2. Next the first address to be moved is duplicated and that number is increased by the number of characters that have been input to **INSBUF**. Remember that this number is stored in the first two bytes of **INSBUF**. Thus, we have pushed a_1 and a_2 of (7-6) onto the stack. We must now compute the total number of bytes to be moved. This is equal to the total number of characters stored in **WORDS** minus those characters that occur before the inserted data. This number is computed in line 10 where the integer stored in **POINT** is subtracted from the total number of characters stored in **WORDS**. Thus, the correct data will be on the stack when <**CMOVE** is executed in line 11. Once this is done, the **WORDS** array will be opened up to allow the text to be inserted. The old data is still stored, but we will write over it. We have used <**CMOVE** rather than **CMOVE** so that we do not write over data before it is moved.

We now move the data from the **INSBUF** array into the space that we have provided in the **WORDS** array. After lines 11 and 12 are executed, but before **CMOVE** is executed, the stack will contain the following three single-length integers: the address of **INSBUF** plus 2 is third on the stack; this is the lowest address of the data to be

moved. The address of **WORDS** plus 2, plus the integer stored in
POINT is the lowest address of the new location of the moved data;
this is the second stack position. The top number on the stack is
the number of characters stored in **INSBUF**. Thus, when **CMOVE**
is executed, the data will be moved into the proper position in the
WORDS array. We could use either **CMOVE** or **<CMOVE** in this case
since the data will not overwrite itself.

The last operation that we must perform is to modify the number
stored in the first two bytes of the **WORDS** array, which specifies
the total number of characters that are stored in the **WORDS** array.
We must increase the original number by the number of characters
that have been inserted. This is done in line 13 where the number
stored in the first two bytes of **INSBUF** is added to the number
stored in the first two bytes of **WORDS**. We have used the word **+!**
here.

Some care should be exercised here. You must be careful not to
add too many characters. The **WORDS** array can only hold 1024
characters. This is because we used **ALLOT** to provide this amount
of storage in Figure 7-1. If you try to insert characters so that there
are more than 1024 characters stored in **WORDS** then part of the
dictionary can be overwritten. You may have to reboot your system
with a resulting loss of data. The program in Figure 7-1 could not
write more than 1024 characters into the **WORDS** array. However,
you can use the program in Figure 7-2 many times. Thus, it is possible
to insert too much data. We could include a check in the **INSERT**
word which would abort the operation if the number of characters
stored in the **WORDS** array plus the number of characters in
INSBUF is greater than 1024.

TYPE—The FORTH word **TYPE** can be used to output strings that
are stored in memory. An example of its use is

WORDS 2 + 15 TYPE

When this is executed 15 characters will be output starting from
the address **WORDS** plus 2. The stack relation for **TYPE** is

a n →

7-2. ADDITIONAL WORDS USED FOR CHARACTER INPUT
We shall now discuss some FORTH commands that are used for
the input of characters. These words may be incorporated in your

own FORTH words. In addition, the words that we discuss in this section are used extensively by the FORTH system for its own management of character input.

EXPECT—Another FORTH word that can be used to input characters is **EXPECT**. A typical use of **EXPECT** is

LETTERS 10 EXPECT   (7-11)

We assume that **LETTERS** is an array that has been established prior to the execution of (7-11). When (7-11) is executed, computation will pause and character input will be expected. In this case 10 characters will be expected since 10 was the single-length integer on top of the stack when **EXPECT** was executed. The characters will be entered into the **LETTERS** array, starting at the address that is pushed onto the stack when **LETTERS** is executed. Input will take place until 10 characters have been entered *or* the RETURN key has been pressed. The stack relation for **EXPECT** is

a n →   (7-12)

In Figure 7-3 we show a simple example of the use of **EXPECT**. The **LETTERS** array is set up which can store 10 single-byte integers. The FORTH word **CHAR** is set up in line 2. Now we use **EXPECT** to input up to 10 characters into the **LETTERS** array. In lines 3 and 4 we output the data from the **LETTERS** array. The data is duplicated and output using both , and **EMIT**. In this way both the

```
0 ( SIMPLE EXAMPLE USING EXPECT )
1 VARIABLE LETTERS    8   ALLOT
2 : CHAR    LETTERS   10 EXPECT   CR
3       10  0  DO    LETTERS  I  +   C@  DUP   EMIT  .
4          LOOP    ;
5
6
7
8
9
10
11
12
13
14
15
```

Figure 7-3. A simple example of the FORTH word **EXPECT**.

letter and its ASCII code are shown. **LETTERS** can store exactly 10 characters. Often, we allocate two additional bytes at the beginning of the array. These are used to store a single-length integer that is equal to the number of characters in the array. Some FORTH systems add one or two special characters to the end of a string of characters stored by using **EXPECT**. Storage space should be allocated for these characters.

Some FORTH systems use a slightly different definition for **EXPECT**. You should check its use in your system.

WORD, >IN, HERE, and BLK—When you enter a sequence of instructions from the keyboard, the FORTH system must be able to break it up into individual words. The actual input is a stream of characters and the individual words must be separated by special characters called delimiters. Usually blanks are the delimiters, but other symbols might be used. The FORTH command **WORD** is used to establish the specific delimiter to be used. In addition, when **WORD** is executed, the input data up to the specified delimiter is stored in the memory of the computer. Consider the following

32 WORD   (7-13)

When **WORD** is executed, the 32 is popped from the stack and used as the delimiter. Since 32 is the ASCII code for a blank, the blank will be used as the delimiter. If the 32 had been replaced by 35 then # would be used as a delimiter.

When **WORD** is executed, the input stream of characters will be scanned until the delimiter is reached. All the scanned characters will be stored. The starting address of the memory locations that store the scanned characters will be pushed onto the stack. In addition to the stored characters, the first stored byte will contain a one-byte integer that is equal to the number of scanned characters. Remember that the input stream is only scanned until a delimiter occurs. If the input stream starts with a series of delimiters, they will be ignored when **WORD** is executed. That is, the stream will be assumed to start when the first nondelimiter character occurs.

There is a FORTH-79 word available called **HERE** which stores the address of the next available dictionary memory location. When **WORD** is executed, the starting address of the stored string is the number stored in **HERE**. (This may not be the case in all FORTH systems.)

The operation of **WORD** is more complex than we have indicated. Suppose that the stream of input characters consists of a series of words and that the delimiter is a blank. As we have described the operation, only the first word would be stored when **WORD** is executed, since the scanning would stop at the first delimiter. However, there is another FORTH word that can be used to change this situation. The word is >**IN** (pronounced to-in). >**IN** is the name of a FORTH-79 variable. The number stored in >**IN** is used to offset the point where the FORTH system starts to scan the input stream of characters when **WORD** is executed. For instance, if the number stored in >**IN** is 3 then the first three characters of the input stream will be ignored when **WORD** is executed. The number stored in >**IN** can range from 0 to 1023.

There is one other FORTH word that we must consider. We have assumed that the input stream of characters comes from the keyboard. However, this need not be the case; the information could come from a disk. When **WORD** is executed, the source of the input stream must be supplied to the FORTH system. This information is stored in another standard FORTH variable called **BLK**. If the number stored in **BLK** is 0 then the FORTH system considers that the keyboard is the source of the input stream. (We shall consider disk operations in the next chapter.)

The word **SCAN** (see Figure 7-4) will help to illustrate the use of the words that we have just introduced here. In line 1 we start by storing 0 in **BLK**. Thus, the input will be from the keyboard. Next

```
0 ( SIMPLE EXAMPLE USING WORD )
1 : SCAN      0    BLK !    5 >IN !      32   WORD   C@      CR
2      1 +                1   DO  HERE  I + C@           EMIT LOOP
3      CR CR         QUIT    ;
4
5
6
7
8
9
10
11
12
13
14
15
```

Figure 7-4. A simple example of the FORTH words **WORD**, >**IN**, **HERE** and **BLK**.

we store 5 in **>IN**. This means that the first five characters in the input stream will be ignored by **WORD**. We shall see the reason for this subsequently. Next 32 is pushed onto the stack and **WORD** is executed. Thus, we have established the blank as the delimiter. After the input stream is scanned, the address that results from the execution of **HERE** will be on the stack. When **C@** is executed the one-byte integer stored in this address will be fetched. This number will equal the number of scanned characters. One is added to ther number of characters and the parameters of a loop are set up. The stored characters are output to the screen. (Note that we have used **HERE** as the starting address for the stored data.) We end with the word **QUIT**. If this were not done in this simple program, any characters in the input stream that were not stored when **WORD** was executed would subsequently be interpreted by the FORTH system as input.

Suppose that the block in Figure 7-4 were loaded and we typed

SCAN THE QUICK BROWN FOX (RETURN)   (7-14a)

The output would be

THE   (7-14b)

The offset number stored in **>IN** is 5; thus the first five characters of the input stream are ignored by **SCAN**. Hence, the word **SCAN** is ignored and the word **THE** is printed. The first delimiter after the offset occurs after **THE** so scanning ceases at this point. When (7-14a) is entered, **SCAN** causes the execution of the program in Figure (7-4). The input **SCAN** is interpreted by the FORTH system as an indication that the word called **SCAN** is to be executed. The text **SCAN** is still in the input stream. For this reason, the offset is included in line 1. If this were not done, the output that results when the program in Figure 7-4 is run would always be the word **SCAN**.

QUERY—In the preceding example we had to set the value stored in **>IN** equal to 5 so that the four letters **SCAN** would not be read each time that the FORTH word **SCAN** is run. There is a FORTH word that can be used to avoid this problem. It is **QUERY**. When it is executed, the next 80 characters input from the keyboard will be input into the input buffer. Thus, only those characters that are input after **QUERY** is executed will be in the buffer. The operation of **QUERY** will also be terminated when a **RETURN** is entered as well as when 80 characters are entered. If the values stored in **BLK** and in **>IN** are both 0, then **WORD** will scan the input buffer. For instance, suppose that we modify the program in Figure 7-4 by replacing the 5 in line 2 with a 0 and writing **QUERY** before the 32 in the same line. When the word **SCAN** is executed, **SCAN** itself will not be in the input buffer when **WORD** is executed. Thus, the modified program will cause the correct input stream to be scanned.

7-3. STRING MANIPULATION

In this section we shall discuss some FORTH words that are very convenient to use when strings are manipulated. Not all of these words are part of FORTH-79. However, they are provided in MMSFORTH and in other FORTH systems. Check the manual for your FORTH system to determine which string manipulating words are available.

String Constants, Variables, and Arrays

We can define constants, variables, and arrays that store strings. In Section 7-1 we discussed how this could be done using standard FORTH words. We shall now consider some nonstandard words that are at times more convenient to use.

A string constant is set up using the word **$CONSTANT** (pronounced string-constant). (The symbol $ is often used to represent a string quantity.) An example of the use of **$CONSTANT** use is

$CONSTANT ALP HOUSE"   (7-15)

Note that there is only one set of quotation marks. In this case we have set up a string constant called **ALP**. It stores the string **HOUSE**. The first byte of **ALP** stores a one-byte integer that is equal to the length of the string. Thus, for the example of (7-15) the data area for the dictionary entry **ALP** consists of six bytes. If **ALP** is executed, the address of its first byte is pushed onto the stack. This is different from a numeric constant.

A string variable is set up using the word **$VARIABLE** which is pronounced string-variable. An example of its use is

20 $VARIABLE ABC   (7-16)

In this case we set up a dictionary entry called **ABC** that has 21 bytes. All the bytes will be filled with zeros when the variable is set up. The first byte is often used to store the length of the string that is actually stored in **ABC**. This is not done automatically. The stack relation for **$VARIABLE** is

$$n \rightarrow \hspace{8cm} (7\text{-}17)$$

String variables and constants are used in the same way. The difference between them is that the value of a string constant is established when its defining statement is executed. However, as we will discuss later, we can fetch or store values from string variables and string constants using the same FORTH words. Again, note that this differs from numeric FORTH constants and variables.

String arrays can be set up using the word **$ARRAY**. As we discussed in Section 7-1, string arrays can be set up using **ALLOT**. It is somewhat more convenient to use **$ARRAY**, but it is not FORTH-79. An example of the use of **$ARRAY** is

$$20 \ 10 \ \$ARRAY \ LETTERS \hspace{5cm} (7\text{-}18)$$

Here we have set up an array called **LETTERS**, which has 11 elements. Each element can store up to 21 bytes. The stack relation is

$$n_1 \ n_2 \rightarrow \hspace{7cm} (7\text{-}19)$$

Note that $n_2 + 1$ is equal to the number of elements in the array, and $n_1 + 1$ is equal to the number of bytes stored in each element. The maximum value of n_1 is 255. The array is initially set up with 0 in all its elements. If we want to put the address of the first byte of the element in row three of the **LETTERS** array onto the stack we would enter

$$3 \ LETTERS$$

We can set up a two-dimensional string array using the word **2$ARRAY**. An example of its use is

$$n_1 \ n_2 \ n_3 \ 2\$ARRAY \ TABLE \hspace{4cm} (7\text{-}20)$$

Here we have set up an array table with $n_2 + 1$ rows and $n_3 + 1$ columns. Each element will contain $n_1 + 1$ bytes. The maximum value for n_1 is 254. The stack relation is

$$n_1 \ n_2 \ n_3 \rightarrow \hspace{6cm} (7\text{-}21)$$

The array is set up with all its initial values equal to 0. If we want to put the address of the element in row 3 and column 5 of the **TABLE** array onto the stack we would enter

3 5 TABLE

Remember that the numbering of rows and columns starts with zero.

Manipulation of String Data

We shall now consider how string data can be stored, fetched, and manipulated. We shall start with the word **$!** (pronounced string-store). Suppose that we have data stored in a string variable or string constant called **ABC** and we want to copy it into another string variable or string constant called **TOP**. The following will accomplish this:

ABC TOP $!   (7-22)

The manipulations using strings are different than those that use numbers. This is because it is often undesirable to push a string onto the stack. Remember that these instructions are not part of FORTH-79 and may vary from system to system. If the string that is stored in **ABC** is longer than the one that is stored in **TOP** then part of the dictionary will be overwritten. This *must* be avoided.

If we want to print a string we use the word **$.** (pronounced string-print). For instance, if we want to output the string that is stored in **TOP** we would write

TOP $.   (7-23)

The address of **TOP** would be popped off the stack and the string stored in **TOP** would be printed. The stack relation is

a →   (7-24)

Remember that **a** represents a single-length unsigned integer.

FORTH maintains an area of memory called the *scratch pad*. This is a group of memory locations that are set aside to temporarily store items such as string data. The starting location of the scratch pad is stored in the FORTH-79 word **PAD**. The location of the scratch pad will change as the dictionary size is increased. When the word **PAD** is executed, the first address of the scratch pad will be pushed onto the stack.

At times we want to form a single string putting two existing ones together. This is called *concatenation*. The word that results in the concatenation of two strings is **$+** which is referred to as string-concatenation. For instance, if we execute

ABC TOP $+   (7-25)

the string stored in **TOP** will be appended to the string stored in
ABC. The resulting string will be stored in **PAD**. The address of **PAD**
will be pushed onto the stack. You should be careful when you
concatenate strings. Remember that the resulting string will be
longer than either of the original ones. Do not attempt to store a
string in a dictionary space that is too small for it. The stack relation
for **$ +** is

$$a_{\$1} \quad a_{\$2} \quad \rightarrow \quad a_{pad} \qquad\qquad (7\text{-}27)$$

A string can be entered directly, using the word **$"**. An example
of its use is

$$\$'' \quad \text{THE QUICK BROWN FOX}'' \qquad\qquad (7\text{-}27)$$

Note the space after the first ''. The string is terminated by the
second quote. If (7-27) were entered from the keyboard followed
by a **RETURN** the string would be stored in memory and the starting
address would be placed on the stack. If **$"** is used in the definition
of your FORTH word then the string is stored in the next available
dictionary entry.

At times it is desirable to have your program prompt the user to
enter a string. This can be done with the word **IN$**. When this is
executed, program pauses and the ? prompt appears. The person
using the program enters the string, which is terminated by a
RETURN. The string is stored in **PAD** and the address of **PAD** is
stored on the stack. The scratch pad is only a temporary storage
area. The data should be removed and stored elsewhere since
subsequent operations may overwrite the scratch pad.

There are times when we only want to use some of the characters
in a string. Suppose that we want to store a string in a variable's
memory location, but we want to make sure that we do not overwrite
the dictionary. In other words we want to limit the number of
characters in the stored string. There are several words that may
be used here. One is **LEFT$** (pronounced left-string). An example
of its use is

$$\text{ABC} \quad 10 \quad \text{LEFT\$}$$

When this is executed the address of **ABC** and the single-length
integer 10 would be popped from the stack. The ten leftmost
characters of **ABC** would be copied into the scratch pad and the
address of **PAD** would be left on the stack. The stack relation is

$$a_{\$} \quad n \quad \rightarrow \quad a_{pad} \qquad\qquad (7\text{-}29)$$

There are two other related words; one is **RIGHT$**. This functions in the same way as **LEFT$** except that n characters from the right are copied into the scratch pad. At times we may want to copy a part of the middle of a string into the scratch pad. The word **MID$** is used for this purpose. The stack relation is

$$a\$ \; n_1 \; n_2 \; \rightarrow \; a_{pad} \tag{7-30}$$

In this case n_2 characters from the string that is stored at a$ are copied into the scratch pad. The copied string starts n_1 characters into the stored string. **LEFT$**, **RIGHT$**, and **MID$** do not change the original stored string.

At times it is desirable to interchange the values stored in two strings. The word **$XCG** which is referred to as string-exchange accomplishes this. Be careful not to move a string into a storage space that is too small. The scratch pad is used as temporary storage when the interchange is carried out. The stack relation is

$$a\$_1 \; a\$_2 \tag{7-31}$$

String Comparison Words

There are comparison words that can be used with strings. For instance, we can search to see if a string contains a particular sequence of characters. This is useful in word processing applications. The word **INSTR** is used for such purposes. An example of its use is

$$\text{ABS TOP INSTR} \tag{7-32}$$

In this case the string stored in **ABS** will be searched to see if it contains the string stored in **TOP**. For example, if the string stored in **TOP** is BOOK and the string stored in **ABS** is THE BOOK IS ON THE TABLE, when **INSTR** is executed the integer 5 will be pushed onto the stack. In general, when **INSTR** is executed, a single-length integer will be pushed onto the stack. If the string that is being searched for is found, then its first starting position will be pushed onto the stack. If the string is not found, then 0 will be pushed onto the stack. The stack relation for **INSTR** is

$$a\$_1 \; a\$_2 \; \rightarrow \; n \tag{7-33}$$

Sometimes we want to alphabetize a list. Each string has a numerical value based on the position that it would have in an alphabetized list. For instance AAA has a lower numerical value than AAB. Similarly AECDEDE has a lower numerical value than ZXE. Note that lower case letters have different ASCII codes from their upper case counterparts. Remember that the numerical value of a string depends upon its value in an alphabetized list. The word **$COMPARE** is used to compare the numerical values of two strings. An example of its use is

ABC TOP $COMPARE   (7-34)

When **$COMPARE** is executed, the numerical value of the string stored in **ABC** is compared with the numerical value of the string stored in **TOP**. The two addresses are popped off the stack and a -1, 0, or 1 is pushed onto the stack. The number will be 0 of the numerical value of the two strings is equal. The number will be -1 if the numerical value of the string stored in **ABC** is less than the numerical value of the string stored in **TOP**. The number will be 1 if the converse is true. The stack relation is

a$_1$ a$_2$ → n   (7-35)

As an example of string manipulation let us write a FORTH program that alphabetizes a list of names. The program is shown in Figure 7-5. It occupies two blocks, or screens. It is assumed that both of these have been loaded. We have distributed comments throughout the program to help explain its operation. Let us now consider the details of the operation. There are three FORTH words defined in this program. The first, **ALPHAIN**, is used to enter the data. The second, **ALPHAOUT**, does the actual alphabetizing and outputs the result. The third word **ALPHA** simply calls up the first two words. In line 1 we define a string array called **LASTNAME**. It has 11 rows and each row can store 20 bytes. We also define a 21-byte string variable called **TEMM**. In line 2 we define a string constant called **Q**; it stores 20 Z's. (We assume here that only upper case letters will be used.) In line 3, two variables **NUMB** and **NUMB1** which store single-length integers are defined.

The FORTH word **ALPHAIN** starts in line 4. In line 5 to 7 the values stored in the **LASTNAME** array are initialized. 20 is stored in the first byte of each element. All the remaining elements are set equal to zero. If the program were only to be run once each time it was compiled, then this last step would be unnecessary. Remember that when a string array is set up, all the values are set equal to 0. However, if we run the program without recompiling it we must initialize the arrays. In line 7 we set the first byte of the **TEMM** variable to 20.

```
0  ( AN ALPHABETIZING PROGRAM   1 OF 2 )
1  20 10  $ARRAY LASTNAME           20 $VARIABLE TEMM
2        $CONSTANT Q  ZZZZZZZZZZZZZZZZZZZZ"
3        VARIABLE NUMB   VARIABLE NUMB1
4  : ALPHAIN    ( INITIALIZE VARIABLES AND ENTER DATA )
5           10 0 DO 20 I LASTNAME C!
6             20 1 DO  0   J LASTNAME  I +   C!   LOOP
7        LOOP          20   TEMM C!
8             ( ENTER NUMBER OF NAMES )
9        CR ." ENTER NUMBER OF NAMES " #IN  NUMB !
10            ( ENTER LIST OF NAMES )
11       CR  NUMB @ 1+  1    DO   ." ENTER NAME NO. " I .
12            CR   I  LASTNAME 1+   20 EXPECT        CR
13       LOOP   CR    ;
14
15
```

```
0  ( AN ALPHABETIZING PROGRAM 2 OF 2 )
1  : ALPHAOUT ( ALPHABETIZING ROUTINE )
2    ( SET TEMM TO ALL Z'S    )
3    NUMB @ 1+   1   DO      Q    TEMM $!
4      ( SET UP INNER LOOP AND COMPARE )
5       NUMB @ 1+  1  DO  I LASTNAME    TEMM     $COMPARE
6         ( FIND NAME )
7         0< IF I NUMB1 !  I LASTNAME          TEMM $!
8              THEN  LOOP
9            ( PRINT NAME )
10             CR   NUMB1 @ LASTNAME  $.
11           ( SET PRINTED NAME TO ALL Z'S )
12         Q   NUMB1 @  LASTNAME  $!
13     LOOP ;
14 : ALPHA   ALPHAIN   ALPHAOUT    ;
15
```

Figure 7-5. An alphabetizing program.

Lines 9 through 13 cause the data to be entered. The execution of line 9 prompts the user to input a single-length integer. This is equal to the number of names that are to be alphabetized. This number should be 10 or less. (Actually, row 0 could be used to store data although we do not do it here.) If you want to alphabetize a longer list of names, then change the 10 in line 1 to the desired number. In lines 11 to 13 a loop is set up that causes the names to be stored in the **LASTNAME** array. We use **EXPECT** here since it can be used to automatically limit to 20 the number of characters that can be entered. Observe that 20 is pushed onto the stack before **EXPECT** is executed. The address that is pushed onto the stack is **LASTNAME + 1**. Thus, the first integer stored in each element of

the **LASTNAME** array will remain 20. The word **ALPHAIN** ends
in line 13.

Now let us consider the second block in Figure 7-5. This is where
the alphabetizing takes place. The word **ALPHAOUT** starts in line
1. There are two nested loops. The outer one is the remainder of
the block. The initial and test values for the loop are 1 and 1 plus
the total number of names. In line 3 **TEMM** is set equal to 20 Z's
so that it will be the last name in an alphabetized list. Next the inner
loop is set up. **TEMM** is compared with each name in the list, in
turn. If the numerical value of any name is less than the numerical
value of **TEMM**, then that name replaces the string that is stored
in **TEMM**. In addition, the value of **NUMB1** is set equal to the
number of the row of the **LASTNAME** array that contains the name
that replaced **TEMM**. Thus, after the inner loop has completed its
first cycle, **NUMB1** will contain the row number of the first name
in the alphabetized list. Line 10 causes this name to be listed. Next,
in line 12 the value of the output name is changed to 20 Z's in the
LASTNAME array. The outer loop then cycles again. Since the name
that was originally alphabetically first has been changed to 20 Z's,
the name that is alphabetically second will be found and output.
Thus, when the looping is completed an alphabetical list of the names
will have been printed. **ALPHAOUT** ends in line 13.

In line 14 we define the word **ALPHA** that calls both **ALPHAIN**
and **ALPHAOUT**. When **ALPHA** is executed the user of the program
will be prompted for the required data and the alphabetized list of
names will be printed.

Some Additional String Manipulating Words

Let us now consider some additional words that are used in
manipulating strings. A string often has many blank spaces. For
instance, suppose that 64 spaces have been allocated for a string
but only 25 have been used. The remaining space may be filled with
blanks. This can be troublesome. For example, if we output this word
on a printer it would be undesirable to print the blanks. The first
byte of the storage space often contains a number equal to the total
length of the string. If we could temporarily reduce this number
so that it represented the length of the string with the trailing blanks
removed then unnecessary operations could be avoided. For
instance, we could use this number to control the number of
characters that are printed. The FORTH word **-TRAILING** pushes
a number onto the stack that is equal to the length of the string

with the trailing blanks removed. An example of the use of **-TRAILING** is

ABC ABC -TRAILING   (7-36)

When **-TRAILING** is executed, the first address of **ABC** will be popped off the stack and the reduced character count will be pushed onto the stack as a single-length integer. Thus the stack will contain the starting address of **ABC** and the revised count of its characters. The revised count will be on the top of the stack. The first byte of **ABC** is *not* changed when **-TRAILING** is executed.

The word **$-TB** actually removes the trailing blanks from a string. For instance if we execute

ABC $-TB

the first byte stored in **ABC** will be reduced so that it contains the count of the characters with the trailing blanks removed.

Numerical String Information

There are FORTH words that supply numerical information about strings. We shall now consider them. The word **LEN** is used to supply the length of a string. For instance, the execution of

ABC LEN   (7-37)

results in the address of **ABC** being popped off the stack and a single-length integer equal to the number of characters in the string being pushed onto the stack.

The word **ASC** supplies the ASCII code for the first character in a string. For instance, the execution of

ABC ASC   (7-38)

results in the address of **ABC** being popped off the stack and the value of the ASCII code for the first character in the string stored in **ABC** being pushed onto the stack. The stack relation for **LEN** and **ASC** is

a → n   (7-39)

The word **CHR$** pops the single-length integer (which must equal a valid ASCII code) from the top of the stack and puts its character representation onto the scratch pad. The present address of the scratch pad is pushed onto the stack. The stack relation is

n → a$_{pad}$ (7-40)

There are times when we have a number that is stored in a string representation. We cannot perform any arithmetic using such numbers. The numbers must be in their binary form to perform arithmetic. The word **VAL** converts a number that is represented by a string to a single-length integer. For instance if **ABC** stored the string 123 then after

ABC VAL

was executed, the single-length integer 123 would be on the top of the stack. The stack relation is

$$a \rightarrow n \qquad\qquad\qquad (7\text{-}41)$$

EXERCISES

The following exercises call for writing FORTH words or programs. Check the programs by running them on your computer. Do nut make any single FORTH word too long. Instead write one FORTH word that calls upon shorter FORTH words.

7-1.   What is the difference between a character and a string?

7-2.   Compare the FORTH words **C!** and **C@** with ! and @ respectively.

7-3.   Set up two arrays. Store integers in the first array. Use **CMOVE** to duplicate the integers of the first array into the second array. The second array must be at least as large as the first array.

7-4.   Repeat Problem 7-3 using **MOVE**.

7-5.   Why could either **CMOVE** or **<CMOVE** be used in Problem 7-3?

7-6.   Write a FORTH word that inputs characters from the keyboard and outputs their ASCII code. The operation should terminate when you enter the symbol %.

7-7.   Write a program that allows you to enter text that is stored in an array. Have it output one sentence at a time.

The operation should pause at the end of each sentence and wait until you input a character.

7-8. Modify the program in Figure 7-1 so that you can change a character in the stored text.

7-9. Modify the program in Figure 7-1 so that you can delete a character from the text.

7-10. Modify the program in Figure 7-2 so that you cannot add too many characters to the **WORDS** array.

7-11. Modify the program in Figure 7-1 so that it uses the FORTH word **EXPECT**. Terminate input with a carriage return.

7-12. Write a program using the FORTH command **WORD** that scans a string and outputs the first word. At this point the program should pause. When the user enters a character, the next word in the string should be output. This should continue until the entire string has been output.

7-13. Repeat Problem 7-12 using the # as a delimiter.

7-14. Contrast string constants and numerical constants.

7-15. Modify the program in Figure 7-1 so that it uses the words in Section 7-3.

7-16. Repeat Problem 7-8 using the words in Section 7-3.

7-17. Repeat Problem 7-9 using the words in Section 7-3.

7-18. Repeat Problem 7-10 using the words in Section 7-3.

7-19. Modify the program in Figure 7-5 so that the original array is preserved.

7-20. Repeat Problem 6-16 including the salesman's name. Do not use the words in Section 7-3 here.

7-21. Repeat Problem 7-21 using the words on Section 7-3.

7-22. Repeat Problem 7-21 but now have the data printed out in alphabetical order according to the salesmen's names.

7-23. Discuss the operation of the FORTH word **$ +** .

7-24. Why shouldn't you use the scratch pad for long-term storage of data?

7 - 2 5 Modify the program in Figure 7-5 so that only the first four characters of each name are used in the alphabetizing routine.

7 - 2 6 Modify the program in Figure 7-1 so that you can search the stored data for a string of characters.

7 - 2 7 Repeat Problem 7-26 without using the FORTH word **INSTR**. Hint: write your own word to perform this function.

7 - 2 8 Compare the words **-TRAILING** and **$-TB**.

7 - 2 9 Write a program that adds two numbers that are stored in character form.

Chapter 8
Disk Operations

In this chapter we will discuss the fundamental ideas of disk input/output. In Chapter 1 we considered some basic ideas of disk operations so that you could store your programs on disk and run them later. We will expand upon these ideas here. In addition we shall also consider the important topic of data storage on disks. Many of the ideas relating to these topics are interrelated. Many of the techniques used for program storage can also be used for data storage. In general, the details that we discuss in this chapter may vary somewhat from system to system.

8-1. BASIC IDEAS OF DISK STORAGE

In Section 1-4 we discussed some elementary ideas of disk storage. We shall now expand upon these ideas. Some of the same ideas that were discussed in Section 1-4 will be repeated here.

Pure FORTH systems come complete with their own operating systems. These are simple when compared with the more sophisticated operating systems that are availiable. However, one advantage of the pure FORTH approach is that you can easily modify it to suit your purposes. For instance, most operating systems have an extensive directory structure. The directory structure in the basic FORTH system is rudimentary. However it can be extended easily into a customized form of directory. Some FORTH systems do come with a directory structure. Usually, these can also be modified by the user. Some FORTH systems use the host computer's operating system, but incorporate their own words for disk input/output.

Let us start by considering the storage of programs on floppy disks. As we discussed in Section 1-4, most FORTH programs are typed

in from your editor program and are stored on disks. The FORTH
system works with blocks of data. Each block consists of 1024 bytes
of data. The number of bytes may vary, but this is a typical value.
Assume that you are entering a program using your editor. The
material that you type in from your keyboard is not entered directly
onto a disk. Instead, it is stored in the main memory of the computer
in block buffers. Remember that a buffer is an area of memory that
is set aside for temporary storage of data. In FORTH the buffer area
is divided into blocks. That is, each 1024 bytes of memory consitute
a memory block. This data can be stored on a disk, in which case
we say that a block of information has been stored on a block on
the disk. Your FORTH system allocates a number of block buffers.
Each block is stored in a buffer block. This number is fixed in some
systems and variable in others. Your FORTH manual should indicate
this.

Let us assume that you have typed in a program and stored it in
a block buffer. Most editing routines have procedures that allow you
to mark the buffer block for update using the FORTH word **UPDATE**.
Suppose that you are working with a long program that occupies
several blocks. It may occupy more blocks than there are buffers
available. For instance, suppose that the program is stored in three
disk blocks, but that there are only two block buffers. If you edit
three blocks, then you must overwrite one of the memory buffers.
If a buffer has been marked for update, and you attempt to overwrite
it, then that block will automatically be written to the proper disk
block before the overwriting occurs. That is, the FORTH system will
protect blocks that have been marked for update. (Check your
FORTH manual to make sure how your particular system works.)

Often, you can mark a block for update while working in the editor.
In this way your changes will be saved even if you accidentally exit
the editor. Many systems allow you to exit the editor without saving
any material by pressing the BREAK key. If you have not marked
that block for update, and you accidentally hit the BREAK key, all
your editing may be lost. You may mark for update a block that you
are editing, and then decide that the changes you have made are
wrong. In this case you may end up saving something that you really
want to eliminate.

We can cause the material in the memory block buffers to be saved
on a disk. Before considering the word that does this, let us look
at some additional editing details. The blocks on the disks are
numbered. (We shall discuss the numbering procedure later.) You

must indicate the number of the block that you want to edit to the editor program. The FORTH word **EDIT** is used for this purpose. For instance, if you wanted to edit block 123 you would type

123 EDIT (RETURN)   (8-1)

When **EDIT** is executed, 123 will be popped off the stack and block 123 will be read from the disk into a memory-block buffer. You will already be in the editor program so you can edit the block. The stack relation for **EDIT** is

n →   (8-2)

The number of the block that is being edited will be stored in a FORTH-79 variable called **SCR**. The system also stores the number of the block on the disk that corresponds to the data that is stored in the buffer. Note that **SCR** cannot be used to store this number since you may work on several blocks at the same time. The number stored in **SCR** will contain the number of the *last* block that has been edited. (We shall modify this statement somewhat subsequently.) Suppose that you have edited one or more blocks and have marked them for update. If you type the FORTH command **SAVE-BUFFERS**, each memory buffer will be saved on the appropriate disk block. In many FORTH systems the word **FLUSH** can be used in place of **SAVE-BUFFERS**.

There may be times when you are experimenting with a program and do not want the program presently stored in the memory buffer to overwrite the program that you have stored on the disk. Remember that this storage sometimes takes place even if you do not give the command. The FORTH word **EMPTY-BUFFERS** can be used to prevent a buffer from being written to disk. When **EMPTY-BUFFERS** is executed, the update marks are removed from all the memory buffers. **EMPTY-BUFFERS** does not delete any material from the memory buffers. Thus, you can still load and edit the material that is stored in the buffers. Remember that once you edit the material you may mark the block for update again.

If you want to mark the last block that you have worked on for update, then **UPDATE** can be used. The execution of **UPDATE** marks only one block for update.

Suppose that you want to obtain a listing of the program that you are working on. There are two FORTH words that can be used. One is **L**. This is executed by simply typing

L (RETURN)   (8-3)

The block whose number is stored in **SCR** will be listed on the screen. (You can use **PCRT** to have the block output to your printer.) The word **L** can only be used to list the block whose number is stored in **SCR**. If you want to list a different block, use the word **LIST**. For instance, if you want to list block 123 you would enter

123 LIST (RETURN)   (8-4)

The number 123 would be popped off the stack and stored in **SCR**. The file would then be listed. The stack relation for **LIST** is also given by (8-2).

Once the appropriate value has been stored in **SCR**, you do not need to use the word **EDIT**. The MMSFORTH word **E** can be used. If you type

E (RETURN)

the block whose number is stored in **SCR** will be edited.

Let us look at program compilation. This must be done before a program can be executed. Remember that compilation does things such as establishing dictionary entries for words and variables. To compile a block, use the FORTH word **LOAD**. When you load a block any instructions that are written in the block are executed. Suppose that you want to compile the program that is stored in block 123. You would type

123 LOAD RETURN)   (8-5)

In this case 123 would be popped off the top of the stack and the specified block would be loaded. Any word definitions would be compiled and any direct statements such as

VARIABLE ABC

would be executed. The stack relation for **LOAD** is given by (8-2).

There are times when you need to load several blocks. In such cases you can use the MMSFORTH command **LOADS**. This is not a FORTH-79 word. Suppose that you want to load block 123 and the following two blocks. Then type

123 3 LOADS (RETURN)   (8-6)

The stack relation is

n_1 n_2 $\rightarrow$ (8-7)

There is another definition for **LOADS** that is used in some FORTH systems. You should check the operating manual for your system to see how to use **LOADS**.

One way to load several blocks is to have the last statement in one block be a load statement for the next block. When the first block is loaded, that statement will be executed and the next block will be loaded. If you want to load blocks 123 and 124 then make the last statement in block 123

124 LOAD

When you load block 123 block 124 will automatically be loaded. This procedure can be repeated. If a single FORTH word spans two blocks, this procedure cannot be used. The simplest way to handle this difficulty is to write shorter words that do not span more than one block. That is, write one word that calls several shorter ones.

Most FORTH systems do not have directories. However there is a word that is found in many FORTH systems that can be used to determine the information stored on most blocks. It is **INDEX**. An example of the execution of **INDEX** is

50 20 INDEX (RETURN)   (8-8)

When this is executed the first lines of 20 blocks starting with block number 50 will be listed on the screen. Since it is good programming practice to put a descriptive comment in the first line of each block, the **INDEX** listing provides the key to the block numbers of the various programs. You can also determine which blocks are empty so that you can use them for new programs. The stack relation is

$$n_1\ n_2\ \rightarrow \qquad\qquad\qquad (8\text{-}9)$$

We have discussed the various blocks on the disk. Let us consider the structure of the material stored on the disk to see how block numbers are assigned. We will only consider the details of disk structure that are pertinent to this discussion. The numbers that we will use are typical for small floppy diskettes. However, the ideas are general and can be applied to other disk systems. Data is stored on tracks in a disk. Some disk drives have 35 tracks; others have 40 to 80 tracks. We shall consider 40 as a typical number. Each track is divided into a number of sectors. The sector is the smallest subdivision of the disk. The number of sectors on a track depends upon the recording technique that was used. We shall assume that there are 10 sectors on each track. Each sector typically stores 256 bytes of data. Thus four sectors are needed to store a block. Usually some sectors are used at the start of each disk as a *boot* program. We need not concern ourselves with the details of this program, we will just assume that two sectors are used for the boot program.

If we are working with a 40-track disk with 10 sectors on each track, each disk will store 99 blocks. There are 400 sectors on the disk. Since two are used for the boot program, and 99 blocks use $99 \times 4 = 396$ sectors, then 398 of the sectors are utilized. The additional two sectors on the disk will not be used.

Now we will assume that we are working with more than one disk drive. FORTH systems generally assign block numbers consecutively. For instance, there may be disks in drives 0 and 1. (Note that the first drive, track, sector, etc., is numbered 0.) Block number 98 will be the last block on the disk in drive 0. Similarly, block 99 will be the first block on the disk in drive 1. The number of a block depends upon the drive in which it is used. Suppose that a particular block is the sixty-first one on the disk. If that disk is put into drive 0 then the block in question will be called block 60. On the other hand, if that disk were in drive 1, then the block in question would be called block 159. Remember that the block in position 61 is called block 60, etc.

To illustrate some of the material that we have been discussing let us write a simple directory program. It is assumed that each disk will have its own directory program. For instance, we could put the directory program on block number 60 of each disk. If the disk were mounted on drive number 0 then the directory program would be loaded by loading block 60. Or, if the disk were mounted on drive 1 the directory program would be loaded by loading block 159, etc.. After the directory program is loaded you can obtain a listing of the programs by entering **DIRECTORY**. The names of the various programs on the disk will appear on the screen. If you want to load any one of these programs, you simply type in its name followed by **RETURN**. The program will be loaded and its starting block number will be placed in **SCR** so that it can be edited or listed.

The directory program is listed in Figure 8-1. In line 1 we define the word **DRIVNO**. This queries the user for the drive on which the disk is mounted. This number is pushed onto the stack as a single-length integer. In this sample directory program we assume that there are three programs stored on the disk. **FACTORIAL** is stored in block number 20, **FACTREAL** is stored in block number 21, and **ALPHA** is stored in blocks number 46 and 47. In line 2 the word **FACTORIAL** is defined. **DRVNO** is called so that the number pushed onto the stack is equal to the drive number in question. This number is then duplicated. Its value is stored in **SCR** and is used to load

```
0  ( DIRECTORY PROGRAM )
1  : DRVNO      ." ENTER DRIVE NUMBER"    #IN       ;
2  : FACTORIAL  DRVNO  99    *   20  +  DUP  SCR !  LOAD  ;
3  : FACTREAL   DRVNO  99    *   21  +  DUP  SCR !  LOAD  ;
4  : ALPHA      DRVNO 99  *  46  +  DUP  SCR  !  DUP
5             LOAD    1+    LOAD  ;
6
7
8
9
10 : DIRECTORY CR ." FACTORIAL          FACTREAL          ALPHA        " ;
11
12
13
14
15
```

Figure 8-1. A simple directory program.

the desired block. Hence the desired results have been obtained. The word in line 3 performs essentially the same operations. In line 4 we define the FORTH word **ALPHA**. When **ALPHA** is executed, two blocks must be loaded. The word **ALPHA** is similar to the two preceding words except that before the first block is loaded, **DUP** is executed, and then **LOAD** is executed. The number remaining on the top of the stack is then increased by one and **LOAD** is executed again. Thus, the required two blocks will have been loaded when **ALPHA** is executed.

In line 10 the word **DIRECTORY** is defined. It causes the names of all the programs to be listed. Therefore, the directory program functions as desired. This is a very simple directory program. Every time that a program is added to the disk, the directory program itself must be updated. If we were to write a complex operating system, tasks such as directory management could be taken care of automatically.

There are two other FORTH words that are related to the management of blocks and block buffers. The first of these is **BLOCK**. A typical use of **BLOCK** is

132 BLOCK   (8-10)

In this case 123 would be popped from the stack and block 123 would be retrieved from the appropriate four sectors of a disk and stored in the memory. This set of consecutive memory locations is called a block buffer. The first address of the buffer would be pushed onto the stack. This location is used by the FORTH system to keep track of the location of the buffer. You can also use it if you are using the buffer to store data. The stack relation for **BLOCK** is

n → a   (8-11)

Another FORTH command that is used for disk input/output is **BUFFER**. A typical use of this word is

123 BUFFER   (8-12)

In this case, when **BUFFER** is executed, 123 would be popped off the stack and 1024 bytes of memory would be assigned as a buffer for block 123. The starting address of this block of memory would be pushed onto the stack. The word **BUFFER** is similar to **BLOCK**. The difference is that when **BUFFER** is executed *no* information is read from the disk. **BUFFER** is only used to reserve a buffer for information stored on the disk in a particular disk block. The stack relation for **BUFFER** is given in (8-11).

8-2. STORAGE OF DATA ON DISKS

We shall now discuss the storage and retrieval of data to and from disks. This is often done during the execution of a program. Some of the words that will be introduced here are not in FORTH-79. However, they are found in MMSFORTH and corresponding words are found in some other FORTH systems.

DWTSECS and DRDSECS—We shall now consider two words that can be used to write to and read from a disk. These are not part of FORTH-79, but are very convenient to use. **DWTSECS** is used to write data to a disk. A typical example of its use is

NUMB 1 23 8 2 DWTSECS   (8-13)

Here we assume that **NUMB** is the name of an array variable. When (8-13) is executed, the information stored in memory at the starting address of **NUMB** is written onto a disk. The information will be written onto the disk that is in drive number 1. Two sectors will be written onto sector 8 of track 23 of the disk. (Remember that the numbering of drives, tracks, and sectors starts with 0.) Since a sector constitutes 256 bytes, this means that 512 bytes will be read from the memory and stored on the disk. When **DWTSECS** is used, it does not matter what type of information is stored in the memory; it merely causes a consecutive number of bytes to be stored. For instance, **NUMB** need not be an array; it could be a variable representing a single-length integer. However, the 512 bytes starting with the address **NUMB** would still be copied onto the disk in drive 1 if (8-13) is executed. The stack relation for **DWTSECS** is

$$a \ n_1 \ n_2 \ n_3 \ n_4 \ \rightarrow \ n\text{flag} \tag{8-14}$$

Note that n_1 represents the drive number, n_2 represents the track number, n_3 represents the sector number on the track, and n_4 is the number of sectors to be copied. A flag is pushed onto the stack. Let us consider its significance. Errors can occur when disk input/output is performed. The FORTH system checks, and if no error has occured then a 0 will be pushed onto the stack. This represents a false flag. If an error has occured a true flag will be pushed onto the stack. You can use this flag to abort the operation, repeat it, or perform any other operation that you wish.

The word **DRDSECS** causes data to be read from a disk and be stored in the memory. It is similar to **DWTSECS**. For instance, if we execute

NUMB 1 23 8 2 DRDSECS   (8-15)

then the information stored on the disk in drive 1, track 23, sectors 8 and 9 will be read into the main memory starting at the address specified by **NUMB**. If we execute (8-13) and then execute (8-15), the 512 bytes of data would be read from memory to disk and the same information would be read from disk back to memory.

When we use **DWTSECS** or **DRDSECS**, an integral multiple of 256 bytes is always transferred. Often, the amount of data that we want to store is not such an integral multiple of 256 bytes. In such cases we must move some extra bytes.

As an example of the words that we have just discussed, consider Figure 8-2. This is a simple program that can be used to write numerical data to a disk and have it read back. In line 1 we set up two arrays, **NUMB** and **NUMB1**. In line 2 we define the word **INPUT**. When it is executed, the numbers 3, 6, 9, 12, . . . 597 will be stored in the **NUMB** array. We have used more than 256 bytes but less than 512 bytes here. In line 4 we start the word **DISKWRITE** that writes 512 bytes to sectors 8 and 9 of track 23 of the disk in drive 1. The bytes are taken from the memory location starting at the address of **NUMB**. If an error occurs during the writing of the disk then the statements between **IF** and **THEN** will be executed.

```
0 ( AN EXAMPLE OF DISK INPUT/OUTPUT )
1 VARIABLE NUMB  512 ALLOT      VARIABLE NUMB1 512 ALLOT
2 : INPUT         200 0  DO  I  3  *  NUMB I 2 * +    !  LOOP    ;
3
4 : DISKWRITE    NUMB  1 23 8   2     DWTSECS
5     IF        ." DISK ERROR"  QUIT   THEN  ;
6
7 : DISKREAD    NUMB1  1 23 8   2   DRDSECS
8      IF       ." DISK ERROR "   QUIT  THEN    ;
9
10 : OUTPUT     200 0 DO NUMB1 2 I * + @  .  ." "    LOOP    ;
11
12
13
14
15
```

Figure 8-2. A simple program for the input and output of data to and from a disk.

These statements will cause "DISK ERROR" to appear on the screen and the operation to terminate. We did not enter any data into the **NUMB** array after byte 400. However, 512 bytes starting with the starting address of **NUMB** will be copied onto the disk. This number is independent of the bytes alloted to **NUMB**.

In line 7 we start the word **DISKREAD**. This causes 512 bytes to be read from sectors 8 and 9 of track 23 of the disk in drive 1. This information will be stored in the main memory starting with the address of **NUMB1**. If a disk error occurs then the words "DISK ERROR" will appear and execution will terminate. In line 10 we list the word **OUTPUT** which outputs the data in the **NUMB1** array. This is done so that you can check to see if the program is working correctly.

When data was written to disk there were some items read from memory locations whose contents we did not know. This is no problem. Each memory location must contain some binary number, even if it is 0, which will be stored on the disk. There will usually be such extra data read since the number of memory locations that are read by **DRDSECS** must be an integral multiple of 256.

Reading of Text Data

Text information can be stored using the previously discussed procedures. In fact, any type of information stored in memory can be stored on the disk. However, the words **DWTSECS** and **DRDSECS** are not FORTH-79. We will now discuss some FORTH-79 words that can be used to read text material from a disk block. Some of the words that were introduced in Chapter 7 can be used here. For instance, in Figure 7-4 we used the words **BLK**, **>IN**, and **WORD**. If the number that was pushed onto the stack before **BLK** was executed was not a 0, then the scanned data would have come from the information stored on a disk block rather than from the keyboard. The number of the disk block is equal to the integer that was on the top of the stack when **BLK** was executed.

We can always enter text material onto a disk block using the editor. This is done in exactly the same way that a program is entered. The procedure discussed in the last paragraph can be used to work with that data. We will consider some additional FORTH-79 words that can be used.

TYPE—The FORTH word **TYPE** is used to output a specified number of characters. For instance,

34500 60 TYPE

would result in 60 characters being output. The characters would be those stored in memory locations 34500 to 34559. **TYPE** is not really concerned with output from a disk, but it is particularly convenient if we want to output text that is stored in a memory block buffer. The stack relation for **TYPE** is

a n →   (8-16)

COUNT—Before illustrating the use of **TYPE** with material stored in a block buffer let us consider another FORTH word, **COUNT**. Suppose that a string is stored in the variable **SENT**. Usually the first two bytes of this variable store an integer equal to the length of the string. We shall assume here that the length of the string is 64 or less bytes and that the string length is stored by an unsigned one-byte integer. When **SENT** is executed, the address that is on the stack would not be the proper one to use for **TYPE** since the first byte would contain an integer. To correct this we could simply add 1 to the number on the top of the stack and then push an integer equal to the number of characters to be output onto the stack. The following would accomplish the desired result.

SENT 1+ SENT C@ TYPE   (8-17)

When (8-17) is executed, both the address of the beginning of the string and its length will be pushed onto the stack before **TYPE** is executed. **C@** pushes the number onto the stack as a single-length integer. The manipulations of (8-17) can be accomplished by the single FORTH word **COUNT**. Instead of (8-17) we could write

SENT COUNT TYPE   (8-18)

The word **COUNT** can be implemented by the following FORTH word.

: COUNT DUP 1+ SWAP C@ ;   (8-19)

Let us now consider the simple program in Figure 8-3 which illustrates the use of **TYPE** in outputting text that is stored on a block. The output of the program consists of the words "THIS

```
0 ( AN EXAMPLE OF THE USE OF TYPE )
1 ( THIS PROGRAM PRINTS THE WORDS SMALL WORD  )
2 : TEST   CR CR    155  BLOCK    66 +    41    TYPE   CR CR
3            ." SMALL WORD "      CR CR     ;
4
5
6
7
8
9
10
11
12
13
14
15
```

Figure 8-3. A simple example of the use of the FORTH word **TYPE.**

PROGRAM PRINTS THE WORDS SMALL WORD" which is then followed by the words "SMALL WORD." Line 1 contains some of the desired text material enclosed in parentheses. This is done so that when the block is loaded, the material in line 1 is neither compiled nor executed. If text material were stored on a separate block that was not to be compiled, then the parentheses would not be necessary. We are assuming here that this program is on block 155. Then, when **BLOCK** is executed, block 155 will be loaded into a memory buffer and the starting address in the buffer will be pushed onto the stack. The text that we want to print is on line 1 of the block. Each line of a buffer contains exactly 64 characters, including blanks. The word "THIS" starts in the third character position of the second line. Thus T is the sixty-seventh character in the buffer. So we add 66 to the starting address of the buffer, which was pushed onto the stack when **BLOCK** was executed. There are 41 characters in the text that we want to print. Hence, 41 is pushed onto the stack. When **TYPE** is executed, the desired text will be read from the buffer and output. The FORTH word ." is used to print the remainder of the desired text. We can use the ideas discussed here to output any text that was stored on a disk.

EXERCISES

The following exercises require you to write some FORTH words or programs. Check the words or programs by running them on your computer. Do not write any FORTH words that are too long. Instead, write one FORTH word that calls upon shorter FORTH words that you write.

8-1.   Discuss some ideas for disk storage.

8-2.   What is a block?

8-3.   What is the difference between a memory block buffer and a disk block?

8-4.   Write a FORTH word that will automatically load the block that you are editing when the word **LD** is entered.

8-5.   Experiment with the words **EMPTY-BUFFERS, SAVE-BUFFERS, FLUSH,** and **UPDATE** to determine their functions.

8-6.   What is the difference between the words **EDIT** and **E**?

8-7.   What is the difference between the words **LIST** and **L**?

8-8.   Determine how the word **LOADS** is used in your system.

8-9.   Use the FORTH word **INDEX** to obtain a listing of the programs stored on your disk. This assumes that the first line of each block was written appropriately.

8-10. Modify the directory program in Figure 8-1 so that the programs will not be loaded unless a proper password is given.

8-11. Write a FORTH word that will perform the directory operations in Figure 8-1 when the following data is supplied for each program: its name, starting block, and the number of blocks to be loaded.

8-12. Modify the program in Problem 6-16 having all the output stored on a disk.

8-13. Modify the program in Problem 8-12 so that the input data can be stored in an array.

8-14. Write a program that computes and stores the first five factorials in an array.

8-15. Repeat Problem 8-14 using double-length integers. Compute the first nine factorials.

8-16. Repeat Problem 8-15 using floating point numbers.

8-17. Repeat Problem 8-15 using double-length floating point numbers.

8-18. Use the words **COUNT** and **TYPE** to output a string that you have stored in memory.

8-19. Repeat Problem 8-14 using **TYPE** to print out appropriate headings.

8-20. Store text on a disk block and then have it output one sentence at a time.

Chapter 9

Some Additional FORTH Operations

In this chapter we will discuss some additional FORTH words. Some of these will concern compilation and the workings of the FORTH system. A knowledge of these words will both increase your programming techniques and further your understanding of FORTH.

9-1. Compiler Control

In this section we will discuss some FORTH words that can direct the operation of the compiler. In all of the FORTH words that we have written so far, the following procedure occurred. During compilation, a word is placed in the dictionary and then it can be executed. If one word calls upon other words essentially the same thing happens. That is, after compilation, the dictionary entry for the calling word contains the addresses of the called words. This enables execution of those called words as part of the execution of the calling word. As an example consider Figure 7-5. There we define the words **ALPHA**, **ALPHAIN**, and **ALPHAOUT**. When the block is loaded, each word is compiled into the dictionary. When **ALPHA** is executed, both **ALPHAIN** and **ALPHAOUT** are called and executed. FORTH provides some words that can modify this procedure.

IMMEDIATE—The FORTH word **IMMEDIATE** can be used to cause a word to be executed during compilation. This idea is illustrated in Figure 9-1. For the moment we will assume that only lines 1 and 2 are present. When the block in Figure 9-1 is loaded

```
0  ( SOME EXAMPLES OF COMPILER WORDS )
1  : TEST  ." PRINT THIS " ;     IMMEDIATE
2  : TEST1 ." ONE "    TEST ;
3  : TEST2 ." TWO "          ;
4  : TEST3 ." THREE " [COMPILE] TEST        ;
5  : TEST4 ." FOUR "   TEST  ;
6  : TEST5 ." FIVE "    COMPILE  TEST2  ;   IMMEDIATE
7  : TEST6 ." SIX "   TEST5         ;
8
9
10
11
12
13
14
15
```

Figure 9-1. Some examples of the FORTH words **IMMEDIATE**, **[COMPILE]**, and **COMPILE**.

the words "PRINT THIS" will appear. This will occur during compilation of the block. This does *not* come about when line 1 is compiled. During loading, **TEST** becomes a dictionary entry for an immediate word. During the compilation of **TEST1** the immediate word **TEST** is encountered. Its address is not compiled into the word **TEST1**, **TEST** is simply executed. After compilation, if we execute **TEST1**, the word **TEST** will not be executed. That is when **TEST1** is executed the words "PRINT THIS" will not appear. If we type TEST (RETURN) then the words "PRINT THIS" will be output. However, remember that if an immediate word is part of the definition of another word, then the immediate word will not be executed when the first word is executed. A word is made immediate by typing **IMMEDIATE** after the semicolon which ends its definition.

   [COMPILE]—There are times when we want to use an immediate word within another FORTH word and have it function as though it were an ordinary word. There is a FORTH word that we can use to accomplish this. It is **[COMPILE]** (pronounced bracket-compile). An illustration of the use of this word is given in line 4 of Figure 9-1. **[COMPILE]** is written within the FORTH word **TEST3**. **[COMPILE]** immediately precedes the word that it is to act upon. For instance, when the word **TEST3** in Figure 9-1 is compiled, the compiler acts as though **TEST** were not an immediate word. When the block in Figure 9-1 is loaded, the compilation of **TEST3** does *not* cause "PRINT THIS" will be printed. Remember that an immediate word following **[COMPILE]** is treated as if it were not an immediate word.

COMPILE—As we have discussed, if an immediate word is included as part of another word, the immediate word will be ignored when the first word is executed. The immediate word is not compiled into the dictionary entry of the "outer" word. We can include words within immediate words and have these words compiled into the dictionary entries of other words that contain the immediate word. For instance, consider lines 3, 6, and 7 in Figure 9-1. The word **TEST6** includes the word **TEST5**, which is an immediate word. Normally when **TEST6** is executed **TEST5** would have no effect on the execution. **TEST5** includes the word **TEST2**, which is not an immediate word. In **TEST5**, immediately preceding **TEST2**, we have the word **COMPILE**. When **TEST5** is compiled within another word, **TEST2** is treated as though it were part of an ordinary word, not an immediate one. On the other hand, the rest of **TEST5** is treated as an immediate word. For instance when **TEST6** is compiled "FIVE" is output. Subsequently, if **TEST6** is executed "SIX TWO" will be output. If the word **COMPILE** were omitted from **TEST5**, then **TEST2** would not affect the execution of **TEST6**. If **TEST5** itself is executed, then **TEST2** will be ignored. That is, the word following **COMPILE** will not be executed when the word containing it is executed. When a word containing **COMPILE** is executed, the address of the following word is compiled into the dictionary so that it can be executed.

In summary, let us look at what takes place when the block in Figure 9-1 is loaded. The compiling of **TEST1** will cause "PRINT THIS" to be output. The compiling of **TEST4** will result in the same output. Finally, the compiling of **TEST6** will result in "FIVE" being output.

Now let us consider the result of the execution of the words in Figure 9-1. If we execute **TEST** the output is "PRINT THIS". When **TEST1** is executed the output is "ONE". The immediate word **TEST** has no effect here. When **TEST2** is executed "TWO" is output. When **TEST3** is executed the output is "THREE PRINT THIS". The word **[COMPILE]** causes **TEST** to be compiled into this word. When **TEST4** is executed the output is "FOUR". When **TEST5** is executed the output is "FIVE". **COMPILE** prevents **TEST2** from being executed here. However it will affect the operation if **TEST5** is included within another word. This is illustrated when **TEST6** is executed. Now the output is "SIX TWO."

LITERAL, [, and]

There are times that we want to use the initial value of a variable throughout the program. However, the value of a variable may change during the execution of the program. Thus, if we simply fetch the value of the variable during execution we would not obtain the initial value. We could define a constant equal to the initial value of the variable and use it, but this involves extra definitions. If there are many such variables, then considerable extra storage space would be used. The FORTH words **LITERAL**, **[** (referred to as left-bracket) and **]** (right-bracket) can be used to resolve these problems. An example of their use is shown in Figure 9-2. Let us consider the operation. In line 1 we define the variable **VAR**. Then we push 5

```
0  ( AN EXAMPLE OF THE WORD LITERAL )
1    VARIABLE   VAR             5    VAR !
2  : SUMM    [ VAR @ ]     LITERAL        +     ;
3  : ANSWER   7   *     DUP    VAR !      SUMM      .     ;
4
5
6
7
8
9
10
11
12
13
14
15
```

Figure 9-2. An example of the use of the FORTH words **LITERAL**, **[**, and **]**.

onto the stack and store that value in **VAR**. In the next line we define the word **SUMM** where the FORTH words that fetch the value stored in **VAR** are enclosed in square brackets. The **[** causes the material following it to be *executed, not compiled* when the block is loaded. This execution continues until the **]** is encountered. Compilation then proceeds. Thus, during the compilation of **SUMM** the value 5 which is stored in **VAR** will be pushed onto the stack. Next **LITERAL** is executed. This causes the single-length integer that is on the top of the stack to be popped off and compiled into the

definition of **SUMM**. It is as though we wrote 5 after the word
SUMM in line 2. The word **SUMM** pops the top number from the
stack and adds 5 to it. The resulting sum is pushed onto the stack.

Consider the word **ANSWER** that is defined in line 3. It pops the
top number from the stack, multiplies it by 7, and duplicates the
result. This value is then stored in **VAR**. Thus, when **ANSWER** is
executed, the number that is output is equal to 7 times the number
that is currently on top of the stack plus 5.

Let us now review the last three words that we have considered.
LITERAL pops the single-length integer from the top of the stack
and causes it to be compiled into the word that is currently being
compiled. The stack relation is

$$n \rightarrow \tag{9-1}$$

when the FORTH words [and] are used within a word definition.
During compilation, any material between the brackets is executed
rather than compiled.

9-2. VOCABULARIES AND THE DICTIONARY.

When a word is stored in the dictionary, one of the items it contains
is the address of the previous dictionary entry. This is called the
link field or simply the *link*. Each dictionary entry, itself, consists
of a series of consecutive memory locations. When the dictionary
is searched, the last entry is searched first. If that name does not
match the desired one then the link is used to find the previous entry
in the dictionary. At times it is desirable to order this searching. For
instance, suppose that you are editing your program using the editor.
It would be desirable if the editor commands were searched first
since this would shorten the time of a dictionary search. At other
times it would be desirable to have other words on the top of the
dictionary.

Let us see how the structure of the dictionary and the order in
which it is searched can be controlled. All the words in the dictionary
are linked together. We can group sets of words together. In FORTH
such groupings are called *vocabularies*. The dictionary does not have
to be a linear string of definitions; there can be several branches.
For instance, suppose that there are three branches. In each branch
the link of one word points back to the preceding word of that
branch. However, two of the branches can ultimately point back
to a common ancestor in the first branch. They do not point toward

each other. Each branch can be considered a vocabulary. In FORTH the main vocabulary is called FORTH. We have, thus far, written all our words into the FORTH vocabulary. As we have discussed, it is sometimes desirable to define separate vocabularies. Let us see how this can be done.

VOCABULARY—The FORTH word **VOCABULARY** is used to set up a new vocabulary. For instance, if we want to set up a vocabulary called **HOUSE**, we would first execute

VOCABULARY HOUSE   (9-2)

(Some versions of FORTH require that **HOUSE** be followed by **IMMEDIATE**.) **HOUSE** is not yet a vocabulary. However, when the word **HOUSE** is executed it becomes the *context* vocabulary. Suppose that a dictionary search is made. The search would start with the context vocabulary. If the word is not found, then the search would go to the FORTH vocabulary. Now suppose that we execute the word FORTH and make it the context vocabulary. Now the search would start with the **FORTH** vocabulary. If the word is not found the *search would not* go to the **HOUSE** vocabulary. By properly defining vocabularies we can conveniently work with two different words with the same name. We could have done this with only one vocabulary. The use of more than one vocabulary may make it more convenient.

CONTEXT, CURRENT, and DEFINITIONS—In addition to the discussion in the preceding paragraph, it is somewhat important to note that dictionary entries are not made into the context vocabulary but into one called the *current* vocabulary. When the FORTH word **DEFINITIONS** is executed, the context vocabulary also becomes the current vocabulary. For instance if, after we execute (9-2), we execute **HOUSE** and then **DEFINITIONS**, any new words that we write will be compiled into the **HOUSE** vocabulary. New words are entered into the current vocabulary while dictionary searches are made into the context vocabulary.

There are two FORTH variables, **CONTEXT** and **CURRENT**, that store pertinent addresses. **CONTEXT** stores the address of the first vocabulary defining word in which dictionary searches are to be made. Similarly, **CURRENT** stores the address of the vocabulary defining word into which new word definitions are to be made. The stack relation for both of these words is

$$\rightarrow \ a \hspace{12em} (9\text{-}3)$$

The execution of **CONTEXT** or **CURRENT** causes their own addresses, not that of the vocabulary defining word, to be pushed onto the stack.

Let us consider some aspects of dictionary searches. Suppose that we work with several vocabularies which are defined in the following order: **FORTH**, **HOUSE**, **BOOK**. If **BOOK** is the context vocabulary, then a dictionary search will encompass all the dictionaries. On the other hand if **HOUSE** is the context vocabulary then **BOOK** will not be included in the dictionary search.

'—Let us now consider the FORTH word ' (pronounced tick) which is the apostrophe symbol. When ' is executed, the address of the next word in the input stream will be pushed onto the stack. For instance, if we execute

' NUMB $\hspace{18em} (9\text{-}4)$

the address of **NUMB** will be pushed onto the stack. If you want to check if a name has been used, then execute ' followed by the name. If an "ok" is output then the name is in use. If the name followed by a question mark appears on the screen then the name has not been found by the directory search. We can use ' to find the address of a constant and then modify the value stored by that constant.

9-3. SOME ADDITIONAL FORTH WORDS.

In this section we shall consider some additional FORTH words. One provides a new programming technique. Some others are involved with memory manipulation.

MYSELF—There are times when it would be convenient for a FORTH program to call itself. This is called a *recursive* operation. The FORTH word **MYSELF** accomplishes this. Let us illustrate this with an example. Figure 9-3 illustrates the FORTH word we call **RECURSIVE** that functions in the following way. It pushes 3 onto the stack and executes **+** . The resulting sum is then pushed onto

```
0  ( A RECURSIVE PROGRAM )
1  : RECURSIVE    3  +  DUP    99   -    0>
2         IF   .  QUIT     THEN      MYSELF  ;
3
4
5
6
7
8
9
10
11
12
13
14
15
```

Figure 9-3. An example of the use of the FORTH word **MYSELF.**

the stack. This sum is then duplicated. Next 99 is pushed onto the
stack and - is executed. Then **0>** is executed. If the resulting flag
is true, then the number on the top of the stack is output and
execution ceases. If the flag is false then **MYSELF** is executed. This
causes **RECURSIVE** to call itself and the operation repeats. Thus,
this same program keeps adding 3 onto a number until the resulting
sum is 100 or more. At that time the sum is output and execution
ceases.

Care should be taken when **MYSELF** is used. Do not write a word
that keeps calling itself indefinitely. The operation will never
terminate and you will have to reboot the system to regain control.
Also be careful that you do not keep pushing data onto the stack
and overwrite all memory.

EXECUTE—Upon execution of the word **EXECUTE**, the word
whose address is on the top of the stack is executed.

EXIT—When the word **EXIT** is executed from within a word,
execution terminates. **EXIT** cannot be used within a loop. If **EXIT**
is in a block and is not part of a word, when the block is loaded
compilation and loading will terminate when **EXIT** is reached.

FIND—This word pushes the address of the next word in the input
stream onto the stack. If the word cannot be found, then 0 is pushed
onto the stack.

Memory Filling

There are times when it is convenient to fill certain consecutive memory locations with repetitive data. For instance, in Section 8-2 we discussed that, in writing information to a disk, some extraneous data might have to be recorded. In such cases it would be desirable to make the extraneous data all 0's so that the disk does not contain meaningless data. In some computers, the video screen of the terminal is *memory mapped*. This means that the screen is divided into segments, each the size of a single letter or punctuation mark. A portion of the memory is set aside in which each location corresponds to one of the screen segments. The character that is output in any segment is determined by the ASCII code that is stored in the corresponding memory location. The memory locations that map the video screen are in a consecutive group. Suppose that we want to clear the video screen. If we could write a 32, which is the ASCII code for a blank, into each of the video screen's memory locations, then video screen would be cleared. FORTH has several words that can be used for the purposes that we have discussed. One such word is **FILL**. An example of its use is

$$26000 \ 1000 \ 90 \ \text{FILL} \tag{9-5}$$

When (9-5) is executed, 1000 memory locations, starting will memory location 26000 will be filled with the ASCII code whose decimal representation is 90. This corresponds to the letter Z. The stack relation for **FILL** is

$$a \ n_1 \ n_2 \ \rightarrow \tag{9-6}$$

If we want to fill the memory with the ASCII representation for a blank, then **FILL** could be used to put 32 in the appropriate memory locations. However, there is a special FORTH word that can be used for this purpose. It is **BLANK**, or in some systems, **BLANKS**. The stack relation for this word is

$$a \ n \ \rightarrow \tag{9-7}$$

In this case n memory locations starting with a will be filled with the ASCII code for a blank.

ERASE—ERASE functions in the same way as **BLANK** except that the memory locations are filled with 0's.

EXERCISES

The following exercises call for you to write FORTH words or programs. Check the words or programs by running them on your computer. Do not write any FORTH words that are too long. Instead, write one FORTH word that calls upon shorter FORTH words that you write.

9-1. Discuss the action of the word **IMMEDIATE**.

9-2. Compare the FORTH words **[COMPILE]** and **COMPILE**. Illustrate your discussion with FORTH words that you write.

9-3. Write a directory program that automatically lists the programs in the directory when the directory block is loaded.

9-4. Modify the program in Figure 7-2 so that when the program is compiled, a period is output each time that a line of text is processed.

9-5. Discuss the use of the FORTH word **LITERAL**.

9-6. Repeat Problem 9-5 for the FORTH words **[** and **]**.

9-7. Write a FORTH program that averages a student's grades in four tests and stores the result in a variable. The program is to output the average and whether or not the student passes. The passing grade should be initially stored in the same variable that ultimately stores the average.

9-8. Write a recursive FORTH program that obtains the sum of twenty consecutive integers, starting with the integer that is on the top of the stack.

9-9. Repeat Problem 9-8 adding twenty consecutive even integers.

9-10. Repeat Problem 9-8 adding twenty consecutive odd integers.

9-11. Write a program using **MYSELF** that computes the factorial.

9-12. Write a recursive program that computes the sum $1/n^2$ where n = 1, 2, 3, ... Use floating point numbers. The program should terminate when $1/n^2$ becomes less than 0.00001.

9-13. Fill 1024 consecutive memory locations with the ASCII representation for X.

9-14. Why may the program of the preceding problem cause you to have to boot your system?

9-15. Write a program that fills a block buffer with blanks.

A Glossary of FORTH Words

In this glossary we shall present a listing of the FORTH words covered in this book. The section in which the word is introduced, the stack relation, and a brief description will be given. Not all the words are FORTH-79. The enhancements to FORTH-79 are found in MMSFORTH and other FORTH systems. For specific information see the sections where the words are defined.

Word	Section	Stack	Description
!	6-2	n a→	Stores a number into address on top of stack
#	3-3	$d_1 \rightarrow d_2$	Used in pictured numeric output for digits of unsigned double-length integers
#>	3-3	d → a n	Terminates pictured numeric output
#IN	3-1	→ n	Prompts for input of single-length integer
#S	3-3	d → 0.	Converts digits to ASCII code in pictured numeric output
$!	7-3	a$ a →	Used for string storage
$ "	7-3	→ a	Sets up a string stored in memory

$-TB	7-3		Removes trailing blanks from string
$.	7-3	a →	String print
$ARRAY	7-3	n_1 n_2 →	Sets up a string array
$COMPARE	7-3	a_1 a_2 → f	Compares string variables
$CONSTANT	7-3		Sets up a string constant
$VARIABLE	7-3		Sets up a string variable
$XCG	7-3	a_1 a_2 →	Exchanges values stored by string variables
'	9-2	→ a	Gives address of next word in the input stream
(	2-3		Begins a comment
*	2-1	n_1 n_2→n	Results in a product
*/	5-2	n_1 n_2 n_3→n	Multiplies n_1 by n_2 and then divides by n_3 with double-length product
*/ MOD	5-2	n_1 n_2 n_3→ n_r n_q	Similar to * / except that remainder is also obtained
+	2-1	n_1 n_2→n	Results in a sum
+*!*	6-2	n a →	Adds to the stored value
+*LOOP*	4-3	n →	Used with variable increment looping
,	6-3	n →	Compiles n into the dictionary
-	2-1	n_1 n_2 →n_d	Results in the subtraction of n_2 from n_1
-TRAILING	7-3	a n_1 → a n_2	Reduces character count
.	1-4	n →	Outputs number
."	3-1		Used for text output
.R	3-3	n_1 n_2 →	Outputs number n_1 in field n_2

/	2-1	n_1 $n_2 \rightarrow$ q	Results in division of n_1 by n_2
/ MOD	2-1	n_1 $n_2 \rightarrow$ r q	Results in division leaving quotient and remainder
0<	4-1	$n \rightarrow f$	True if n is less than 0
0 =	4-1	$n \rightarrow f$	True if n = 0
0>	4-1	$n \rightarrow f$	True if n is greater than 0
1 +	2-7	$n \rightarrow n_1$	Adds one to integer on top of stack
1-	2-7	$n \rightarrow n_1$	Subtracts one from the integer on top of the stack
16*	2-7	$n \rightarrow n_1$	Multiplies the number on top of the stack by 16
2!	6-2	$d\ a \rightarrow$	Stores a double-length integer
2$ARRAY	7-3	n_1 n_2 $n_3 \rightarrow$	Sets up a two-dimensional string array
2*	2-7	$n \rightarrow n_1$	Multiplies the integer on top of the stack by 2
2 +	2-7	$n \rightarrow n_1$	Adds 2 to the integer on top of the stack
2-	2-7	$n \rightarrow n_1$	Subtracts 2 from the integer on top of the stack
2 /	2-7	$n \rightarrow n_1$	Divides the integer on top of the stack by 2
2@	6-2	$a \rightarrow d$	Fetches a double-length integer
2ARRAY	6-4	n_1 $n_2 \rightarrow$	Sets up a two dimensional array
2CONSTANT	6-1	$d \rightarrow$	Used to establish a double-length constant
2DARRAY	6-4	n_1 $n_2 \rightarrow$	Used to establish double-length integer array
2DROP	2-5	$d \rightarrow$	Drops a double-length integer from the stack

2DUP	2-5	d →d d	Duplicates the top double-length integer onto the top of the stack
2OVER	2-5	$d_1 d_2$ → $d_1 d_2 d_1$	Duplicates the second double-length integer onto the top of the stack
2ROT	2-5	$d_1 d_2 d_3$ → $d_2 d_3 d_1$	Rotates the third double-length integer to the top of the stack
2SWAP	2-5	$d_1 d_2$ → $d_2 d_1$	Swaps top two double-length integers
2VARIABLE	6-2		Used to set up a double-length variable
:	2-3		Used to start a FORTH word definition
;	2-3		Used to end a FORTH word definition
<	4-1	$n_1 n_2$ → f	Flag is true if n_1 is less than n_2
<#	3-3		Starts pictured numeric output
< =	4-1	$n_1 n_2$ → f	Flag is true if n_1 is less than or equal to n_2
<>	4-1	$n_1 n_2$ → f	Flag is true if n_1 is not equal to n_2
<CMOVE	7-1	$a_1 a_2 n$ →	Duplicates n bytes of memory starting at a_1 to a_2; move starts from high memory
=	4-1	$n_1 n_2$ → f	Flag is true if n_1 is equal to n_2
> =	4-1	$n_1 n_2$ → f	Flag is true if n_1 is greater than or equal to n_2

<IN	7-2	→ a	Variable containing character offset
>R	2-6	n →	Transfers an integer to the top of the return stack; must be matched by R>
?DUP	4-5	n → n n	Duplicates the top single-length integer unless it is zero
@	6-2	a → n	Fetches the single-length integer stored at address
ABS	2-7	n_1 → n_2	Replaces the top single-length integer by its absolute value
ALLOT	6-3	n →	Adds n bytes to a variable's storage area
AND	5-5	n_1 n_2 → n_3	Performs logical AND operation on a bit-by-bit basis
ARRAY	6-3	n →	Used to set up an array
ASC	6-3	a → n	Pushes the ASCII value of the first character in a string starting at a onto the stack
BASE	2-7	→ a	Variable containing the numeric base used for output
BEGIN	4-4		Used in BEGIN-UNTIL or BEGIN-WHILE-REPEAT forms
BLANK	9-3	a n →	Fills in bytes of memory starting at a with the ASCII code for blanks
BLK	7-2	→ a	Variable containing the block used for an input stream

BLOCK	8-1	n → a	Transfers block n from disk to memory and pushes the starting address of the block onto stack
BUFFER	8-1	n → a	Similar to block but the data is not read from the disk
c!	7-1	n a →	Stores the least significant byte of a single-length integer
c@	7-1	a → n	Fetches one byte and stores it as a single-length integer
CASEND	4-6		Used to end the CASE statement
CHR$	7-3	c → a	Converts a one-byte integer to its ASCII representation and stores it in PAD; puts the address of PAD on the stack
CMOVE	7-1	a_1 a_2 n →	Copies n bytes of memory starting at a_1 to a_2, beginning with low memory
COMPILE	9-1		Compiles value into a word
CONSTANT	6-1	n →	Sets up a constant with the value n
CONTEXT	9-2	→ a	Variable containing the address of the context vocabulary
COUNT	8-2	a → a_1 n	Pushes starting address of string and string count onto stack $a_1 = a + 1$
CR	3-1		Outputs carriage return
CREATE	6-3		Sets up a dictionary entry
CRT	3-1		Routes output to the video display

CURRENT	9-2	$\rightarrow a$	Variable containing the address of current vocabulary
D#IN	5-1	$\rightarrow d$	Queries for input of double-length integer
D*	5-1	$d_1\ d_2 \rightarrow d_p$	Takes product of double-length integers
D* /	5-2	$d_1\ d_2\ d_3$ $\rightarrow d$	Takes product $d_1\ d_2$, then divides by d_3 to obtain the quotient of double-length integers; the intermediate product is quadruple length
D* / MOD	5-2	$d_1\ d_2\ d_3$ $\rightarrow d_r\ d_q$	Same as D* / except that a remainder is also obtained
D +	5-1	$d_1\ d_2 \rightarrow d$	Obtains the sum of two double-length integers
D-	5-1	$d_1\ d_2 \rightarrow d$	Obtains the difference d_1 minus d_2 for double-length integers
D/	5-1	$d_1\ d_2 \rightarrow d$	Obtains the quotient of d_1 divided by d_2 for double-length integers
D/MOD	5-1	$d_1\ d_2 \rightarrow$ $d_r\ d_q$	Similar to D / but the remainder is also pushed onto the stack
D.	5-1	$d \rightarrow$	Outputs a double-length integer
D.R	5-1	$d\ n \rightarrow$	Outputs a double-length integer in a field of n characters
DO =	5-1	$d \rightarrow f$	Flag is true if the double-length integer is equal to zero

D<	5-1	$d_1\ d_2 \rightarrow f$	Flag is true if d_1 is less than d_2
DABS	5-1	$d_1 \rightarrow d_2$	Gives the absolute value of a double-length integer
DARRAY	6-3	$n \rightarrow$	Sets up a double-length array
DECIMAL	2-7		Sets output to base 10
DEFINITIONS	9-2		Sets ccurrent vocabulary to context vocabulary
DEPTH	2-2	$\rightarrow n$	Gives the number of equivalent single-length integers on the stack
DMAX	5-1	$d_1\ d_2 \rightarrow d$	Gives the larger of two double-length integers
DMIN	5-1	$d_1\ d_2 \rightarrow d$	Gives the smaller of two double-length integers
DNEGATE	5-1	$d \rightarrow -d$	Gives the negative of the double-length integer on the stack
DO	4-3	$n_1\ n_2 \rightarrow$	Sets up a loop
DRDSECS	8-2	$a\ n_1\ n_2\ n_3$ $n_4 \rightarrow nf$	Reads disk sectors
DROP	2-2	$n \rightarrow$	Drops top single-length integer from the stack
DUP	2-2	$n \rightarrow n\ n$	Duplicates the top single-length integer
DWTSECS	8-2	$a\ n_1\ n_2\ n_3$ $n_4 \rightarrow nf$	Writes disk sectors
E	8-1		Causes editing of the screen specified by SCR contents
EDIT	4-2	$n \rightarrow$	Starts editing of block n; stores n in SCR
ELSE	4-2		Used in IF-ELSE-THEN construction

EMIT	7-1	c →	Outputs a character
EMPTY-BUFFERS	8-1		Mark all buffers as empty
ERASE	9-3	a n →	Sets memory at zero for n bytes starting at byte a
EXECUTE	9-3	a →	Executes dictionary word whose address is on the stack
EXIT	9-3		Terminates execution
EXPECT	7-2	a n →	Inputs characters to memory starting at address a, for n characters or until carriage return
FILL	9-3	a n n$_c$ →	Fills n bytes of memory (starting with address a) with the ASCII equivalent of n$_c$
FIND	9-3	→ a	Finds address of the next word in the input stream
FLUSH	8-1		Saves marked buffers on disk
FORGET	2-4		Deletes all words up to and including the following word
FORTH	9-2		Name of first vocabulary
HERE	7-2	→ a	Gives the address of the next available dictionary byte
HEX	2-7		Converts numerical output to hexadecimal
HOLD	3-3	c →	Used to insert a character into pictured numeric output
I	4-3	→ n	Pushes the loop index onto the stack

I'	4-3	$\rightarrow$ n	Pushes the loop test value onto the stack
IF	4-2	f $\rightarrow$	Used in conditional operations
IMMEDIATE	9-1		Alters compilation and execution
INDEX	9-1	n_1 n_2 $\rightarrow$	Outputs the first line of n_2 screens starting at block n_1
J	4-3	$\rightarrow$ n	Pushes the index of the next outer loop onto the stack
KEY	7-1	$\rightarrow$ n	Pushes the ASCII code for the next input character onto the stack
L	8-1		Lists the screen whose number is stored in SCR
LEAVE	4-3		Causes the loop to terminate
LEFT$	7-3	a n $\rightarrow$ a_1	Obtains n leftmost characters from string started at a and stores them in PAD
LEN	7-3	a $\rightarrow$ n	Pushes the length of a string onto the stack
LIST	2-3	n $\rightarrow$	Lists block n and puts n in SCR
LITERAL	9-1	n $\rightarrow$	Causes the stack value to be compiled as literal during compilation
LOAD	2-3	n $\rightarrow$	Loads block n
LOADS	8-1	n_1 n_2 $\rightarrow$	Loads n_2 blocks starting with n_1 (alternative definition in some systems)
LOOP	4-3		Increases the index of a loop by one
M*	5-3	n_1 n_2 $\rightarrow$ d	Double-length product of single-length integers

M*/	5-3	d_1 n_2 n_3 $\rightarrow d_2$	Multiplies d_1 by n_2 and stores the product as a triple-length integer; divides by n_3; a double-length quotient results
M +	5-3	d_1 n $\rightarrow$ d_2	Mixed precision addition
M-	5-3	d_1 n $\rightarrow$ d_2	Mixed precision subtraction; n is subtracted from d_1
M /	5-3	d n_1 $\rightarrow$ n_2	Mixed precision division; d is divided by n_1 to obtain a single-length quotient
M / MODD	5-3	d n_1 $\rightarrow$ d_r n_q	Similar to M/ except that a quotient and remainder are obtained
MAX	2-7	n_1 n_2 $\rightarrow$ n	Gives the largest of two values
MID$	7-3	a n_1 n_2 $\rightarrow$ a_1	Copies to a_1 a substring of n_2 characters starting at n_1 characters into a string starting at a
MIN	2-7	n_1 n_2 $\rightarrow$ n	Gives the smaller of two values
MOD	2-1	n_1 n_2 $\rightarrow$ n	Results in a remainder of n_1 divided by n_2 being pushed onto the stack
MOVE	7-1	a_1 a_2 n $\rightarrow$	Moves n 16-byte memory words starting at a_1 to a_2
MYSELF	9-3		Allows recursive programs
NCASE	4-6	n $\rightarrow$	Beginning of CASE statement
NEGATE	2-7	n $\rightarrow$ -n	Replaces a number by its negative

NOT	4-5	$f_1 \rightarrow f_2$	Replaces a flag by its complement
OCTAL	2-7		Sets output number to base 8
OTHERWISE	4-6		Default in CASE statement
OVER	2-2	$n_1\ n_2 \rightarrow$ $n_1\ n_2\ n_1$	Duplicates second number onto the top of the stack
PAD	7-3	$\rightarrow a$	Variable containing the starting address of the scratch pad
PAGE	3-1		Clears the terminal's screen
PCRT	3-1		Causes output to both the screen and the printer
PRINT	3-1		Causes output to the printer only
QUERY	7-2		Used for character input
QUIT	3-1		Clears return stack and returns control to printer without output of "ok"
R>	2-6	$\rightarrow n$	Pops the top single-length integer from the return stack and pushes it onto the stack; must match >R
R@	2-6	$\rightarrow n$	Duplicates the top single-length integer from the return stack onto the stack
RANDOMIZE	2-7		Randomizes random number generator
REPEAT	4-4		Used in BEGIN-WHILE-REPEAT form
RIGHT$	7-3	$a\ n \rightarrow a_1$	Moves n rightmost characters from the string at a to

			PAD; stores the address of PAD on the stack
RN1	2-7		Generates a random number and stores it in SEED
RND	2-7	$n_1 \rightarrow n_2$	Generates a random number that lies between 1 and n_1
ROLL	2-2	$n \rightarrow$	Moves an n deep single-length integer to the top of the stack
ROT	2-2	$n_1\ n_2\ n_3 \rightarrow$ $n_2\ n_3\ n_1$	Rotates the third single-length integer to the top of the stack
SAVE-BUFFERS	8-1		Marks all buffers as updated
SCR	8-1	$\rightarrow a$	Variable storing the address of the most recently edited or listed screen
SIGN	3-3	$n \rightarrow$	Inserts the ASCII code for the minus sign into pictured numeric output, if n is negative
SPACE	3-1		Outputs the ASCII code for a blank
SWAP	2-2	$n_1\ n_2 \rightarrow$ $n_2\ n_1$	Exchanges the top two integers on the stack
THEN	4-2		Used in IF-ELSE-THEN construction
TYPE	3-3	$a\ n \rightarrow$	Outputs n characters starting with address a
U*	5-4	$u_1\ u_2 \rightarrow u$	Unsigned single-length integer multiplication
U.	5-4	$u \rightarrow$	Outputs an unsigned single-length integer

U.R	5-4	u n →	Outputs an unsigned single-length integer in an n character field
U / MOD	5-4	u_d u_1 → u_r u_q	Unsigned division with double-length dividend; quotient and remainder are on the stack
U<	5-4	u_1 u_2 →	Flag is true if u_1 is less than u_2; numbers are unsigned
UNTIL	4-4	f →	Used in BEGIN-UNTIL construction
UPDATE	8-1		Marks all buffer blocks as updated
VAL	7-3	a → n	Converts the ASCII representation of an integer to binary form
VARIABLE	6-2		Used to define a variable
VOCABULARY	9-2		Used in the establishment of a new vocabulary
WHILE	4-4	f →	Used in BEGIN-WHILE-REPEAT construction
WORD	7-2	n → a	Inputs characters from the input stream; uses a character whose ASCII code is n as a delimiter
XOR	5-5	n_1 n_2 → n	Performs the XOR operation on each bit of n_1 and n_2
Y/N	4-5	→ f	Queries for Y or N input; N gives true
[	9-1		Ends compilation and starts execution; used within word definition
[COMPILE]	9-1		Causes compilation of an IMMEDIATE word

|] | 9-1 | Ends execution and restarts compilation; used with [|

Index

About the Author . . .

Dr. Paul M. Chirlian is a professor in the Department of Electrical Engineering at Stevens Institute of Technology. He is one of the most prolific technical authors in the world today. His fifteen books cover a wide range of electronics and computer topics, including all three popular computer languages: BASIC, FORTRAN, and Pascal.